About the Author

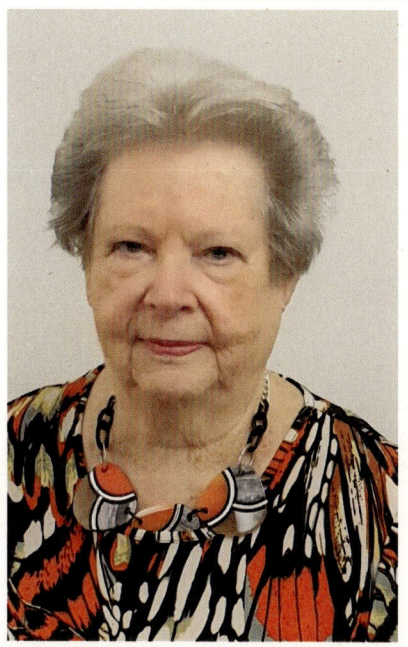

Noreen Kemp was born in 1939 in Arbroath, Angus, Scotland, but, as her father was employed in the Jute Mills in Calcutta, she was brought up in India and was at school in Darjeeling. She met her husband in Calcutta, where he worked for the Chartered Bank. After their marriage, she accompanied him on his assignments overseas until his retirement in 1986. She now lives with her family in Dorset, England. This is her first book.

To Bill,
I hope you enjoy the book.
Regards
Noreen
20/7/25

HAVE BANKER WILL TRAVEL

Noreen Kemp

HAVE BANKER WILL TRAVEL

Vanguard Press

VANGUARD PAPERBACK

© Copyright 2025

The right of Noreen Kemp to be identified as author of
this work has been asserted by her in accordance with the
Copyright, Designs and Patents Act 1988.

All Rights Reserved

No reproduction, copy or transmission of this publication
may be made without written permission.
No paragraph of this publication may be reproduced,
copied or transmitted save with the written permission of the publisher, or
in accordance with the provisions
of the Copyright Act 1956 (as amended).

Any person who commits any unauthorised act in relation to this
publication may be liable to criminal prosecution and civil claims for
damages.

A CIP catalogue record for this title is available from the British Library.

ISBN 978-1-83794-693-8

*Vanguard Press is an imprint of
Pegasus Elliot Mackenzie Publishers Ltd.*
www.pegasuspublishers.com

First Published in 2025

**Vanguard Press
Sheraton House Castle Park
Cambridge England**

Printed & Bound in Great Britain

Dedication

To Jamie, my love, and for all those women who have followed their menfolk all over the world.

Acknowledgements

My thanks are due to my friends, Rev. Canon Kenneth Noakes and Philippa Daffern, both of whom read my original manuscript and encouraged me to write this book; Emma Farrell, who assisted me with the IT technology; my family, who supported me throughout my journey; my production editor, Lesley Perry, and her team at Pegasus, who all helped bring this book into being.

CHAPTER 1
HONG KONG (1961–1962)

Before he retired in 1986, my husband was employed by the Chartered Bank of India, Australia and China (the Chartered Bank for short), as a member of their foreign cadre. This meant that during the course of your career, you moved from country to country, wherever the bank posted you – rather like being in the foreign service. You had to be twenty-one before you joined the expatriate cadre and male. There were no expatriate female staff.

My husband, Jim Kemp, joined the bank in 1955 after doing his national service and, after his training in London, he was posted as a sub-accountant to Calcutta, where we met in 1956.

A sub-accountant's first tour of duty was for a period of five years, during which the bank did not allow their employees to get married – they said you could not afford it, which was true, junior bank employees being notoriously badly paid in those days. This also allowed the bank freedom to move you easily and quickly round their branches. Most sub-accountants were moved at least once during their first tour. Jim moved twice, from Calcutta to Chittagong and finally to Hong Kong before he went on his first leave. After six months' Home leave, your subsequent tours lasted for three years, followed by six months' leave.

There was a career path which you followed. You started out as a sub-accountant and stayed at that rank for about ten to fifteen years, moving up from a junior to a senior sub-accountant. During that period, you learnt your 'trade' working in all departments of the bank and sometimes having charge of a small to medium branch, where you were designated as a 'Manager'. This was sometimes hard for customers to understand, as to them – particularly the Chinese in Hong Kong – a 'Manager' was a 'Manager', and they did not really appreciate the difference between 'Manager' of a small branch like Tsuen Wan and a large branch like Hongkong, or why large loans needed to be referred by Tsuen Wan to the manager of Hong Kong before being granted.

After your long stint as a Sub-Accountant, you could progress fairly rapidly, first to the rank of assistant accountant, then accountant, then deputy manager and finally manager, and sometimes chief manager for a large area, e.g. Hong Kong, Singapore (small area, lots of money), Malaya (latterly Malaysia), India, Pakistan Indonesia and so on – some went to London, where there were several general managers, presided over by a chief general manager – a very big bug indeed!

Most large expatriate firms had similar terms of service and career paths for their expatriate officers – all the banks, Hong Kong and Shanghai, National and Grindlays, Barclays and Standard Bank of South Africa, all the big agency houses like Jardines, Borneo Company, Mather & Platt, Mackinnon Mackenzie, Unilever and Guthrie Bousteads – under whose umbrella were all sorts of mills (jute, cotton, sugar and paper…), plantations (tea, coffee, cotton, cocoa, rubber…) and insurance firms, throughout Africa, India and the Middle and Far East.

It was compulsory for all expatriate bank officers to learn the language of the country you were posted to on your first tour, after which you were encouraged to learn as many more as you wished to. The bank provided a local teacher, a *munshi* and after you had successfully passed an exam, refunded your fees plus a bonus. Jim could speak fluent Hindi, a smattering of Cantonese and Malay. All expatriate firms expected their staff to do this.

You were allowed to get married on your second tour and many bachelors did. In the Chartered Bank, permission from the Court of Directors was required before you could do so. Before permission was granted, your fiancée was required to travel to London to be approved by the Court of Directors as a fit and proper person to become a bank wife. Once you had run this gauntlet, permission to marry – or not – was then granted. I can understand this in a way, as I have lost count of the number of times when being introduced in a new posting, Jim's customers would say, 'This is Jim Kemp, new manager of the Chartered Bank, and this is Mrs Chartered Bank' especially by the Chinese, both in Malaysia and Hong Kong.

I was fortunate indeed that I did not have to jump over this hurdle, as before I was married, I worked in the British High Commission in Calcutta, where I was the Deputy High Commissioner's Social Secretary. In effect, this meant that I was his PA's assistant. At that time, the PA happened to be Joyce Hobbs, the wife of the assistant manager of the Chartered Bank.

Tom Hobbs left Calcutta to become one of the general managers of the bank in London, and apparently, Joyce vouched for me, so I was spared the Board ordeal, passing the test as a fit and proper person to be a bank wife.

Jim came home on his first leave in January 1961, and we were married in Arbroath, Scotland, on June 10th. On June 15, I had my twenty-second birthday, and ten days later, we flew to Hong Kong, where Jim had been appointed as manager of the Tsuen Wan branch in the New Territories.

When we arrived, we had a fortnight's 'hand over' period from our predecessors, the Kilpatricks. We stayed at the five-star Peninsula Hotel in Kowloon, in a large room which had an ensuite bathroom in avocado, with a sunken bath. I was terribly impressed with the sunken bath!

In 1961, Tsuen Wan was just being developed but had already grown into quite a large industrial town. A new five-storey bank building had been proposed, and the temporary premises were in a small building sitting at the bottom of a hill, just below the New Territories Police Headquarters. Unkindly, it was known locally as the *'cheesaw'* (piss house) to the Hong Kong Bank, which had a handsome, new building some two hundred yards from the temporary Chartered Bank building. There was a great deal of friendly rivalry between these two major banks in Hong Kong.

We lived in the bank house at Ting Kau, five miles up the Castle Peak Road. This was a flat-roofed bungalow that sat on the tip of a headland looking out to Tsing Yi, Lantau and some smaller islands. We had a spectacular view of the islands from our veranda, looking out onto the deep blue sea, with junks in full sail, lorchas, fishing boats and an array of various other craft sailing past. There were two government bungalows behind us on the headland, but our house definitely had the prime position.

Most of the bank expatriate personnel lived in flats, so to have a house was a tremendous bonus. We were also far enough away from other bank personnel to afford us a great deal of privacy – no one in the bank knew what we were doing, unless we specifically told them – another bonus! Living in a block of company flats can sometimes be quite claustrophobic.

Our bungalow was built by a Chinese millionaire as his weekend holiday home and overlooked a Chinese graveyard at the back. This was very bad feng shui. According to Chinese custom, all buildings are built on a dragon, and unless built on the dragon's back, they are considered unlucky. Usually, before being built, the feng shui man is consulted and will tell you whether the site has good feng shui or not. If not, he can perform a ceremony to drive away the evil spirits. Overlooking any kind of graveyard is very bad feng shui. I cannot think why the Chinese millionaire let his bungalow be built there – perhaps that is why he sold it.

When the bank first bought the bungalow, it was impossible to get servants to work in it. Eventually, the feung shui man was called in to drive away the evil spirits, and the problem was solved.

A big bonus for the house was that it had its own local water supply – a huge boon in the days of water shortages in Hong Kong, where people on the island and mainland Kowloon, in times of drought, only received water for a limited period every three or four days.

A steep concrete drive swept down the hill to the bungalow and bellied out in front of the L-shaped house, disappearing into the garage. There was a retaining wall round the front of the headland, on which sat several large pots of bougainvillea.

A passage led from the garage into the house, through about eight shower rooms, up the backstairs, past two amahs' rooms, up some more stairs to the kitchen and then up to a corridor running down one side of the house. Off this were the dining room, one bedroom and bathroom, stairs down to a large downstairs bedroom, and the master bedroom and bathroom, which straddled the end of the house. The downstairs bedroom was an odd room. It had no en-suite bathroom or cupboards, but the wall by the stairs was pockmarked with little lockers – presumably where, if you were a guest, you could keep your swimming costume and towel.

There were steps leading up the front of the house to the veranda, which ran down the opposite arm of the L. There was a hollow wall in front of the veranda filled with miniature fairy roses. The front door led into the hall, with the lounge window looking onto the veranda. There was a small lawn at the far side of the veranda with a tall hibiscus hedge enclosing it at the back, in front of the retaining wall belonging to the next house – a bungalow owned by the Government Land and Surveys Department, in which lived Paula and Des Moore, who became one of our lifelong friends.

It was a very hot house. The lounge and corridor were lined with large picture windows looking out to Tsing Yi Island, but these did not open. Two small side windows at either side did open and let in a bit of air, but the house was really built for air conditioning. Bank officers of Jim's seniority at that time were only allowed to have one air-conditioned bedroom per house. This we had.

We had our own beach – a few rocks with steps leading down to the sea with a bit of rock you could swim off. We never did. Too dangerous! The back of the house was rocky and hilly – we tried unsuccessfully to persuade the bank to step it so that we could have a garden.

All bank houses, unless you were very unlucky, were well and fully furnished. This one was newly furnished, our predecessors, the Kilpatricks, being the first occupants. We had a large cane suite in the lounge, a full set of Stuart crystal glasses, a canteen of Community Plate silver cutlery and a Noritake china dinner service for twelve. You were supposed to be able to walk into a bank house with just your clothes and some personal knickknacks and pictures, and this I was always able to do. They were furnished with everything – sheets, towels, beautiful table linen, dinner services, right down to the pots and pans, wooden spoons and dusters in the kitchen and ashtrays in the lounge.

My mother insisted we take our wedding presents with us; these were never unpacked, as they included a set of crystal identical to that supplied by the bank. These trunks travelled with us from Hong Kong to Sarawak and then back Home to live in my mother's attic until we bought a house of our own, at which point it was transferred to *our* attic until we retired in 1986.

Enid Kilpatrick looked after me very well, despite having to pack and see to two toddlers. We were out every day meeting the rest of the bank wives at lunches and having dinners with customers at night.

The day after we arrived, Joyce Reynolds, the Hong Kong Manager's wife, invited Enid and me to lunch – a farewell for her and an introduction to the rest of the wives for me. I remember this event very well, as I was very shy and feeling very young and gauche compared to the sophisticated other bank wives. I was dressed in a bright red cotton dress with cream 'sunbursts' on it, a dropped waist and gathered skirt, which made me look about fifteen. All the other wives were dressed in sophisticated, straight-skirted linen shifts in pastel colours – I decided I would have to do something about my clothes. But how? We certainly could not afford to buy me an expensive new wardrobe.

After a delicious lunch, we adjourned to the sitting room for coffee and liquors, and one of the wives beckoned me over. "Come and sit by me," she said. I obediently did so. Just then, there was a lull in the conversation, and I heard her say in a loud, carrying voice, "And now, my dear, tell me – what kind of contraceptives do *you* use?" The whole room turned to look, and my face went as scarlet as my dress before the conversation quickly started up again, and Enid came and rescued me. When I got back to Jim, I asked, "Are all bank wives like that?" He assured me they were not.

I was very lonely after Enid left, marooned on my headland as I could not drive, and both the government wives who lived behind me worked. We took over the Kilpatrick's two 'black and white' amahs (that is to say, they wore black trousers and a white shirt): fat, jolly, motherly, middle-aged, Ah Soy, and her young niece, the thin, Ah Lan, the two of them basically ran the household. I did the shopping, Ah Soy did the cooking and Ah Lan did the laundry, and they split the cleaning between them. The house ran like clockwork, and I did not really have anything to do with it. They were noisy! After a couple of days I said to Jim, "I don't know if I can keep these two."

"What do you mean?" he asked.

"Well, they keep shouting and fighting with each other," I said. Jim laughed.

"No they're not," he replied. "They're just talking– it just sounds as if they're fighting – that's the Cantonese language!"

Our garden consisted of a wooden slatted, stepped shelf affair that Jim had built under the veranda, on which we had about four tiers of flowerpots, plus small flower beds going up the sides of the stairs and a hollow veranda wall planted with fairy roses. I spent much of my time gardening, reading and playing the piano – a lovely new upright Yamaha bought by the Kilpatricks from the Tsang Fook Piano Company.

This piano was a godsend to me. I think it is very important if you are an expatriate wife to have a hobby – or several; it does not matter what it is – knitting, needlework, bridge, golf, mahjong, tennis whatever anything with which to pass the often long, tedious and lonely hours spent by yourself in some out of the way places, where you cannot work – indeed *often* cannot work because you need a Work Permit. My all-absorbing hobby is music – specifically singing. I am passionate about it. So having a piano is really important to me and keeps me happy.

We had a tall red hibiscus hedge at the end of a tiny lawn by the back wall of the house and were plagued by legions of small red biting ants. You couldn't have a cup of coffee or a plate of biscuits on the veranda table without them being covered in ants within about five minutes. I could not understand where they came from, until a Chinese friend persuaded me to cut down the tall hibiscus hedge, after which they miraculously disappeared. Red ants apparently love hibiscus. I have never grown hibiscus near a house since.

Together with the two amahs, we took over the Kilpatricks' dachshund, called Lulu – a black, fat grumpy bitch, whom we were going to send on to the Kilparticks' next posting. Lulu was thoroughly spoilt and used to have a saucer of tea or coffee mid-morning and afternoon – a custom which I soon stopped. She disliked children, her nose having been put out of joint when the Kilpatrick children arrived on the scene. We used to take her for a walk most evenings along the banks of the nearby reservoir. She was so fat that, at first, she would walk about one hundred yards, then flop down and wait for our return. But gradually, she lost weight and became fitter and better-tempered and was soon accompanying us on long walks all the way along the top of the reservoir.

Jim asked me what I wanted for a wedding present, and I said, "A Scottie," as my family had always had one. This was easier said than done in Hong Kong. However, one day, there was an advertisement in the South China Morning Post saying, *'Scottish terrier pups for sale at the Jockey Club'*. They were far too expensive, but we decided we would go and 'just have a look'. This was fatal, as, of course, once we saw the pups, we had to have one. The seller placed the five pups on the flat roof of the kennels and I chose the one that came to me when I called – a little black dog whom we called 'Fergus'. The Chinese kennel owner gave him to me to take home in a brown paper bag – he was eight weeks old and really, I think, too young to have been parted from his mother.

Not having intended to buy a pup we were unprepared for him, and somewhat apprehensive about what Lulu would say when we took the pup home, so that night we put him to bed in our bathroom in a cardboard box with the front cut out and shut the door. Lulu whined and scratched at the bottom of the door until, in exasperation, I let her in, whereupon she climbed into the box and lay across the opening.

The pup snuggled up to her, and they both went off to sleep quite contentedly. Lulu took over Fergus completely. She housetrained him, taking him in her mouth out to our pocket-handkerchief lawn, and depositing him on the grass to do his business. She would then pick him up again and bring him back indoors. It was not unusual to see her trotting along the passageway, carrying Fergus in her mouth, going from A to B.

When Fergus was about nine months old, I decided to enter him for the Hong Kong Dog Show at the Jockey Club. I had never even been to a dog show before and hadn't got a clue as to what I was supposed to do.

Fortunately, we met a lady who was a regular entrant and showed Pekinese. She invited us to her flat and showed me what to do. The flat was filthy! She had about a dozen Pekinese there, all wearing bootees so that they did not step in their own puddles or pooh. I rehearsed Fergus on a lead at home and practiced, mostly unsuccessfully, parading him round our veranda and lawn.

On show day, we turned up at the club at about nine a.m., where we were shown to half a horsebox. It was very hot and there was a lot of straw about, which got up my nose and it wasn't long before I had a massive dose of hay fever. Fergus was entered for the Scottish terrier class, which was not until two p.m. Whilst we were waiting, I walked Fergus around the show, where he took exception to an Irish wolfhound, who must have been the largest dog there, and started barking at him. The wolfhound just looked round lazily as if wondering where the noise was coming from. I don't think he even saw Fergus, who was just beside his feet.

When we eventually got into the show ring, I managed to walk him once round the ring before he just sat down and refused to budge. I think the judge was hard put to it to contain his mirth. Eventually, he gave me a first rosette. Having won that, Fergus progressed to 'Best Terrier Pup' in show – so we received another certificate and rosette. Did I mention that he was the only entrant in both classes?

We had been in Tsuen Wan for about a month when I was lucky enough to get a job at the police headquarters as secretary to the assistant commissioner, New Territories and Marine. I thoroughly enjoyed this, as I had been very bored sitting at home, and it was also extremely convenient. Jim dropped me off at work, went into his temporary office, whilst I climbed up the steps into the police headquarters. Nothing could have been better! We went home for lunch, and I went down the stairs to collect him from the bank at five o'clock. The pay was good too – without my salary, we would have been hard put to it to make ends meet, but with it, I bought myself a suitable new wardrobe and, of course, Fergus.

My job was not normally very arduous. I worked as PA to the assistant commissioner, originally a man called Cluny, then an ex-Palestine policeman called Turner and the senior superintendent of police, a very large Scotsman called Dougie Taylor, who must have been six foot six and dwarfed most of the Chinese. Dougie would visit Jim at the bank for a coffee some mornings and had a habit of sitting at Jim's desk, removing his hat and absentmindedly stroking the nap with his swagger stick. It looked very menacing. Jim's Chinese customers always gave him a wide berth, until one morning, Jim said to Dougie, "Do you mind not doing that, Doug? You're frightening all my customers."

One of my main tasks was to take the superintendent's daily reports for my boss over the telephone. They were a fascinating glimpse into the Hong Kong underworld: 'Three sampans containing twelve illegal immigrants, two raids on mahjong schools leading to the arrest of three Triads (the Chinese mafia – an illegal society), two fishing boats dynamiting fish, raids on five opium dens' and on one memorable occasion, 'murder of two women and one man on a high-rise building staircase – all blind – including the murderer'.

We would often have junks dynamiting fish on the rocks below Ting Kau and woke up one night hearing someone running on our flat roof, then jumping down onto the rocks below. The next morning, we discovered that someone had been trying to burgle the houses above us but had run away when the occupants switched the lights on, escaping across our roof, onto the rocks below and finally onto a waiting sampan.

During my tenure with the police, Hong Kong experienced a major influx of immigrants from China. This was the first time it had happened. Normally, the Chinese border control guards were extremely strict and would shoot immigrants trying to cross over from Canton into Hong Kong. However, suddenly, they were letting everyone through. No one ever found out why. Thousands of desperate Chinese were pouring undeterred over the border, both by land and by sea.

The army was drafted in to assist the police in stopping them, as Hong Kong just could not cope with the massive influx. The government set up detention camps in the New Territories, where they imprisoned those they caught, fed them and sent them back into China as soon as they could. However, many got through, and once they had made their way into the crowded streets of Hong Kong and Kowloon, they were soon absorbed into the local society. Almost all of them would have had some relatives that they could go to, just to get them started in a new life.

This was particularly upsetting for the Chinese policemen, who may well have come across some mainland relatives whom they were then supposed to arrest and return. On one occasion, Dougie Taylor returned to the headquarters, visibly upset. "What's wrong?" I asked. He had caught a couple of teenagers, the same age as his own children, who had escaped but got separated from their parents in the general melee. He then had to arrest them and send them off to one of the camps to be interned and returned across the border. I don't suppose they would ever have found their parents again.

Jim's secretary's sister, was one of those who came to Hong Kong during this incursion. Jeannie and her husband had one of the flats in the new bank building just above the office, and Jim met Jeannie and her sister on the staircase one day. Jeannie started to explain how her sister came to be there. "Don't tell me," said Jim. "I don't want to know. Just disappear her!" Jeannie did.

Our lives soon took on a steady pattern. We would work all week, and on Saturday afternoon, after the bank closed at one o'clock, we would go into Kowloon to do our weekly shopping. After our shopping spree, we would have supper at a restaurant called Rikkis, share a huge 'Suzie Wong Salad', large enough for two and then go to the cinema.

The first time we went to the cinema, I wanted to visit the ladies and asked Jim where it was. He pointed to an usherette and said, "Go and ask her – say, *'Chee saw hai, bin do nai'*" (which literally translates as 'where is the piss house?'). My Cantonese must have been perfect, as she replied in Cantonese, and of course, I hadn't a clue what she said.

On Sundays, we would explore the New Territories in Susie, Jim's white Sunbeam Alpine, which was his pride and joy.

I found summer in Hong Kong city and Kowloon unbearably hot and humid, due, I think to the heat being reflected back into the city streets by all the concrete skyscrapers, as, temperature-wise, it is not nearly as hot as, say, Borneo – you just felt much hotter. As the New Territories were not so built up, Ting Kau felt slightly cooler. The Hongkong and Kowloon streets were narrow, crowded, noisy and full of people. As you passed between the high-rise buildings, you could hear the click of the mahjong tiles coming from the overcrowded flats day and night. Many small businesses were run out of these flats – people making plastic flowers, toys, paper goods – Hong Kong people are very industrious and always keen to get on in life.

In winter, the weather is delightful. The skies are a clear, cloudless blue, and the air is crisp and clear. It is cold enough in the evenings to have a fire, and indeed most houses were built with reversible air-conditioner/central heating systems. You can wear jersey dresses and suits, sports jackets and autumn/light winter clothing, and grow all the lovely early summer flowers. We used to drive to a nursery in the New Territories that grew sweetpeas up their border garden wall by the road. The perfume was fantastic, and you could buy a large bunch of flowers for one Hong Kong dollar.

We often went to dinner with Jim's customers, and I quickly learnt some of the Chinese customs. At one of our first dinners, I was wearing a light blue dress and my hostess had on a huge blue ring. "What a pretty ring you're wearing," I said, making conversation. "Look! It's the same colour as my dress!" Whereupon she took it off her finger and put it on mine. I nearly died of embarrassment, not knowing that you should never admire someone else's jewellery, or else they feel obliged to give it to you. Fortunately, it was not a valuable ring, and the stone was just a piece of glass.

On another occasion soon after we arrived, we were invited to a wedding dinner at a big hotel in Kowloon, hosted by Mr Chong. Jim had only met him once. We were ushered into a room full of guests, had a lovely meal and an enjoyable evening. Next day at the bank, a different Mr Chong arrived and said to Jim, "Where were you last night? You did not come to the wedding."

"Yes, I did," said Jim, to discover that we had been to a wedding dinner by a different Mr Chong, whom Jim did not know at all. Jim's customer's wedding party had been in the room next door. Our hosts had been so polite that they had never let on! Fortunately, our Mr Chong thought it was a huge joke.

My most memorable Chinese dinner was, however, one in Kowloon, which I attended by default. Invitations had gone out to several bank couples addressed to 'Mr & Mrs...', but all the other wives who lived in Kowloon and the island had decided not to go. Communication between us was obviously not very good because I did not know this.

We arrived at the dinner, and I was very taken aback to find I was the only woman there. I sat quietly in a corner, whilst all the men ate and drank liberally, and virtually forgot I was there. As the dinner progressed and everyone got more convivial, with the Chinese faces getting redder and redder due to the amount of alcohol consumed, it became time for party tricks. Everyone seemed to have one – whether it was turning somersaults, standing on their head, walking on their hands on the table and generally horsing around. I was thoroughly entertained and had a much livelier time than at a staid normal dinner, sitting through about nine courses of who knew what – better not to ask sometimes – the Chinese maxim being 'if it moves, you can eat it'.

At our first Christmas in Hong Kong, we decided to ask all the bank bachelors and anyone else without children for Christmas lunch, ending up with about twenty squashed round our extended dining room table plus an extra table. There were ourselves, our neighbours Paula and Des Moore, Rae and Margaret Fulton, who was the Kowloon manager and his wife and the bachelors. We had ordered a fifteen-pound ham, and about a twenty-five-pound turkey from the Dairy Farm, which we stuffed with chestnut and sausage meat.

We started lunch with grapefruit, then went on to the serious business of eating the turkey, ham, roast and boiled potatoes, peas and Brussels sprouts – we ran out of the latter, and I had to send Ah Soy up to Paula's to get another packet out of her freezer – then Christmas pudding with brandy butter, mince pies with cream, biscuits and cheese, coffee and chocolates and brandy and liqueurs.

I have never seen people eat so much. If I close my eyes, I can still see Hamish McWilliam, one of the bachelors – a small, thin, wiry young man, known by the Chinese as *Sai quat sin* (a skeleton), gnawing his way through one of the huge turkey legs, totally demolishing it. At about four o'clock, I asked if anyone would like tea. "Yes!" was the reply, so we had homemade Christmas cake, scones and Scotch pancakes, with butter and jam. Come eight o'clock, the guests were still there, so we had scrambled eggs and the remains of the turkey and ham (not much of that left) in sandwiches. All we had left in the house next morning was a couple of pieces of bread for some toast and tea.

One of the bachelors bought Fergus a little mechanical dog on a leash, at the end of which was a rubber tube. You squeezed a bulb at the end of the tube, and the dog jumped about yapping. What fun we had with that! Fergus also had a party trick. I used to play Beethoven's Sonata Pathetique (1st Movement), and for some reason, wherever he was, as soon as I played the opening bars, Fergus would rush in, run slap up to the sounding board of the piano, and start to sing, howling his way all through the first page, after which he would stop singing and wander off again. He did that all his life. Only to that piece – nothing else! He really was a most discerning dog. It was one of the best Christmases we have ever had.

I wish now that I had kept a diary of all our travels as one forgets so much, but I didn't. Once a month, we would go to 'Jimmy's Kitchen' on Hong Kong island with the Moores. Paula always had snails which smelt delicious – all that garlic – however, I could never bring myself to taste them.

After we had been in Hong Kong about a month, we decided to have a buffet supper for Jim's customers and some of the senior bank staff from Hong Kong. This was my first dinner party, and we were eager to make a good impression. We had a guest list of about thirty, and Jim decided that, as the catering would be beyond our amahs, he would ask his ex-cookboy Cheng, to come and do the cooking. Cheng was a fantastic cook, whom Jim had inherited when he first was in Hong Kong, before we were married.

Unfortunately, Cheng contracted some sort of nervous illness and could no longer work as a full-time cook. Jim got him a job as a doorman at the bank, but he was still available to come and cook for a party. We (or at least Cheng) decided on the menu.

Jim sent Lau Wing the bank driver in the bank van to pick up Cheng, who did all the shopping for the dinner and arrived at Ting Kau with the food and his bag of tricks in the morning. He promptly commandeered the kitchen, and Ah Soy and Ah Lan, who skivvied for him were in awe at his talent.

I can't remember what else we had to eat, but the centrepiece on the table was a huge whole thick-lipped garoupa (a large fish), which Cheng cooked and had sitting up on its tummy, swimming in a sea of blue chopped aspic to resemble waves. It really was quite magnificent.

After admiring his skill, I took the ladies off to wash their hands before dinner, only to find, when I returned, that he had further improved on his handiwork – and the garoupa now looked most fearsome, with big flashing eyes! Cheng had inserted small battery light bulbs into its eye sockets.

Amazing. I was the talk of the town. The party was a great success. Everyone agreed that Cheng had surpassed himself, and the whole household – Ah, Soy, Ah Lan and me (undeservedly) – had all gained much face in the neighbourhood.

We had no TV in Ting Kau, so every Sunday night, we would visit the Fultons in Kowloon, together with most of the bachelors. We would sit on the floor of their family room and watch a serialised programme of Churchill's memoirs. I cannot remember what it was called, but it went on for most of the year we were in Hong Kong. During the evening we would have 'pot luck', which consisted of tinned Oxford sausages, fried egg and chips – a very enjoyable Sunday evening.

I have always loved to sing and have had lessons since I was a teenager. While in Hong Kong, I was able to have singing lessons and we joined the local operatic society, The Hong Kong Singers.

I found a good singing teacher – a charming old Italian gentleman called Signor Gualdi. He had a choir, and I sang at several concerts with him – notably one in which I sang the role of Amneris in a programme of operatic excerpts mixed with Chinese folk songs, which he had transcribed. "You will come next week and sing Amneris with me," he said at my singing lesson one Saturday morning. Maestro Gualdi used to get quite carried away on the rostrum during rehearsals, and I think often thought he was conducting at the opera house in Milan or somewhere. He would join in the aria with you, which could be quite disconcerting at times – particularly when you were least expecting it.

I also sang in my first radio show – can't remember how I came to be invited to do that – accompanied by the official Hong Kong radio accompanist Moya Rea. I can't remember what I sang, except that there were some Scottish folk songs in the programme. Several of my friends in The Hong Kong Singers heard the broadcast and said to me later, "I didn't know you could sing!"

The Hong Kong Singers produced *'Chu Chin Chow'* whilst I was with them, and I had the part of the slave girl – a main part, but no singing. The show was very successful and was the first show produced at the newly opened concert hall on the island.

Being the first show in the hall, there were inevitably a few teething problems that required solving, the most immediate being that there were no weights for the props which held up the scenery. At the dress rehearsal, the poor stagehands physically held up the scenery to prevent it from falling on the performers, who spent the entire rehearsal watching it warily as it swayed about while the supporting stagehands got progressively more and more tired. Fortunately, struts and weights were produced in double-quick time for the first performance the next evening.

More drama! The actor playing the villain of the piece, Abanazar, fell ill with kidney stones, for which he was prescribed strong antibiotics. The stage manager played his part for the whole week, except on the last night, when Abanazar decided he was well enough to perform. Just before curtain up, someone gave him a strong brandy to calm his nerves, and this, coupled with the antibiotic, made him as drunk as a coot in double-quick time! Come the scene in the magic cave, where Abanazar is surveying the gold and the jewels littering the floor of the cave, he lay on the couch, saying drunkenly, "Open ses… ses… ses – open se… s… s… ses." He could not quite say 'Sesame'. As he was on stage on his own, there was not much anyone could do to help, and the door to the cave remained firmly shut. The producer and backstage staff were getting quite frantic after the third or fourth attempt failed. Eventually, the stage manager shouted, "Sesami!" and the genie was pushed onto the stage to finish the sentence and allow the cave to open and the show to proceed.

Jim supervised the building of the new bank in Tsuen Wan. This was a large five-storey, glass-fronted modern edifice, very smart inside. It was the first of many bank buildings the erection of which Jim supervised during his career. We had a grand opening, with Willie Pullen the Chief General Manager in London and his wife, flying out to perform the ceremony. There was a big party in the bank after the official opening.

Not long after the opening, Typhoon Wanda descended on Hong Kong. This was my first typhoon. When the warnings went out, we took all the precautions we could at Ting Kau – lifting the plant pots off the sea wall and wooden flowerpot stand and putting them in the garage, together with anything else that wasn't battened down.

We went to work as usual with the wind strong but not too high. By about ten, the wind had increased considerably and was roaring round the island, tossing large planks and everything else in its way about as if they were matchsticks. Rain lashed down. All the police officers were in the operations room trying to send men out to assist people where they could.

Halfway through the morning, I had a call from Jim to say that the wind had sucked out the whole of the large bronze-framed plate glass front windows of the new bank building, together with all the concealed plastic lighting shades, and could the police please come around as the bank was now insecure. How my policemen laughed. It was a long time before the bank lived that down – especially as their advertisement at that time featured the slogan 'Big, Strong and Friendly'.

Once the front of the building was down, the wind, of course, made its way inside, and several of the doors were twisted off their frames. There was a stairway down the back of the building, leading from the flats on the top floor. The wind took off the back door of this and then came howling down the staircase like a funnel, carrying away anything that stood in its way, and there was a four-foot flood in the basement. A large piece of plate glass hurtled past Jim and Jeannie, who were standing by the staircase, missing them both by inches.

Conveniently, the eye of the typhoon came over the city at about one o'clock, and Jim and I returned to Ting Kau for lunch. We had a large creeper of Quisqualis in a flower trough hanging over the veranda wall. Wanda had sucked it clean out of the trough and it disappeared somewhere into the wind. I was very sad about this, as Quisqualis, or 'Drunken Sailor', as it is known in Bombay, is one of my favourite tropical creepers, with a beautiful perfume, especially at night. The legend of how it got its name is that one evening down by the Bombay Port Trust, where there was a large plant of it hanging over the wall, a sailor, somewhat worse for the wear, was overcome by the heavy fragrance of the flowers as he weaved his way back to his ship and fell asleep beneath it for the rest of the night, so it became known as 'Drunken Sailor'. Fortunately, that was our only casualty.

We celebrated our first wedding anniversary with a romantic dinner at the Miramar Hotel, which was to have dire consequences. I had been suffering badly from hay fever, and Margaret Fulton suggested I go and see an American chiropractor in Kowloon, who was supposed to be able to cure allergies. So the next Saturday, Jim and I set off to consult him. Yes, he assured me, he could cure me, as I had a vertebra in my neck slightly displaced, which was irritating the nerve on the way to my nose and giving me hay fever.

He made me kneel in front of a velvet-covered piano stool with my head hanging over the seat – a bit like an executioner's block – I could imagine how Anne Boleyn must have felt. He gave me an almighty blow on the back of the neck which made me see stars for several minutes. He then ran his fingers down my spine and assured me that the vertebra was now in place, and I would have no more trouble.

Slightly dazed, I rose off my knees, and off we went for our weekly dinner at Rikkis. Before we got there, however, I started feeling decidedly queasy, and eventually said to Jim, "I feel awful – we shall have to go home." As soon as we got to Ting Kau, I had to rush upstairs with violent diarrhoea and vomiting.

After being up all night, Jim sent for the doctor, who took one look at me and said, "You have infective hepatitis – jaundice."

"I can't have," I cried. "I'm not yellow!"

He laughed. "But you soon will be – it will take about ten days. Once you are yellow, you will feel a lot better. This is highly infectious," he said to Jim. "So tell your amahs to mark all her crockery and cutlery, and keep them separately. And see she gets plenty to drink." He never came back to see me. He left instructions with Jim that I should not drink alcohol for a year (no hardship, as I rarely drink alcohol), and could not eat fried food (more difficult, as I love chips). However, I found that the mere smell of fat made me feel quite queasy, so that was no bother either.

I don't think I have ever felt so ill. Ah Soy was a great nurse. Every morning, Jim would place a jug of barley water on my bedside table with instructions to Ah Soy to see I had drunk it by lunchtime. She would come into the bedroom at intervals during the day and see I had not drunk anything – "*Dlink, missee! Massa say, missee must dlink! You dlink!*" she would say, standing over me until I did so.

"*I no wanchee dlink!*" I would tell her querulously, as all that happened was that I would then be running at both ends. Besides, all I really wanted was my mother. However, she persisted. As the days went by, I got more and more yellow – until finally, I was a brilliant shade of orange. I was off work for about six weeks and thought I would never return to my normal colour.

No sooner had I returned to work than I discovered, much to our delight, that I was pregnant. Fortunately, government servants in Hong Kong get free medical care, including pregnancy, which the bank health insurance plan termed 'a self-inflicted injury', and having a baby in Hong Kong was an expensive business if you had to foot the hospital bill.

I was about six weeks pregnant when Jim rang me one day to say that we had been posted to Miri. "Where's that?" I asked.

"In Sarawak," he replied.

"Where's that?"

"In Borneo!" At least I knew where that was!

Sadly, I resigned from my job. We packed up the house and started on a round of farewell parties. Having just recovered from jaundice and being newly pregnant, I developed the disconcerting habit of falling asleep in the middle of the party. I definitely could not stand the pace.

Poor Fergus, who was only ten months old, had to spend a month in quarantine at the Jockey Club, the only quarantine kennels in Sarawak being in Kuching – a plane journey away from Miri at that time. The Kilpatricks wrote to us saying that they were unable to take Lulu in their new posting, and as we could not afford to take two dogs with us to Miri, we very regretfully had to find a new home for Lulu. This we did with a lovely family who had two boys of about eight and ten and lived on Tsing Yi Island. She went off with them without a backward glance. I was quite upset.

We had purposely kept our last evening free, but one of the bank's largest customers heard about this, andcollaring Jim at a party, invited him to dinner, saying, "I know you are keeping it free, so you have no excuses and must come!" There was not much Jim could do but agree.

As the flight the next morning was at six a.m., and we had to be at the airport at five, we arranged to spend the night in Kowloon with the Fultons, knowing that the dinner would be very late. We said a sad farewell to Ah Soy and Ah Lan, who were in tears and presented me with a parcel of beautiful baby clothes.

Sure enough, we did not get to bed until about one a.m. and were hardly asleep before it was time to get up again. Margaret came to the airport with us, but Rae, who had valiantly '*yam singed*' (a Chinese toast meaning 'bottoms up') for Jim most of the evening could not make it. Margaret said she had tried her best to wake him but without success. We were just going through customs, when he appeared, looking very much the worse for wear, having made a heroic effort to come and see us off.

We fell into the plane, having put our luggage and Fergus, who was travelling in quarantine with us, into the luggage compartment, and set off to fly to Brunei via Manila on our way to Sarawak.

CHAPTER 2
MIRI (1962–1964)

The history of Sarawak, the Land of the Hornbill, and the realm of the White Rajah, reads is just like a romantic historical novel.

Sarawak was ruled for a time by the very eccentric Brooke family, who came from the village of Sheepstor in Devon, where they are all buried. There are some fascinating books written about them.

The first Rajah, James Brooke, was born in 1803. He inherited some money from his father and bought a schooner called *'The Royalist'*. In 1839 he sailed to Singapore, where the Governor Sir Stamford Raffles, commissioned him to take some gifts to the Raja Muda Hashim (Raja Muda means heir apparent in Malay) of Brunei. Sarawak, at the time, was a part of Brunei.

When James landed in Brunei, the country was in the midst of an uprising by local Malays its coastline being ravaged by pirates. The Raja Muda asked James for help, offering him sovereignty over Sarawak should he lead the Sultan's forces to victory – which he did.

Brooke was made the Rajah of about three thousand square miles of swamp, jungle and river, which was sparsely populated by the head hunting Dayaks, who marked important events in their lives by taking the heads of other people in their community. James outlawed such acts.

Shrunken skulls were made by removing the brain from the skull, then smoking the head over a fire until the skin shrank and stuck to the skull bones.

Rajah Brooke ruled wisely and paternalistically. He suppressed piracy, arranged peace between the tribes and instituted a simplified British code of law, making himself available to all his subjects at all times, day or night. Indeed, right up to the time when Sarawak joined Malaysia, any Sarawakian could see a government official at any time, either at their office or at home – their door was required to be always open to the people. James said that Sarawak belonged to the people, and he ruled for them. He never married and was knighted by Queen Victoria.

He was succeeded by his nephew Captain Charles Johnson, who changed his name to Brooke. Charles extended the boundaries of Sarawak into the interior until it became about the size of England. He abolished slavery, built roads, waterworks and a railway. He also encouraged his British officers to take native women as lovers in order to make them proficient in the local language by becoming 'sleeping dictionaries'.

The Brookes ruled Sarawak until 1946 when Sarawak became a Crown Colony, against the wishes of the local Dayaks and Malays, who preferred to remain under the Rajah. They felt so strongly about this that when the first governor-general arrived by sea at Sibu, he was stabbed in the stomach by a young Malay and died of his wounds a week later.

On 16 September 1963, Sarawak joined with Malaya, North Borneo (now known as Sabah) and Singapore, to form a federation named Malaysia.

We arrived in Sarawak from Hong Kong in September 1962 after a memorable journey. I was about six weeks pregnant and still recovering from infective hepatitis. First, we flew to Brunei Town via Manila, then came a tedious journey by road, across two ferries and some miles of sand road to Miri. Both Brunei (now known as Bandar Seri Begawan) and the 4th Division of Sarawak, owed their prosperity to oil, which meant they were very dependent on the oil company, which was Shell.

As Fergus was travelling in quarantine, the Miri Agricultural Department had dispatched their ancient Land Rover with doubtful springing to meet us and convey us to Miri. The Malay driver and his mate were supposed to see that Fergus remained in his kennel until we reached Miri. Malays, being Muslims, do not like dogs much – they are *'haram'* or unclean. They were terrified of Fergus, who, at eleven months old, was still a puppy and wagged his tail furiously at us, asking piteously to be let out of his wooden box.

It was late afternoon when we piled into the Land Rover, and Jim, aware that the ferries at Kuala Belait stopped running at dusk, asked the driver whether we should stay overnight in Brunei. He was assured we would be in plenty of time to catch the ferry – I think the driver had a girlfriend in Kuala Belait.

Brunei is about eighty miles from Kuala Belait. We rattled for ages down the endlessly straight tarmacked road, eventually arriving at Kuala Belait at about ten at night. The ferries had long since stopped running, and there were no hotels. Jim asked the driver to go to the Chartered Bank to see if he could find out from the night watchman where the manager lived. Just as we arrived, Tom Watson, our man in Kuala Belait and his wife Jenny, returned from the cinema at the Shell Panaga Club. Jim explained our plight, and the Watsons took us up to their flat, which was on the top of the bank, to discuss what to do.

The flat had two bedrooms: one for the Watson children and the other for Jenny and Tom, so Jim and Tom set off to the Panaga Club to see if they could find us a bed for the night. Our driver and his mate were dismissed to find their own accommodation, Fergus released to spend the night in the Watsons' kitchen and the driver assured that the dog would not go nowhere else.

After an exhausting fortnight of farewell parties in Hong Kong and an all-day journey, I was completely done in – and very hungry. Jenny was about seven months pregnant, and I can dimly remember sitting up in the Watsons' bed beside her, eating bananas. Jim and Tom eventually returned to say that Geoff Shepherd, one of the Borneo Co bachelors, had a spare bedroom we could have. By this time, both Jenny and I were fast asleep. Jim shook me awake, and Tom drove us to Geoff's bungalow. I don't remember much about him (or the bungalow), apart from the huge breakfast he gave us the next morning.

Geoff, with me still half asleep, drove us back to the Watsons where the agricultural department driver was waiting. We picked up Fergus and went off to catch the ferry.

The ferry was like a huge raft, which ran on cables and was mechanically winched across the stream. The Land Rover drove up the ramp, and we were soon across the river and driven down the other side onto the sand road.

The sand road traversed for the most part through primary jungle on either side. When it rained, which it did heavily at least twice a week, it was virtually impassable – the rain gouging great potholes into the surface – and when it was dry, you drove through clouds of dust. Shell had a grader which they periodically ran up and down the road, ironing out most of the bumps. We bounced endlessly down this potholed road for what seemed like hours, the dense green jungle lining both sides. We could hear the birds and animals in the jungle, but the vegetation was packed so closely together that we saw little – apart from a massive wild boar that ran across the road at one point. Eventually, the second river was crossed, and at about noon, we arrived in Miri tired and scruffy.

Miri, a small town in those days, had approximately six streets. The bank was situated at the corner of the main intersection in the middle of the town square. It was the only bank in town. We stopped to pick up the manager, Denis Page, who cheerfully told us we had been expected the day before, and there was a welcoming party arranged for us that evening at the house.

Joy Page was waiting for us at the house. We stayed with the Pages and spent the next ten days, whilst Jim took over the bank and the Pages left, in an unending circle of farewell/welcoming parties! I would last out until about ten o'clock and then fall fast asleep in a chair wherever I happened to be – goodness knows what people must have thought of me. When I went to see the doctor John Menon, he just laughed and said that, what with recovering from hepatitis and the bumpy journey from Kuala Belait, it was a wonder I hadn't lost the baby, let alone falling asleep at parties.

Despite the fact that they were trying to pack, Joy and Denis made us feel really welcome, and introduced us to everyone. They had two boys: Michael the elder was about two, and the younger nearly one. Joy left me quite a few baby things. There was a cot, which went with the house, and we inherited the house dog – an Alsatian/ 'tanker dog' (which means mongrel) mix, a bitch, called Judy. Fortunately, Judy and Fergus got on all right.

The Miri house was situated on the top of a hill called The Tanjong – which means 'hill' in Malay. The Tanjong was flat-topped with houses set round the edge of a large grass field, or *padang*. The first house as you came up the hill was the residency. It was the largest house on the Tanjong, where the Resident John Fisher and his wife, Ruth lived.

We were between the educational department bungalow (the Knights) and the field force house on stilts (the Lewises). Further along, there were the police force superintendent's bungalow (the Parrs), then a couple of agricultural department houses (the Dowsons and the Carradices). The medical department bungalow (the Menons) was just opposite us on the *padang*.

It was all open plan. There were no gardens as such, but you were welcome to cultivate as much of the large expanse of grass/jungle around you as you wished. The jungle proper started about a hundred yards away from our servant quarters at the back of the house. This was beneficial, as less wildlife was inclined to intrude into the houses – be it monkeys or, more likely, snakes and other creepy crawlies – if there was no cover for them to hide in between the jungle and the houses and if the grass was kept cut short. I never saw either a monkey or a snake in all the time we were in Miri.

The government houses were a mixture of bungalows and Malay-style houses – most were built well off the ground, an excellent design, as with all the windows open, the house could catch whatever breeze was going. Cars could be parked on the concrete floor underneath the house, which acted as a sort of open garage.

The bank house was a large three bedroomed bungalow, which was raised about two feet off the ground – an error made by the architect and/or builder. It was actually supposed to be well off the ground. Under the bungalow was just sandy soil.

After we had been there a couple of months and had a plague of mosquitoes, we asked Shell to send their eradication squadron up to the house. The Shell men came and gave us the full treatment, using what I think was almost neat dieldrin. You would not believe what crawled out to die – huge scorpions, spiders, centipedes, millipedes and all sorts of other creepy crawlies – but, thank goodness, no snakes! I was horrified, and thought of young Michael, the Page's two-year-old, who, when scolded, would crawl beneath the house to sulk where no adult could reach him. Luckily, he was never stung or bitten by anything.

Michael was not the only one to seek refuge under the bank house. Judy had been sterilised, but unfortunately, the operation had not been entirely successful, meaning that she could not have puppies but came on heat. Consequently, when in season, all the dogs in the neighbourhood, including Fergus and Lucky the Menon's setter, normally the best of friends, gathered under the house to howl and fight. It was impossible to get at them, and we would use a hose to try and dissuade them, but usually without much success. Fortunately, Judy did not come on heat too often, and only for a couple of days.

The front steps of the house led into a large lounge/dining room, which ran the length of the house. The front door consisted of two big folding-back louvred doors, which we only closed at night. Anyone passing during the day could easily see into the whole of the lounge/dining room – not exactly very private, but there weren't that many passersby. Two ensuite bedrooms were built on the right side of the reception area, with the master bedroom suite and the kitchen on the left. The rooms were all very large and airy. Attached to the back of the house by a covered walkway was the garage and large servants' quarters.

The house was full of what estate agents call 'character'. The L-shaped master bedroom, for instance, had a solid teak and net mosquito screen that shut off the sleeping area in one leg of the L. These screens were extremely heavy, and it took a man some effort to slide them open, so once behind them, you had to stay put till morning – very inconvenient if you wished to visit the loo halfway through the night.

We soon dispensed with these. Fortunately, the windows were all mosquito-proofed, so if you closed the door and gave the room a good going over with the flit gun just before sunset, you could sleep with the fan going, and that kept most of the mosquitoes at bay. There was no air conditioning. When Jim requested one, to which we were entitled, the |manager in Kuching said that we did not need one as it was cooler in Miri than Kuching. Jim pointed out that actually it was a couple of degrees hotter in Miri, but was told 'Perhaps it is but it appears cooler!'

In the kitchen, the American designed floor-standing cooker had the grill placed under the oven, which meant you had almost to lie on your stomach to see whether the chops/toast were burning or not. We invested in a toaster.

One of the rooms in the servants' quarters (or *depa*, as they are called in Malay) was occupied by an enormous gas water heater. Gas was free for us, being installed, operated and managed by Shell. This heater was positively dangerous. If it went out, which it quite often did with the brisk monsoon wind blowing through the door, you relit it by turning the gas on, lighting a long paper spill and standing well back. Then, boom – the gas lit! The secret was to close the door and not allow the thing to go out.

The hot water pipes ran from the *depa* along the monsoon ditch, across the top of the drive, lying in the drain surrounding the house and branching off it underneath the floors. When it rained, which it did at least once a week, the water soon got cold as the unlagged pipes were lying in cold water. The master bedroom and kitchen, fortunately, always had hot water, but the other two bedrooms were not so lucky and only got a lukewarm supply. The plumbers had obviously never heard of pipe connections, and whenever a pipe went round a corner, they just bent it, so the flow of water got gradually less to the furthest bathrooms. We never managed to solve the problem satisfactorily, as it would have meant replumbing the whole house and that meant pulling up the wooden floor to get at the pipes.

Our sea baggage eventually arrived from Hong Kong. As Miri is on a continental shelf, the crates had to be transhipped onto a lighter at sea. Unfortunately, the crate containing our new gramophone/radio/tape recorder cabinet was dropped, and the cabinet badly damaged. We tried unsuccessfully to get the insurance to pay for this and eventually had to get it repaired, but it was never quite the same.

In 1962, Miri was a very isolated spot. Sarawak's Fourth Division was connected to Kuala Belait by a sand road, and there were some twentyfive miles of tarmacked road around Miri and the Shell township of Lutong. There was a road under construction to connect Miri to Kuching, but only ten miles of it had been completed.

The three main streets of the town were laid out in a sort of H-grid with another two streets running parallel to the main vertical arm of the H. The streets were lined with Chinese shophouses, including Kiat Siangs, a general store, Ming Ming, which had frozen food, a bookstore, an open-air market and an air-conditioned ladies' hairdresser, which did a roaring trade.

There was one Chinese restaurant, the Tai Tung, and one hotel, the Miri Hotel (restaurant on top, brothel underneath). We normally only ate in Miri when invited out by Jim's Chinese customers, otherwise, we entertained at home, were entertained in friends' houses or had supper at the Miri Club. When we dined at the Miri Hotel, we did so in the restaurant on the flat roof; however, on a wet evening, we would all adjourn downstairs and join the girls from the brothel and their customers having dinner – much more fun.

Chinese meals in the East differ from those in Britain. At an eastern Chinese meal, you have about seven or nine (always uneven numbers) courses – sometimes many more, the most I have ever had was twenty-five at a wedding in Hong Kong.

You only take a small portion of each course – especially if you don't know how many are going to follow. The first course is always a very nice cold course – prawns, lobster, various other cold meats and salad. Then probably a soup – chicken and sweetcorn or shark's fin with chicken – these are the only two Chinese soups I really liked. Most of the rest, to me, tasted like dirty dishwater and tasted similar.

There is chicken's feet soup – the chicken's feet used to arrive in Hong Kong from America in cartons marked 'Unfit for human consumption'. Melon soup – really tasteless, and perhaps worst of all, and a great delicacy, bird's nest soup. In Miri, this was always served, as the Niah Caves, where the birds' nests were gathered, were just up the road (or should I say jungle) from us. These nests are built in the caves by swifts, using spit to glue together their various building materials – twigs, leaves, etc.

Unfortunately, the cook rarely cleaned the nests properly, so you were inclined to get the birds' nests, plus a few feathers and other unidentifiable bits and pieces floating round in your soup. During the course of the meal, there would be two or three soups. The other courses usually include delicacies that you would not normally get in a private house. These were sometimes very strange, but usually covered in some sort of sauce, and you often happily did not know what you were eating.

There was abalone – my personal pet hate. If not sliced thinly and cooked properly, it is like eating a piece of rubber. It keeps bouncing up in your mouth – very chewy. There were rice birds – small birds, served whole with beaks, eyes and feet, which you put in your mouth and chew, spitting out the bones.

These were candidates, which, with slight sleight of hand, you could deposit on the dish of your male neighbour – usually Jim. Fish in ginger, cooked whole again with eyes, tail, skin and a few scales – put me off fish for life. Various meats – wild boar, chicken, sea slugs, pork – all cooked in a variety of ways.

The meal ends with a large plate of fried rice or noodles and then a platter of fruit. I do love Chinese food – just not their 'specialities'.

Miri was connected by tarmacked road to the Shell townships of Lutong, where the Shell refinery, offices and commissariat were. It was also connected to Piasau, where there were the Shell bungalows and a small school for the expatriate children, which was run by two British schoolteachers.

We were honorary members of the commissariat, where we did most of our grocery and cold storage shopping. All their supplies were shipped in from Singapore and were fresher, better stored and with more variety than anything available from the local store, Ming Ming, whose stock may have defrosted on the sunny quayside and then refrozen when it was put into the shop freezer.

The grass airstrip was at Lutong, where a small plane landed twice a week from Kuala Belait with the mail and passengers. If it was too wet, of course, the plane could not land. Beyond Lutong, there was the sand road to Kuala Belait.

There are two tidal rivers, the Baram and the Miri, up and down which you could travel by speedboat, Chinese launch or *kungpit*. A *kungpit* is the local *prahau* or canoe-type boat, which you either pole or row, or which had an outboard motor attached. You could travel to the various longhouses and to the townships of Bintulu and Marudi.

Both rivers are treacherous, and great care needed to avoid hazards like submerged logs floating down the river and occasional crocodiles, which often look like logs. Past the rivers into the interior, you walked through impenetrable jungle with an experienced Dayak guide, which is what all the medics, district officers, forestry officers and so on did.

There were two clubs in Miri, the Gymkhana and the Recreation Club, both with swimming pools, a golf club with a nine-hole course, and a motor club, all sponsored by Shell. There was also an excellent government ex-Shell hospital across the Miri River, which you got to via Lutong or reached by a car ferry. Almost everything was run by Shell. The Chartered Bank and Borneo Company were the only two large non-Shell businesses.

Sarawak was still a British colony when we arrived. It was divided into five divisions: 1st, 2nd, 3rd, 4th and 5th. Miri was in the 4th division, known as the 'Independent Republic', and at that time, separated from Kuching by virgin jungle. There was an expatriate population of about one hundred – Shell, government officers, Borneo Company and us, the Chartered Bank. Each division was run by a resident, under whom there were about three district officers. There was a British Police Superintendent Gerry Parr, in overall charge of the police, a Superintendent of Special Branch who came from the Hong Kong Police, Albert Hung or Hung Hung Chung, to give him his Chinese name, and an Inspector of Field Force Barry Lewis, who was a Welshman.

We had been in Miri about a month when I was asked if I would like a job with the police, as secretary to Albert Hung. I jumped at the chance. I loved my job, which was mornings only, not very taxing and just what I wanted – I would have been very bored if I had not been working. I had no piano in Miri, so could not amuse myself, could not drive and would have been stuck on the Tanjong all day whilst Jim was at work.

During any lulls in the office, I tried to teach myself Malay, so I bought myself a book called *'Teach Yourself Malay'*. I was trying to make sense of some of the grammar one day when Barry Lewis, the Field Force Officer, came in. "What are you doing?" he asked.

"Trying to teach myself Malay," I replied. "But I'm struggling with the grammar!"

"Oh, don't bother with that," said Barry. "Just turn to the vocabulary and learn as many words as you can, then listen to the way the locals put them together in a sentence and you'll soon pick up how they go. Malay is an easy language to learn." So this is what I did, and it was very good advice as I was soon able to make myself understood at the market and in the house.

In Miri, Jim came home for lunch, so he just collected me from police headquarters and took me home. The dress code in Borneo was very simple and practical. All the men wore white shorts, white short-sleeved shirts, long white stockings and shoes – so much more comfortable and practical than lounge suits.

Our predecessor, Dennis Page, was keen on amateur dramatics and produced several plays during the three years he was in Miri, and I was asked if I would like to have a go. I had never produced a play before but had done plenty of acting, so I said that as long as I could get someone to build the scenery and make the costumes, I would do it. Particularly as, being pregnant, I could not act.

I had a conference with Jim, and we decided to produce *'Dry Rot'*, one of the Whitehall farces, for which we had a script and which we felt would appeal to everyone. We put together a cast and rehearsed twice a week, from eight to ten after supper. Bill Findlay, who worked for the public works department, offered to build the scenery and built a superb set, and there were really no costumes to speak of, which made life easy. The only essential prop was a bowler hat with a hole in the brim, and this my father-in-law sent us by sea, having acquired it at the lost property office at King's Cross Station. We put the hole in the brim ourselves.

In 1962, the Miri resident was an old Rajah man called John Fisher who had been in Sarawak for many years and spoke fluent Malay and Iban. He had been dropped behind the lines in Sarawak during the war and spent it living in the jungle with the Dayaks, with whom he had a great rapport. I think they went Japanese headhunting together.

He knew everything that went on in his residency. I don't know whether or not he had bad feet, but John always wore open-toed sandals with no socks and khaki shorts. He used to turn up to greet VIPs at the airport, resplendent in his grand white drill uniform and solar topi with white plumage on top, and sandals. I don't think I ever saw him wear shoes.

I used to deliver secret and confidential documents to him at his office when the diplomatic bag came in from Kuching and always think of him sitting with his sandaled feet on his desk, sipping a cup of coffee. "Bung 'em in the safe," he would say, and I would open the door of the small safe he had in his room, and loads of buff envelopes, all marked 'Secret' tied up with red tape and seals, would fall out on the floor. I don't know if he ever opened any of them, but he seemed to know what was in them. *I* certainly never saw him open any.

I had not been working long when, in about November, we had the Brunei Rebellion. This was an insurrection organised by the Clandestine Communist Organisation (CCO), an outlawed mainly Chinese political party with affiliations to Indonesia, who, of course, own the rest of Borneo, called Kalimantan. The Indonesians were keen to get their hands on Brunei, Miri and Limbang, with its oil – preferably before Sarawak joined Malaysia. The rebellion, as such, came as a complete surprise to the authorities. Not so to John Fisher.

One morning, Fisher arrived at the bank and said to Jim, "Like to have a word with you in private, old boy! I'm going to ask you to do something very unorthodox. I need you to give me a loan of ten thousand dollars on a signed personal note – not a government one!" Poor Jim. Ten thousand dollars in 1962 was well over his unsecured overdraft limit.

"This is very secret information," said John.

"But I've received a phone call from a man saying he has some very important information for me – a matter of life and death – and asking me to meet him with ten thousand dollars in cash. So I would like you to go with me to meet him. We'll go in your car, as it is not as well-known as mine. Hope that is all right, old boy!"

Well, Jim knew that Fisher's word was his bond and that he would get the money back eventually. Jim gave him the money and drove John up to Well No 1. This was the first well sunk by Shell and was largely dry by now. However, it was of sentimental value and had a largish area cleared round it, with a notice on the rusty oil donkey, which still went up and down, telling 'tourists' all about the well. We often took Fergus there for a walk. It was surrounded by deep jungle, the sort that you go fifty yards into and get thoroughly lost.

They waited there for about ten minutes, and then a man appeared at the edge of the jungle. Fish got out of the car with the money and went to meet him. They talked for a while and then went into the jungle. After about half an hour, they reappeared, talked for a further minute, Fish handed over the envelope to the man, who promptly disappeared back into the jungle. Fish ambled back to Jim, and they drove back to Miri.

Fish was deeply perturbed – he told Jim that his informant had said that the next morning, there would be an armed insurrection. The CCO would invade Brunei, Kuala Belait, Seria, Miri and Lutong, simultaneously and take over all the Shell installations and the government. Fish did not know whether this information was genuine or not.

For extra security, Fish phoned Shell in Kuala Belait who pooh-poohed the idea and hinted he was drunk. He then phoned Kuching, who likewise scoffed at him and was dismissive of the whole idea. Eventually, he phoned his brother-in-law, who just happened to be Brigadier-General Walker, commander of the forces in Singapore, saying, "If you want to see your sister alive and safe, you had better send your boys across here tonight!"

He then sent a message to the government doctor, John Menon, via his chief clerk, asking him to come and see him urgently. John was in the middle of operating, and said to the chief clerk, "Must I come after this operation, or can I finish my list?"

Fisher replied, "Come as soon as you can!"

So, John abandoned his list and turned up at the district office to find Fisher with his feet on the desk. He said, "There's going to be an insurrection at four in the morning tonight, old boy. This is secret information."

John said, "What do you want me to do about it – can I tell the staff?"

Fisher said, "Well, you do what you like – either tell them and say they can choose to believe what I'm saying, or say, 'There's old John Fisher pissed again!" This is what Kuching was telling him. John returned to the hospital and got things ready for the reception of casualties. John's wife Mary was stuck in Kuching, where she had taken her eldest daughter, Jane, who had toothache as there was no decent dentist in Miri and John was left looking after the other two, Sara and Nicky. Nicky was two, Sarah four and Jane six.

Sure enough, the rebels arrived in Brunei the next morning. During the evening, it started to rain very heavily, with an accompanying electrical storm. Johannesburg is the only other place I have been where I have seen electrical storms to equal those in Borneo. The rain comes down in sheets. There are great rumbling crashes of thunder right above your head, and sheets of forked lightning zigzag into the ground. It is electrifying and can be very frightening – especially if you are out in it.

The first troops helicoptered into Lutong. It was too wet for a plane to land, and the airstrip was flooded. But they took off again and went on up to Kuala Belait, where the rebels had already landed. As the place was full of local characters, many are the tales told of the rebellion. Most of them are true – particularly the more farfetched sounding ones.

Communications at the beginning of the insurrection were terrible. No one in authority appeared to know what was going on. After the Green Jackets departed for Brunei, the commandos arrived from Singapore via the ship the *'Tiger'* and landed in landing craft, with difficulty at Lutong, all in assault gear with machine guns, just by the hospital.

They met the hospital staff going to work – "*Salamat tuan, apa baik?*" they called out to the commandos as they passed. "Good morning, sir, are you well?" The commandos had a doctor with them, who, of course, had no idea that we had a hospital at Miri with two master surgeons, one of them titled, and a highly qualified anaesthetist. John Menon asked him what he required, and the doctor asked if he could borrow the government hospital Land Rover with some supplies to take up to the *Ulu* (the interior). The answer was 'No', as the Land Rover would not get very far into the *ulu*! He would have to go by boat or walk.

Communications, as I said, were strange and unreliable, and there was no telephone contact with Brunei. John and the girls came for lunch, and John was bemoaning this lack of news. Jim said, "Let's try phoning the bank flat." He dialled the number and got straight through to Walter Dodgeon, our man in Brunei. "How's it going, Walter?" asked Jim. With much colourful language, Walter told us he was lying face down on the floor behind the sofa, as bullets were whizzing around the main street outside the flat. The line was crystal clear, and we could hear the bullets zinging round! Thereafter, we communicated through the bank for a few days until the rebels were defeated in Brunei. Miri was saved by the continuous rain, her tidal rivers letting the floodwaters flow into the sea, and John Fisher's information.

Though it rains all year round in Borneo, October is the start of the rainy season – the *Landas*, as it is called. This year, it rained and rained for weeks. Everything was damp, mould grew on shoes and I had a large mushroom growing on my sitting room wall. Up in the ulu, there were thirty-foot floods, and you could paddle along in a kungpit and pick the coconuts off the top of the palms. Miri was flooded in places, but because of the rivers, we were not too badly off, and it was dry on top of the Tanjong.

At the start of the rebellion, all women and children were told to pack a suitcase and keep it under the bed, ready to be evacuated to Singapore. This we did, but it was impossible for us to get out – except by helicopter. The sand road to Kuala Belait was impassable, and of course, the rebellion there was worse than in Miri. The airstrip was waterlogged, and no planes could take off or land. Shell diverted some oil tankers that anchored off the continental shelf to take us off, but it was so rough that no lighters could get out to the tankers. Behind us was the jungle, which is always impassable, so we were stuck.

As it happened, the biggest fright we had was about two weeks into the insurrection, when I received a frantic call from Jim. He said, "Get the Menon girls and anyone else on the Tanjong and go in the house and bolt all the doors; the rebels are in town."

Nicky and Sarah were with John at the hospital, and I was just closing our front doors when my neighbour, Pat Lewis, the field force officer's wife, came rushing in. "Come over to my house," she said. "We are all collecting there – the rebels are in town." Off we went, though I did wonder what we were going to do in her wooden house on stilts – thought we were safer in our large brick-and-mortar bungalow – though we had wooden front doors. There were about a six of us there with about a dozen children.

About half an hour later, Jim rang up to say that it was a false alarm – a loose shutter on one of the Chinese shophouses had banged in the wind and sounded just like machine gun fire. Within seconds, the town had cleared of people – just shows how jumpy everyone was. The wives all went back home.

About twenty minutes later, Jim appeared. "I've come for my fishing rod," he said.

"What on earth do you want your rod for in the middle of an insurrection?" I asked. "Surely, you're not thinking of going fishing!" He looked a bit sheepish and explained that when everyone had thought that the rebels were in town, he had shut and locked the iron grilling inside the strong room doors, flung his keys into the far corner of the room, through the bars, so that the rebels could not get them to gain entrance into the safe and then slammed the strongroom door shut! Now, of course, he had to try and retrieve the keys and thought the best way to do that was to attach a strong magnet to the end of the fishing rod, cast it between the bars of the strongroom and hope he could hook up the keys.

They were a huge bunch of keys, and we were the only bank in town. If he could not do that, he would have to contact Chubbs in London to send out one of their men to open the safe, which would not be too popular at head office – not to mention the fact that no one would be able to get any cash in Miri – perhaps for days.

Goodness knows how long it would take the Chubbs man to arrive, given the fact that the only way in and out of Miri was by army helicopter, and at that time, it took twenty-one hours to fly from London to Singapore. Luckily, Jim managed to hook the keys in a couple of casts.

I was still working at the beginning of the rebellion, and one of my tasks was to take the minutes of the meeting of the strategy committee, whose members included the colonel of the regiment, the resident, district officer, police superintendent, head of special branch, the manager of Shell and me. I recall, at about the third meeting, when the previous minutes were read out, the colonel saying, "That's not what I said!"

I opened my mouth to say, "Yes, it is!" and received a sharp kick in the shins from the district officer, who shook his head at me.

Later, I said indignantly to Gerry Parr, "He *did* say that!"

"Yes, I know," said Gerry. "But he's the colonel!" A lesson in diplomacy!

We had a procession of regiments in and out of Miri mopping up the rebels further up in the *ulu*. First, there were the Green Jackets, then the KOYLIs (King's Own Yorkshire Light Infantry) the Gurkhas, and then the Argyll and Sutherland Highlanders. They did not stay in town all that long but moved up and down the rivers.

Before they left, each regiment 'beat the retreat' in the middle of town. With the regimental band and the marching troops, all in their colourful uniforms, this was a wonderful sight for the local population, who had never seen such an impressive ceremony before, and besides being entertaining, it was a 'show of strength' for any would-be rebels who happened to be watching.

The army also organised a concert given by the singer David Whitfield of *'Cara Mia'* fame. We were all invited. It was a marvellous show, and he sang *'Cara Mia'* directly to me, who was vastly pregnant and sitting not far from the front, to my acute embarrassment and the great amusement of all the troops.

Everyone had a story to tell about the troops. There was the mad major in the Green Jackets, whose party trick, when drunk, was to kick a fridge to death with his steel-toed heavy army boots and then sit down and write out a cheque for a new one. He was not very popular when he did that to the fridge at the club, as, being Miri, not Singapore, it was difficult to supply another one immediately. He was posted out very quickly.

We lived next door to the education officer, Bernard Knight, and his wife, Amy. A very kind couple of about fifty. Amy was tall and thin, rather correct and a bit schoolmarmish. They asked some of the squaddies over for a Christmas drink and invited us to go along. As we came up the path, we heard her say to them "… and we've asked the bank manager and his wife to join us." I could almost hear the dismay that these young soldiers felt – what on earth were they going to say to a bank manager!

When we went in the door, there were about twelve young squaddies sitting on the edge of their seats, gingerly nursing glasses of sherry in Amy's best Waterford crystal glasses, and Amy was going round with the decanter, asking, "More sherry?"

I think they were very relieved to see that we were as young as they were, and even more so when they heard Jim ask for a beer. They quickly followed suit, and it was not long before they were telling me all about their experiences in the jungle, where they had stayed in Dayak longhouses.

Dayak women normally go stripped to the waist, and this obviously impressed one of them. He said they had a marvellous feast, with rice wine –tuak, which is about one hundred per cent proof – and all these bare-breasted beauties. "Cor," he said to me. "What an orgee! What an orgee!"

The press soon arrived and propped up the bar at the club, where they garnered most of their information – the exception being the American from *Time* magazine, who appeared hung about with cameras and chomping a large cigar. He got some money from Jim, hired a Dayak guide and disappeared up the *ulu*.

A couple of the forestry officers, known as Ivan the Terrible and Gerry Noales, appeared from out of the jungle where they had been directing a group of Ibans to fell trees across jungle paths to hold up the rebels and had rescued Tom Harrison, the Sarawak Museum curator, and his second wife from advancing guerrillas. A long article appeared in the papers about how the Harrisons had rescued Ivan and Gerry, with a picture of the wrong Mrs Harrison – Tom having been married twice. They were not amused.

In the middle of all this, we staged '*Dry Rot*', which was very popular, especially with the Chinese, who love slapstick. Shell management decided the play was just what they needed in Seria to take their staff's minds off the rebellion for a while. This was my first taste of the power of big business. We were to perform in Seria on Saturday evening, and by this time, it was late March and the baby's arrival was imminent.

So, Shell in Seria put on an extra flight on Saturday afternoon – the bank was open on Saturday morning – to take up the scenery and Jim and me. However, they did not think they could justify putting on a return flight on the Sunday (Jim had to open the bank on Monday morning) as the pilot would have to be paid about three times overtime or something. Instead, they provided a specially sprung Land Rover to take us back to Miri.

Alan Garside the Lutong refinery manager, terrified that I would have the baby in the middle of the jungle, drove us gingerly back from Seria down the potholed sand road with me sitting in the front seat. However, nothing happened, and I struggled on until the bitter end of the pregnancy, despite Jim driving me up the bumpy Riam Road several times to see if we could get things going.

Eventually, a very long and boring AGM of the Motor Club for which I was taking minutes, sitting on a hard wooden seat, started me off. The baby, our first son, Roderick, was born in Miri Hospital forty-eight hours later, on April 26.

We were lucky to be blessed with a wonderful government cottage hospital in Miri. As I said previously, we had two master surgeons, Sir James Fraser and John Menon, (who was also a newly qualified ophthalmic surgeon) who also delivered all the babies and was a regular jack of all trades and Dyson, the Shell doctor and anaesthetist. They were a great team.

John looked after me during my pregnancy, which meant he saw me once a month officially, and I was lucky that I had a very normal pregnancy. But it was extremely lonely. There were no antenatal classes as such. It was my first baby, and rightly or wrongly, I felt too shy to ask anyone anything – even John, or perhaps particularly John, who was such a good friend – without appearing extremely ignorant, which, having no medical background whatsoever, I was. Besides, I was quite terrified. However, all went well, in spite of me pushing almost from the word 'go' (courtesy of Hollywood) and wondering when the boiling water would appear (not quite – I wasn't *that* ignorant). I managed to get through it.

"What are you doing?" John asked me when he appeared on a visit to see me pushing away.

"Pushing," I replied.

"Oh my God!" he answered. "You don't have to do that yet – you've hours to go – you'll be worn out. Don't worry about it – you'll know when to push when the time comes." I did.

Five days after Roderick was born, he had an infantile convulsion. Fortunately, he was still in hospital, and it was spotted by one of the nurses. In those days, the mother and baby stayed in hospital for ten days. Being a new mother, I don't suppose I would have noticed as it was very slight. Roddy went on to have several more and stayed in hospital for the next six weeks until he had been clear of fits for ten days. It was a worrying time.

When the Pages left Miri, unfortunately, their houseboy and wife, who were extremely efficient, retired to Hong Kong, which left us without servants. These were not easy to replace, and we had a procession of Malay amahs who were not really satisfactory. However, soon after Roderick's birth, the Frasers returned to Britain, and their servants became available. They were a Chinese couple. Ah Choo was the amah – a black-and-white amah, who reminded me of Ah Soy in Hong Kong. She was fat, smiley and a good plain cook – and her '*laki*' or husband, who was slightly simple but an excellent gardener. He had green fingers and soon dug a plot beside the *depa,* where he grew Chinese vegetables with great success. I was so pleased to have Ah Chu, who took charge of Roddy with delight.

We had not done much gardening, apart from me sticking a lump of purple bougainvillea into the grass in front of the house, where it grew into quite a large bush within a few months. This always reminded me of Mother Antoinette, an old nun who taught me botany when I was at school at Loreto Convent, Darjeeling.

She walked with a stick and told us that one day she 'planted' her stick in the ground, and lo and behold, a miracle occurred, as after a time, up grew an enormous magnolia tree. Well, my bougainvillea stick was like that. After three years, it was enormous! Things grow quickly in the tropics. Apart from that, there was a trough at the side of the house, which we kept planted with flowers.

Not long after we arrived, Jim received a letter from an Australian, asking 'the manager' to send him some stamps for his collection. Jim obliged and, by return, the Australian sent him four packets of seeds. Two of these were for creepers – the cup and saucer plant and mina lobata, a short annual orange and yellow creeper – and two packets of seeds for 'Ortho Polka Zinnias'.

We emptied our trough, went to the beach and collected a load of seaweed in the car. This, we emptied into the trough after rinsing it with clear water, topped it with soil and planted the zinnias. Up grew the most amazing large striped flowers – I have never seen zinnias like them before or since.

Willie Geekie, who lived at the bottom of the Tanjong, had some wonderful orchids, and so did John Bagley's wife, who was a Dayak. John was the government mosquito eradication officer. When I asked her what she put on her orchids to make them so beautiful, she replied, "Water them with half a can of water and half a spend-a-penny!" She collected the urine in a closed Chinese egg jar, which she then filled with water to put on the plants. This treatment resulted in spectacular blooms.

One day, John Menon noticed that Judy had developed a large cyst on her side.

"*Hummm*," he said, and veterinary care being a bit patchy (viz her sterilisation), "Come down to the hospital on Sunday morning, and I'll cut it out!"

On Sunday morning, Jim, Judy and I went off to the hospital, to see John talking outside to Jamie Fraser and Keith Dyson. "Oh," they said when they heard of the problem, "we'll come and assist!"

Off they went – two MScs, a consultant anaesthetist and the patient, Judy the dog! About an hour later, when Jim and I were starting to wonder what was happening, they all staggered out, dragged along by Judy on her lead.

"We had trouble anaesthetising her," they said, "and managed to get a slight whiff of anaesthetic along the way." We departed with the lively patient.

"By the way," said John a week later, "I sent a specimen of that cyst off to the lab at Kuching for investigation as I didn't know what it was. I labelled it 'Miss Judy Kemp' – it's back benign!"

There was no television in Miri, so everyone made their own amusement. There was golf, sailing and special dinners and dances organised by the club committee. After producing the play, we decided to produce cabarets for these special nights instead of a full three-act stage production. I had a collection of musical skits and sketches which I had gathered before we were married in Calcutta and had been used in several rugby revues. These went down very well with the community and were easier to produce than a play, especially what with the rebellion, etcetra, many of the men spent a lot more time out of town – especially the government officers.

There was a Roman Catholic church in Miri, and we had our own bishop. He was a lovely man, Bish. Galvin, who had his own 'Papal Watchdog' – a monsignor from Rome! We also had a Dutch Jesuit, Father Schoor – quite a stern man – and Father Tommy, a shy, quiet and holy man. I sometimes went with Jim to church, but not often.

Bishop Galvin liked to spend most of his time up the *ulu*. He would disappear for months at a time (uncontactable except by a rather doubtful radio connection – no mobile phones in those days) with his religious paraphernalia in one case, and a large kit of medical supplies in the other, though I don't think he was a medic. Some of the Dyaks were Christians, mostly Catholics, or Seventh-day Adventists.

Our neighbour Willie Geekie, who was half Dyak, swore at the latter, as he said they prevented the locals from planting tobacco – one of their main cash crops – smoking being against the church. Instead of farming other crops, the locals just sat around. Bishop Galvin went far into the interior, first by Chinese launch, then by kungpit (dugut) and finally on Shanks' pony, until he came to the remotest of longhouses, where he dispensed religion and medicine in equal measure, as far as I can gather, and was universally looked up to and admired.

He was a very brave man who, in 1970, was one of the men who foiled the attempted assassination of Pope Paul VI at Manila International Airport on 27 November 1970. *'A veritable colossus of a man from Sarawak'*, the newspaper cutting said! I don't recall him as particularly tall, but that perhaps is because Filipinos are generally quite short. However, that was long after we knew him in Miri, where he came to dinner at the house and presented me with a lovely carved Dyak bowl, made out of the root of the billion tree – a very hard wood. I have it still, and it is one of my most prized possessions.

The Motor Club was really all about go-karting. This was when go-karts consisted of a steering frame with a seat and a lawnmower engine at the back. John Menon, Gay Dowson (an agricultural officer) and Jim owned one between them, which seemed to spend most of its time in bits on our garage floor. Every now and then, the club organised a race meeting in town. The T-shaped track went down the two main streets in the centre of town, which was closed to the public, and the monsoon ditches were bordered by straw bales for safety. The karts whizzed round and round the T for so many laps. The noise was horrific, but the locals loved the races and there was a fair amount of money riding on the winners of the race, as both the Chinese and Ibans liked a flutter.

Occasionally, Jim had to venture up the *ulu* (upcountry). Unfortunately, what with being pregnant and then with a young baby, I was never able to go. He went up by Shell launch, then kungpit, staying at a longhouse overnight. You slept upstairs in a communal room – families had their own places curtained off – on the floor, with the dogs, cats and fleas, whilst the chickens, pigs and other animals slept downstairs. Ablutions and toilet facilities were in the river, keeping a wary eye out for crocodiles and other nasties.

Breakfast was fried eggs, swimming in grease, on a tin plate, and tea with condensed milk. One of the little girls went down to the river to fill the kettle, which she did upriver, whilst taking advantage of the opportunity to squat and have a pee at the same time – still, I guess the water was boiled. Dinner was pork, washed down with arak or tuak – a kind of rice wine brewed on the premises in a large barrel. When you removed the lid, fermentation had been helped along by several *cheechaks* (house lizards), drowned mosquitoes and other stray bodies floating around on the top of the liquor. It was about ninety-eight per cent proof, which I guessed killed any germs and gave you a terrible headache the next morning. The Dayaks are very hospitable, and I guess he could have had a sleeping companion for the night if he so wished (apart from the dogs, that is).

On one occasion, Jim took the wife of one of the Shell doctors and a visiting friend up with him, and they had a very nasty experience on the return journey. The launch was out at sea when a nasty storm brewed up, and as the *serang* (captain) insisted on hugging the coast and refused to go further out to sea, the launch nearly capsized. I was at the pictures at the club when they got a radio message from the launch, and Ron Gribble the Shell manager, was very worried when he came over to tell me. He asked me whether I would like him to take me home, but I said no. I would prefer to stay and see the end of the film, there being nothing I could do about it. However, they all got home safely.

Sarawak joined Malaysia on 31 August 1963. Jim and I were at the ceremony to watch John Fisher take down the Union Jack and hoist the Malaysian flag. This was done to the tune of the new Malaysian and Sarawak national anthems, which were recorded on our tape recorder and played over the tannoy system.

We were in Miri for six months over our end of tour date, the bank having forgotten about us – "We thought you liked it there!" they said! We did but really needed our leave. By then, Roderick was nearly two years old. We packed up our trunks, bid a sad farewell to all our friends and flew off to Singapore to collect the flight back to Heathrow to be reunited with our parents, who were dying to see their latest grandchild.

At Singapore, we landed in the middle of a curfew, imposed by the government because of the 1964 race riots between the Chinese and Malays, caused by religious and political tensions, following Singapore's merger with Malaysia.

We were driven in a police-escorted bus to Raffles Hotel, where their emergency staff supplied us with dinner and breakfast the next morning, before we returned to the airport to catch the flight to Heathrow. So, you could say we had an eventful tour all round – never a dull moment. Did we attract trouble? we wondered. Our parents were very grateful to have us back without any further excitement.

CHAPTER 3
SINGAPORE (1965–1966)

We arrived in Singapore in 1965, after six months' leave in St Albans, and were met at Changi Airport by Peter and Varian Brown, from whom we took over.

The bank owned flats in a compound at Shelford Road, and we lived in one of these. There were three two-storeyed blocks of flats, each containing four spacious apartments, going round three sides of a large square compound, with a tennis court and a garden in the middle of the buildings.

The front door of the building led into a spacious hall, off which were the front doors into the ground-floor flats, one on either side of the hall, with a staircase leading up to the two second-storey flats. Each flat had two bedrooms with en-suite bathrooms, a large sitting/dining room, kitchen and two amah's rooms at the side of the dining room, a small entrance hall, bathroom and study with a door onto the veranda. We had a downstairs flat, which had a small private piece of garden just beyond our veranda. The flats were, as usual, well and comprehensively furnished.

However, we discovered the walls of our flat were 'live'. If you touched the sitting-room walls, you got an electric shock. On investigation, we found that the electric wiring for the flat, which had been recently rewired, had been rewired with cloth-covered flex plastered into the walls. It was not long before the cloth rotted, leaving bare wires in the wall. All that was removed, and the wiring was redone.

As well as the flat, we took over the Browns' two amahs, Yuet Sue and Ah Lan, who were both young and efficient. Yuet Sue was a good cook whose speciality was a gorgeous lemon meringue pie.

During our stay in Singapore, there were only four wives in the complex, two of whom were working. However, my neighbour, Maggie Turner, had two young children, one on either side of Roderick – Wendy, who was four, and Neil, who was two. Rod was three. Wendy, Neil and Rod were soon an item and played very happily together – either at

Maggie's flat or at ours. Most afternoons, Maggie and I would take the children either on an outing to somewhere like the Tiger Balm Gardens at Haw Par Villas, a picnic at the Botanic Gardens or swimming at the Tanglin Club.

Tiger Balm Gardens was a fantastic wonderland for children, with grottoes full of highly coloured painted Chinese mythical figures and scenes from Chinese mythology, folklore, legends and history. The garden had lots of steps to climb, as it was built on a hill, and huge, larger-than-life statues of tigers and mythical beasts children could clamber over and around. Best of all, it was free – built for the amusement of the citizens of Singapore by the fabulously wealthy Chinese millionaire, inventor of the famous Tiger Balm ointment, a cure for all ills.

A picnic at the Botanical Gardens was also very popular. We would take a cold drink and some sandwiches and drive down Cluny Road, which had monkeys living in the trees, into the spacious, wonderful gardens. My favourite spot was a grove of frangipani trees with their fleshy, velvety flowers – all colours – white, cream, red, pink, yellow, cream with yellow throats, all with the most heady and heavenly perfume.

The bank had some houses in Cluny Road – I remember the accountant's house was there. They were pestered by the monkeys, which were a great nuisance and terrible thieves. I remember once someone tried to deter them from coming into the houses by laying out some chocolate Brooklax – a type of laxative – in a couple of sandwiches for them. This had the desired effect and kept them away for a while, but gave them violent diarrhoea, so they left a fearful mess behind them. I suppose you could call it 'the monkey's revenge'.

Swimming at the Tanglin Club was also popular, but we would go to the pool in the late afternoon, so that when the requests for drinks, ice cream or chips came up, we could say we had to go and get Daddy and did not have time for a drink. Neither of us could afford to have a monthly bill for about Singapore forty dollars for ice creams.

One afternoon, as we were on our way out of Maggie's flat on one of these expeditions, Maggie suddenly took hold of Roddy's arm and jerked him down the last two steps – this was within the vestibule of the flats. Looking down, I saw a thin black snake like a shoelace lying on the inside of the step, looking balefully up at us. We screamed for the *kebun* (gardener in Malay), who came rushing in and killed the snake. That is the first and only time I have ever seen a snake in a house, in all my years in the East.

Of course, the kebun said it was poisonous, though I have no idea whether that was true, for to me, all snakes are poisonous, and I am afraid I don't take the time to see whether they have a curved or diamond-shaped head, which tells you which is which, or so my naturalist friends tell me. Just shows how much wildlife you can get in the middle of a city, though I would never dream of walking on the grass in the dark anywhere in the East – but this was in the middle of the day.

One night at about two a.m., Fergus, our Scottie, started barking madly. We both woke with a start, as it was most unlike him, and Jim went off to investigate. On the way to the front door, he picked up one of our heavy Indian silver candlesticks from the sideboard. "What are you going to do with that?" I asked him.

"Hit any would-be burglars!" he retorted.

"For heaven's sake, put it down! If you hit anyone on the head with that, you will probably kill them and land in gaol!" I replied.

He put it down, put all the lights on and went into the study to see what could be seen. Nothing! We made our way back to bed. However, the next morning, we discovered our neighbours had been burgled. The clever thieves had put chloroform through the air conditioning vent into the bedroom, jemmied the front door, gone into their bedroom, opened the wardrobe and taken all Alan's suits and his wife's evening dresses, plus her jewellery, and generally cleaned them out. At that time, this was a regular modus operandi for burglaries in Singapore.

On closer inspection, we discovered that someone had tried to jemmy the door from the veranda into the study in our flat but had failed. We must have disturbed them by putting on all the lights and generally making a noise. So Fergus had heard someone after all. I thought this was such a clever burglary. We gave Fergus an extra-large dinner that evening – we thought he deserved it.

Every Sunday, we went to Mass at a lovely modern church close by. I think it was called St Mary's, but I cannot remember. They had a children's Mass there at nine a.m. It was a very simply decorated church, and the children's service only lasted half an hour. There was a two-minute sermon, and a young nun called Sister Mary, who played the guitar, which was very novel in those days. The hymns were catchy, played to a fast modern beat, and everyone sang. Sister Mary was known as the Singing Nun and was quite famous in Singapore. It was very popular service, not least because of the short sermon.

The wooden altar rail was carved with the early Christian sign of a fish, interspersed with the round host, and we would go up to the choir loft so Roddy could look through the rails and get a good view of the service going on down below. The first time we went up, just before the Service started, he piped up in a carrying little voice, "Oh, look, Mummy!" pointing to the altar rail. "Fish and chips!" to the muffled amusement of the packed congregation.

At Christmas, the children put on a Nativity play. Before the play started, the Canadian Jesuit parish priest Father Robert Prendergast, warned the congregation, "Now, this play has no script. The children know the story, and they are going to act it out using their own words, so anything could happen."

All went well, until Mary and Joseph came to the inn and knocked on the door. The innkeeper came out – "Hallo," he said. Joseph explained how Mary was 'with child' and they needed somewhere to stay for the night – was there any room at the inn?

"Oh yes!" said the innkeeper expansively, "there's plenty of room – come right in!" The play ground to a halt.

"No, there's not!" said Mary.

"Yes, there is," said the innkeeper.

"There's not!" said Mary. "You're supposed to say there's not!"

"Is," said the innkeeper.

This went on for a few minutes until Father Robert eventually intervened and said to the Innkeeper, "You must say there's not!"

Mary stuck her tongue out at him. "Oh, very well," said the innkeeper grumpily. "There's no room here!"

Mary and Joseph marched off in triumph, and the innkeeper said in a loud whisper aside as they went off, "But there is really!"

I found Singapore large, impersonal and boring. Part of this was due to Jim's job at the time – he was in charge of the accounts department, which is a 'backroom boy' job. This meant he never met any customers. He worked very long hours, leaving the flat at about seven thirty in the morning and not reappearing until about six at night. It was also expensive, and we never seemed to have any money.

In an effort to placate me, he came home one night with a large television set. I was infuriated, telling him I would rather he came home at a reasonable hour than buy me televisions.

We were not in Singapore long before I became pregnant, so could not do any of the things I would normally have done – music or amateur dramatics.

I did, however, learn to drive at last. I had made a couple of half-hearted attempts to learn before – once in Hong Kong and once in Miri, but without success. I have never had any desire to drive, but now found that it was inconvenient and expensive to have to rely on taxis all the time, especially as I wanted to take Roddy swimming and on outings, so decided I had better seriously try to learn. I was very nervous about getting behind the wheel.

I had lessons with a very patient young Singaporean Chinese man, and when I was about seven months pregnant, I sat my test. Singapore has always had a very good but strict driving test. First, you had to pass a written/oral test, which, as well as questions on the Highway Code, included the examiner setting a board on a table with roads drawn on it and toy cars. He would place these in different positions on the board – at crossroads or roundabouts, and ask which had the right of way, etc. Only once you had passed this were you allowed to take your practical.

The practical test ended in the middle of Chinatown, where you could only go at about 10 mph and included backing into a parking space between four posts, with a monsoon ditch on one side. Should you touch a post (or go into the ditch), you failed the test. I was so enormous I could just squeeze behind the wheel. By some miracle, I passed. I think the examiner must have been petrified that if I did not pass, I would have the baby on the spot.

Once I was able to drive, Roddy and I used to take Jim to work in the morning so we could have the car for the rest of the day. I was terrified on the roads. I did not realise how terrified until one afternoon on the way to the Tanglin Club, Roddy shouted out of the window to a man peacefully overtaking us on his scooter, "Stupid idiot!" much to the man's surprise, causing him to nearly fall off his scooter. I realised that I had been muttering under my breath all the time I was driving around. However, I soon got over my terror and was whizzing around in our British racing-green Austin 1100.

On 9 August 1965, Singapore seceded from Malaysia to become an independent sovereign state. The separation was the result of deep political and economic differences between the ruling parties of Singapore and Malaysia, creating communal tensions that resulted in racial riots in July and September 1964. Despite dire prophecies as to how she would never be able to go it alone, Singapore has gone from strength to strength.

At about ten o'clock one night just before the baby was born, I had a terrible yearning for a Mars Bar. "Oh!" I said to Jim, "I'll never be able to sleep unless I have a Mars Bar."

So he got the car out, and off we went driving round Singapore looking for Mars Bars at ten at night. This proved difficult. Eventually, we found a cinema kiosk open near the bottom of Shelford Road that sold Mars Bars. Jim bought me six.

I think it only took us ten minutes to get back to the flat, and as we drew up, Jim said to me, "I'll have one of your Mars Bars."

"What Mars Bar?" I asked – I had eaten the lot. I didn't even really like Mars Bars.

Early in August, Jim rang me from the office to say we had been posted to Penang as soon as his work permit came through, and to start packing. I said I would not start packing until he got his work permit, and just as well. The months rolled on, and at last, it was January when the baby was due. I went into Mount Alvernia Hospital and had the baby on January 6th.

Mount Alvernia Hospital is run by the Franciscan Missionaries of the Divine Motherhood order of Catholic nuns. I remained in hospital for five days this time and had ante natal classes run by a lovely young nun physiotherapist, called Sister Crucifixion. What an apt name for a physio! When I had Roddy in Miri, there were no ante-natal classes, so this was something new for me.

As Roddy had had infantile convulsions, I spent all my time in the labour ward, telling the doctor to watch out for the convulsions as they are hereditary. I had a lovely little girl, seven pounds eight ounces, and we called her Mhairi (pronounced 'Varee') Vivienne.

Five days later, I brought her home. As I was feeding her that evening, she had a seizure and turned navy blue on me. I quickly called Maggie Turner, who was an ex-nurse. She called the hospital, and back the baby went. She was in hospital for a further ten days. She had to be free of fits for five days before she was allowed to come home. Apparently, she had had a convulsion in the labour room, but the doctor had put it down to too much mucus. I was not pleased.

Mhairi was due out of hospital on the Saturday. On Friday night, Jim rang up to say his permit had come through, and we were due in Klang (not Penang) on Tuesday! Klang is a town some twenty-five miles out of Kuala Lumpur. So, on Saturday morning, we had the packers in and the new baby out of hospital. It was quite stressful.

We also had to see whether our Scottie, Fergus, could travel with us. To do this, he had to have an exit permit from Singapore and an entry permit into Malaya, two newly separated countries. Off we went to the agriculture department in Singapore and got an exit permit for Fergus within about ten minutes, but when we said we had to get an entry permit into Malaya within the same time, they laughed at us.

We drove to the Singapore/Malaya border at Johore Bahru and asked to see the vet from the agriculture department. "What for?" they asked. We explained.

"He is on holiday," they said.

"Well, can we see his deputy?" we asked.

"No, only the vet can give the permit," the police said. "Anyway, why are you worrying – put him in the back seat with a blanket over him and bring him through." So, of course, we dared not do so, just in case we were stopped and Fergus was discovered crouching under a blanket.

So, Fergus was left behind to travel by air at vast expense to Kuala Lumpur. Jim, Rod and I got in the car with the baby in her basket in the back seat, and off we set for Klang on Tuesday morning.

It was a long, hot drive – our Austin 1100 was not air-conditioned – and we were very worried about whether the baby would have another fit. However, she didn't, and we arrived in Klang tired but all well. When we got there, the Cordens, whom we were taking over from, said, "Oh, you needn't have hurried; we are only going down the road to Seremban." I was speechless!

CHAPTER 4
KLANG (JANUARY 1966–1968)

I loved Klang (now called Kelang). We lived in a flat on the roof of the bank building, right in the middle of town. The branch was built in 1808 on the corner of the main crossroads going out of town from Kuala Lumpur to Port Swettenham (now called Port Kelang), on the corner of Jalan Istana and Jalan Hamza. '*Jalan*' means 'road' in Malay. The bank building is now part of the 'Klang Heritage Site', because of its distinctive features, especially the four Dutch-style gables.

It was a two-storey building, with two flats on the first floor. We lived in the bigger flat, the slightly smaller one being unoccupied whilst we were there. It was a massive, L-shaped flat, with large rooms and very high ceilings.

To enter the doorway to the flat, you drove off the street onto a small parking lot, in front of the garage at the side of the building.

The garage was originally part of the stables. There was a wrought iron gate on the right of the car park as you faced it, which led into an L-shaped garden full of rows of ground orchids, going round what used to be the stables and the back of the building, the ground floor of which was now storerooms. The servants' quarters were on top of the stables at the back. An archway led from the parking lot down by the storerooms to a staircase up to the back of the top floor, and a small, discreet doorway on the other side of the archway led into the flat.

Inside the door, there was a large, black-and-white-tiled floored inner hall, with a staircase leading up to the flat and a side door going into the manager's office. This was great, as Jim just went downstairs and through the door to work, and for the first time since we had left Miri, he could come home for lunch.

Upstairs, there was a smaller hall-cum-passageway, leading into the sitting/dining room, which straddled the length of the flat, with a door leading off the hall into the pantry and kitchen. A door also led into the pantry from the dining room.

Beyond the lounge, a veranda ran round the rest of the flat with a four-foot-high, pillared balustrade, which looked down into the street. One arm of the veranda had a couple of bedrooms with bathrooms leading off it, and it bellied out at the corner of the L into a veranda sitting room/study. This had a desk in it, which I used for writing letters and sorting out my stamp collection. You could look over or through the balustrade onto the crossroads and see everything that was happening in the town.

I was the only one who ever sat on this veranda, which I did in the mornings, when I was working at the desk. Being open, it was extremely dusty and noisy. The smaller arm of the L led round the corner to the very large master bedroom suite. All the back doors of the bathrooms opened out onto the *godown* roof behind the flats.

The bathrooms were extremely antiquated, with large claw-footed iron baths. The floors were of red quarry tiles, and the toilet was built up on a red quarry-tiled throne. There was a grilled drainage hole in the floor by the bath to get rid of the water. A few mothballs placed on this grill prevented cockroaches and other unwanted creepy-crawlies from coming up the drain.

The flats went round two sides of the roof. The central area, which was the roof of the bank *godown* (warehouse) underneath, was glass and built up into a sort of glass point. There was a broad walkway all around the roof, which we used as a roof garden. An open drain ran all the way around, allowing the torrential monsoon rain to fall away.

Outside the kitchen back door, the roof garden was connected by a covered bridge/walkway to what used to be the first floor of the stables, presumably originally the grooms' quarters, and now the servants' quarters. There were a lot of rooms, so the servants had plenty of space. Our staff lived in some style!

When we first moved in, there was no entrance from the house to the garden. You had to go downstairs, across the car park and into the garden via the locked wrought iron gate. After we had been there a while, Jim had a staircase built going from the back of the servants' quarters directly into the garden, so that the children, dog and I, did not have to cross the car park which was always packed during banking hours and could be quite dangerous with irate, hot, sticky customers looking for a parking space.

I loved the flat, though our Chinese friends often asked if I got 'a bad feeling' from it, the bank having been the Kempetai headquarters during the war. Prisoners were taken up to the flats for questioning – and possibly tortured. However, I never experienced any bad vibes, thank goodness, and fortunately did not learn about this until we had lived there for some time, or my imagination could well have run riot.

We had a lovely Chinese couple to look after us, thin and wiry Ah Poon, the cookboy, who was in his fifties, his plump, smiley wife, Ah Choo, and a young baby/wash amah, Ah Lan, who I think, was Ah Choo's niece.

Ah Poon was a good cook. It was difficult to find out exactly what his specialities were, as when you asked him what he cooked, he would reply, "What you like, mem?"

One of my friends, Nancy Cunningham, told me that he cooked a lovely *coq au vin*, but when I asked him, he shook his head and said firmly, "No!"

"Yes, yes," I replied. "Mem Cunningham, she tell me you make number one *coq au vin*."

"No," he said.

I then explained, "Yes! First you cut chicken, then make brown, then put in pot with vegetables and wine to cook."

"Oh!" he replied scornfully. "Mem mean chicken estoo in wine! Why you not say!" It was delicious!

We lived next door to the Istana – the Sultan of Selangor's palace – which was on a hill surrounded by a lovely, large, grassy *padang* (a large lawn), open to the public. Ah Poon loved taking Roddy there after tea either to play football or to fish in the monsoon ditch for tadpoles. Off they would set with Ah Poon in his natty navy blue shorts and white shirt. Navy shorts, according to him, were only worn by Tuan Besars – big bosses – and Roddy in his shorts and T-shirt with a football and fishing net. "Come, Loddy," he would say. "We go! Play football." They would appear an hour or so later with a couple of jam jars full of tadpoles and other ditch life. I don't know who enjoyed themselves more, Ah Poon, or an often reluctant Roddy.

We also had a Tamil kebun (gardener) called Pitchay. Pitchay was officially employed as the bank sweeper, the garden being his subsidiary job. He loved growing orchids – he was not really interested in anything else, but his eyes lit up at the sight of a new orchid – and once he knew we were both interested in gardening, the bank's bill for manure quadrupled overnight. When we first arrived, there were only a couple of rows in the garden, plus a huge purple bougainvillea tree in the middle of the lawn. Jim bearded Pitchay, who was a bit of a character. "Call yourself a gardener," he said in Malay.

"There's nothing in the garden."

"Ah tuan," said Pitchay. "That is because Tuan Corden would not give me any manure. He said it was too expensive."

"Well," said Jim, "how much do you need and how much will it cost?"

"One buffalo cart a month, tuan, and it will cost five dollars."

"Okay," said Jim, "but I expect to see lots of flowers in future."

Pitchay grinned from ear to ear. *"Bunyak bagus, tuan!"* he said. "Very good, sir!" One bullock cart soon grew into a few more.

Within a few months, the garden was a picture – things grow very fast in Malaya. The bougainvillea tree was in almost constant bloom, and Pitchay planted row upon row of ground orchids – the common or garden purple Vanda, the white Diana, red Singapura, the striped tiger and spider orchids. The house was full of them, and I supplied all my friends, much to Pitchay's delight. I understand he also had a thriving local business selling orchids for weddings and other local occasions. I did not really mind, as long as I had plenty for the house and to distribute to my friends whenever I wished. He inspired me to start collecting orchids, and I began collecting hanging orchids. We soon had them hanging all over the bougainvillea and transferred them to the roof garden when they were in bloom. Knowing we would not be in Klang for longer than three years, I refused to pay more than five dollars for an orchid, but that bought me a lot of the more common dendrobiums, and we had a good collection of Lady Hamiltons and White Foam crosses, and my friends would give me some of their orchid *anaks* (babies) once they knew I was interested.

The main garden became a tourist attraction, as you could see the tops of the rows of orchids over the wall and through the wrought iron gate. Tourist buses going from Port Swettenham to Kuala Lumpur would often stop, park in the car park to the annoyance of the bank customers and ask if the passengers could have their picture taken outside the gate. The garden has now been dug up, and there are tall buildings at the back. How sad – but that's progress for you.

The bank flat was very cool. Only the bedrooms were air-conditioned. The sitting room-cum-dining-room was very large and airy, with huge windows looking onto the street and windows at the back of the dining room looking onto the roof garden, so there was a through draft.

The lounge was furnished with a big, heavy three-piece suite. The frame was made of solid teak, with cushioned back and seats. The wide wooden arms of the suite were partitioned down the sides into little shelves – one for your drink, one for your book, one for your ashtray, (most people smoked in those days), one for your glasses, etc. – very practical and very ugly.

I understand it was custom-built and designed after the war, by the then manager, who had two artificial legs, so that he did not have to continually get up and down but had everything he wanted within easy reach. It took two people to move any of the chairs, and the three-seater settee was even heavier. However, as it was the type of suite that would never wear out, we were stuck with it. The floors were polished wood, with a big beige Indian carpet in the middle of the lounge. Two large columns formed an arch dividing the dining room from the sitting room.

There were two cats in residence when we arrived, and though we told our predecessors that there was no way we could keep them as our Scottie killed cats, they left them anyway. No sooner had Fergus arrived than they disappeared, and despite Ah Poon leaving food by the servants' quarters for them, we never saw them again.

The evening after Fergus arrived from Singapore, we were sitting watching television, which was in the corner of the lounge, and I said to Jim, "The mosquitoes are terrible tonight. I'm being badly bitten." When I looked down at my legs, my feet and ankles were covered with black fleas, and the dog was scratching crazily. The fleas must have been on the cats and gone into the cracks between the floorboards to breed. Once the cats had gone, they transferred themselves to us. I had always understood that dog and cat fleas do not go onto humans, but I can assure you that they do. The lounge was full of them. The pest control was in the next day, fumigated the place, and no more fleas.

We had been in Klang a couple of days when Jim rang and said, "Come on down – I have someone here who would like to meet you." Down I went to the office, to be met by a large man with a lived-in face and black curly hair. "Noreen, this is Reg Collins," said Jim.

Reg looked me up and down, and I could hear him thinking, "She could be a bit thinner!" – but I had just had a baby!

He said, "*Humph*! Riona and I are having a dinner party tonight, as I'm thinking of producing a play – come along!"

We duly went along, met Riona, Tony Blumer, who worked for Guthrie Bousteads, managing an agency house, and John Bolland, a rubber planter. After dinner, we read John Osborne's *'The Entertainer'*. When we had finished, Reg asked us what we thought of the play. A bit depressing was the general opinion, including Riona's. "Well," said Reg, "I've cast it now, and we'll be producing it at the Klang Club in eight weeks' time." And we did.

The Klang Club had seen better days. During the 1950s and earlier, t had been a lively planter's club, but with the fall in the price of rubber andMalayanisation, there were not that many expatriate planters left. Many of the rubber estates were defunct, and others were going over to oil palm. Reggie was chairman (or was it president?) of the club and planned to regenerate it.

He had already overseen the opening of a new restaurant called 'The Smugglers Inn', which he hoped would be patronised by people from Kuala Lumpur as well as local Klang people. The decor of the restaurant was quite atmospheric, with fishing nets and floats, lobster pots and all things seafaring hanging on the walls, seafaring pictures and subdued lighting. However, it was not making much money, and the club was still in the red. Reg hoped to draw in a crowd with good-quality theatre and dinner nights and having had a taste of the restaurant and the newly refurbished club, perhaps Kuala Lumpur society would patronise it.

The Klang Club was on two floors, the restaurant and bars downstairs, and on the top floor, a sprung ballroom, complete with stage. *The Entertainer* was an easy play to stage – only one set required. Reggie enrolled Leslie Atkinson, a well-known local pianist and teacher in Kuala Lumpur, who played for the local opera society, as musical director. The stage badly needed reflooring, and Jim and Reggie enlisted the help of some local timber merchants (for free wood) and contractors.

We soon had a new stage and a removable raked auditorium built. This was made of differently sized platforms, which could be easily moved, and the room cleared for use as a ballroom again. We had a little stage lighting – a follow spot and some basic foot and ceiling lighting, and that was it. We ran for three nights to full houses, and the play was a great success, especially after we got a good crit in the *Straits Times* and the *Malay Mail,* and the Klang Theatre Workshop was born.

Our next production was *'Billy Liar'*, by which time we had acquired better lighting and new chairs for the auditorium. Finally, we staged Brendan Behan's *'The Hostage'*. This time, we played for a whole week with a cast of twenty and now had a superb little theatre, with some very sophisticated lighting and the beginnings of a wardrobe. Aspiring actors from Kuala Lumpur now wanted to join the cast, and the audience were certainly coming out to Klang for the evening.

One of our members and co-producer was a young Frenchman called Francois Bocquet, a pupil of the famous French mime artiste Marcel Marceau, a gifted performer, who taught us all a lot of stage craft. I'm not sure how he landed up in KL, but he was brought along to the workshop by Reggie, who was half French and probably met him at the French Consulate. I guess Francois must have been on the hippie trail around Southeast Asia and, having met Reg, decided to stay in KL for a while. It was fascinating to watch Francois getting out of an imaginary cardboard box. Unfortunately, our tour ended after this production, but the Klang Theatre Workshop went from success to success.

When we did *The Entertainer,* I asked Leslie if he knew of a good singing teacher in KL. He certainly did and put me in touch with an English lady called Kathleen Beveridge. I drove up to Jalan Ampang every Tuesday morning for lessons with her. She lived at the far end of Ampang Road, a very long street in KL.

I would drop Rod off at school just before nine o'clock and beetle down the Federal Highway to reach Kathleen's house just before ten. Have my lesson, then race back down the highway to be back in Klang before noon in order to collect Roddy from school. The journey took me an hour door to door. Jim's customers used to say to him, "Saw Noreen driving fast down the highway this morning, going somewhere in a hurry."

Kathleen really taught me how to sing. In two and a half years, she doubled the size of my voice, enlarged my repertoire, taught me to sing in Italian, German and French, and showed me how to interpret and analyse a song. As there was no music shop in KL and the only lieder book I had was for a soprano/tenor (I was a mezzo contralto), I had to transpose most of my lieder into a lower key, writing the music out by hand. This was a laborious and painstaking task and very good for me.

As well as being a gifted teacher, Kathleen was a most accomplished singer. She had a very clear light soprano voice and was a consummate musician. I remember hearing her perform Arnold Bax's exquisite *'Cradle Song'* at a concert in KL. When the last note of the song died away, there was a deep, lingering silence in the concert hall, which is, I think, the ultimate accolade for any performer. You could have heard a pin drop. She was accompanied by Elinah Ahmed, a Malay lady who was one of the official accompanists for the Royal Academy in London when she studied there and was now married to Tunku Ahmed, one of the Malay princes. She was a most sympathetic and wonderful accompanist. She breathed with you. Elinah played for all our concerts.

I loved my lessons, and they were never long enough. At the time, there were several good classical singers in KL, most of whom were pupils of Kathleen, and the standard of music was very high. I had opportunities to sing the alto solos from the Christmas Oratorio, lots of lieder – especially Brahms, Italian opera, English art songs and at one memorable concert, sang the whole of Elgar's *Sea Pictures*, which was very satisfying.

We had no piano in Klang, but our neighbours Joan and George Labrooy, had one, and they kindly let me use it. Their bungalow was next door to the bank, so I would go over most mornings to practice. Granny Labrooy and her friend Miss Jans, who lived with the Labrooys, would be there. I would stay for an hour, do my exercises and the rest of whatever I was studying, but always end my practice with some Victoriana or Negro spirituals for them, as I knew they liked those. The Labrooys also collected orchids and had a wonderful garden full of them. Joan was our doctor, and George owned Caxton Press, a printing business in Klang.

We made many good friends: Nancy and Bill Cunningham, from Midlands Estate, who had two little girls, Anne and Margaret; Winnie and Bill Brown who had two slightly older girls and had come to Klang from Cochin, worked for Harrisons & Crosfield; Tony and Mary Blumer, who had two boys; and Colin and Cathy Davy, who had two girls. There were also two lots of Jenkins, who had four children between them and many more.

There were quite a few couples with children the same age as Rod. During the school holidays, Nancy and I ran a playgroup for three mornings a week at the bank flat to keep the children entertained. It was hard work, trying to hold their attention from nine to twelve, but it kept Rod, Anne and Margaret from getting bored at home.

We had many Chinese friends too, amongst whom were the Yeoh Tiong Lays and the Yap Chin Leongs. Tiong Lay was then a medium-sized building contractor, and Chin Leong a builder who specialised in building wooden houses. The six of us would often go for dinner at the Federal Hotel in KL, where we always sat near the band – a lovely table, but very noisy and not always conducive to conversation. Of course, Tan Sri Dato Dr Yeoh Tiong Lay (as he later became) went on to become one of Malaysia's foremost businessmen, and his firm, YTL, is now a large family international conglomerate, with many and varied interests. We remained good friends and in contact with both the Yaps until they died and the Yeohs, long after we retired, are still in contact with the family. It was not always easy staying in touch, considering the peripatetic type of life which we led.

There was a lovely small kindergarten in Klang, which all the children attended – I suppose there must have been between fifty to one hundred children at it, both local and expatriate. They had a sports day every year and always started the day with a march past of the children. The first year Roddy was there, he trudged round the square playground during the parade, all hunched over to one side. "What was wrong with you in the parade?" I asked him later. "You were marching round all hunched to one side."

"Oh yes, Mummy," he replied. "I had to go round like that, you see, so I could go round the corners." There's really no answer to that.

As we lived in the middle of town, there was always something to see from our corner veranda. Most Saturday mornings, there would be a funeral procession down the main street, past the bank. Rod and I would rush to the veranda to see it pass when we heard the band playing, Rod sitting on the floor looking through the space between the pillars of the wall and I hanging over the top of the balustrade.

If it was a large Chinese funeral, it was always quite spectacular. There would be the hearse with the coffin, surrounded by the professional mourners dressed in white Ku Klux Klan-type robes, with hoods, and sackcloth over their shoulders, the band, men walking on stilts, others carrying models of fully furnished houses, models of cars, false money and whatever else his family thought the deceased would need whilst he was in the netherworld. When we asked Roddy what he would like for his fourth birthday, he replied, "A Chinese funeral." I said I did not think we could afford one, as they are extremely expensive – would a pirate's party do instead?

I enlisted the help of Nancy Cunningham, and we cut out pirate trousers (sewn by Nancy, as I'm no needlewoman), waistcoats and bandannas and scarves for the children – only the trousers needed sewing. I think there were about ten children, and we all had a wonderful time. We went down into the garden and played all the old nursery games of my youth, which were unknown to the little guests. As well as Pass the Parcel and a Treasure Hunt, we played Blind Man's Buff, Pin the Tail on the Donkey, Farmer's in His Den, I Sent a Letter to My Love (which ends in a chase), Oranges and Lemons (ending in a tug of war), Here We Come Gathering Nuts 'n May, and all the old favourites. The children loved all the games. I wonder why they are not played today.

Malaysia has a lovely array of local holidays. As well as *Hari Raya* (Eid – at the end of Ramadan), there was Christmas and Easter, Chinese New Year, Thaipusam (a South Indian festival), Diwali (Hindu New Year and the Festival of Lights), and my favourite, the Chinese mid-autumn Mooncake or Lantern Festival. This festival is celebrated with a family get-together, eating mooncakes, and a lantern parade. I always went to Petaling Street in downtown KL to buy a couple of Chinese lanterns.

Petaling Street was the most fascinating street in KL. A narrowish street in the middle of Chinatown, lined with shophouses with multi-coloured electric signs hanging up outside the shops, packed with street hawkers pushing barrows, shouting their wares, selling all sorts of satay, Chinese snacks and a myriad of T-shirts, souvenirs, haberdashery, cheap toys and lanterns for the festival. These beautiful lanterns are made of multi-coloured cellophane paper in all sorts of shapes and sizes.

There were ships, planes, all sorts of animals and flowers. I remember buying a butterfly for Mhairi and a wonderful fire-breathing dragon for Rod, which lasted for two years! All the lanterns had holders inside them where you placed a lighted candle. Nancy, Ann and Margaret came for tea, and once it got dark, the children all lit their lanterns, and we all paraded round and round our roof garden.

Thaipusam is also a spectacular festival but in a different way. This is a South Indian Hindu festival in honour of Lord Murugan, god of war and a son of Shiva, which is celebrated by Tamils and some Keralites, and culminates in a day of penance and prayers. It commemorates the occasion when Parvati, Shiva's wife, gave Murugan a special spear or '*vel*' so he could vanquish the evil demon Soorapadman. Preparations start forty-eight days before Thaipusam, during which followers cleanse themselves of all mental and physical impurities by observing penances such as control of the senses, complete fasting or eating only one simple vegetarian meal a day or fruit and milk. Many shave their heads and go on a pilgrimage to the temple at Batu Caves in Kuala Lumpur, carrying *kavadis* (burdens) which they offer to the god.

For weeks before the festival, *kavadi* carriers observe celibacy. During the ordeal, many experience a state of trance. The most common *kavadi* is a pot filled with milk, carried on one's head, but there are also impressive bamboo structures shaped like a peacock or chariot, ornamented with symbols evocative of Murugan. Some are heavy structures many feet tall.

After these preparations, *kavadi* carriers may ask a priest to pierce their bodies with small spears, usually through the cheeks and tongue. Other acts of penance include walking on hot coals and wearing nail shoes. There is no blood. I do not know why. An ornate chariot of wood and silver is built for the god and pulled with huge ropes by his followers from the heart of the city to the shrine at the Batu Caves, fifteen kilometres away. This takes eight hours and ends with the god being carried up two hundred and seventy-two steps to the shrine inside the cave.

Each Christmas, the Klang Club held a children's fancy dress party. Every year after Roddy was born in Miri, I used to make a gold fairy castle out of cardboard boxes, vim tins, etc., for the house. When we were in Klang, we enlarged that for the club and made an enormous silver one that took up most of the stage. Both Christmases, we were there, Roddy won first prize at the fancy dress – first as a clown and then as *Gigantor*, who was a Japanese robot on TV. Mhairi was toddling around at the second Christmas and went as a rosebud, a costume made at the local dressmakers. George Labrooy made the *Gigantor* costume out of cardboard boxes painted silver – it was not very user friendly, and Rod just wore it for the parade.

The Davy children also used to win prizes – one year Siobhan went as a sugar lump, which was very imaginative – she was standing in a large cardboard box painted white, suspended from her shoulders with white ribbons – she was Rod's age. Most of the fancy dress costumes were discarded right after the parade in favour of the cooler, more comfortable shorts and T-shirts and party dresses, which allowed the children freedom to charge around the ballroom.

The Sultan of Selangor's son was in Roddy's class at school, and the whole class was asked to his birthday party at the *Istana* (children only). We drove up, and Roddy, normally the friendliest of children, suddenly decided he did not want to go. Eventually, I left him with the Tuanku Ampuan, the Sultan's wife, wailing down her well-upholstered front. "You go," she said. "He will soon be all right!" He was and thoroughly enjoyed the party.

St Andrew's Night and Burns' Night are usually celebrated with gusto by expatriate Scots, of whom there were many in Kuala Lumpur. The sultan always attended both celebrations, where there would be Scottish country dancing and haggis (courtesy of BOAC) in November, and all the ritual of the Burns supper (haggis again) in January. A piper would pipe the haggis in for the supper, setting it before the chieftain, who would stab it and recite Burns' poem *'Address to a Haggis'* before pouring whisky all over it.

His Highness also attended the St George's Day celebration in April, and the last year we were there, Tony Blumer, who was organising the dinner, decided he was going to get up a team to do some Morris dancing, which he did. Jim was one of the dancers. This was, unfortunately, for men only, as I would have loved to have had a go.

They learnt about four dances for the evening, including a sword dance and a handkerchief dance, which they rehearsed to tapes, until one evening, Tony appeared with a fifteen-year-old American boy, the son of the American consul, who was an accomplished fiddler. He listened to the tape and picked up the tunes within minutes and played for the dancing. At the dinner, the dancing took everyone by surprise – no one in Kuala Lumpur had ever seen Morris dancing before, and it was a sensation. His Highness was absolutely fascinated by the whole display.

On another fund-raising dinner at the Klang Club, we had a striptease show – the artiste being Annie Chia, a well-known local stripper and a pupil of Rose Chan of Penang fame, who I think, did her act with a python. Annie, unfortunately, didn't have a python but gave us a first-class show. She was booked for the club by the wife of one of the local doctors, also a doctor, Dr Chan. The Theatre Workshop had, by that time, acquired a blue spotlight, and Jim had the arduous task of climbing up to the rickety lighting platform to operate it. I'm told he had the best seat in the house.

The evening started at The Smugglers with dinner, then up to the theatre for the show. The ballroom was packed, and Annie was horrified when she discovered half the audience were women. Panicking, she told Dr Chan she would perform a censored version of her show. No, she would not, said Dr Chan, if she wished to be paid! So we had the full unexpurgated version, which I found to be very educational and an unforgettable experience. Annie was a first-class entertainer, and it was one of the most successful evenings the Klang Club had had for many a year.

About halfway through our tour, we lost Fergus, our Scottie, who suddenly started having fits. First, just occasionally, and then repeatedly, one after the other. No one knew what caused them. His fur became lank and stringy, his eyes dull, he did not eat and was plainly very distressed and unhappy. We took him to see the vet in Petaling Jaya, and unfortunately, he had to be put to sleep. We were all very upset, as he was only seven, and decided that we would not have any more dogs. Moving around as we did, it was very expensive and not very fair to the animal, who in some places had to do quarantine – we would just look after dogs for people who were going on Home leave and return them afterwards.

But, we reckoned, a cat was different. It more or less went with the house. So, we acquired an adult Siamese cat, which Roddy called Martin – I don't know why! Martin was a large, very good-looking seal point Siamese – very affectionate, and more like a dog than a cat.

We had Martin for a few months, and he seemed very happy with us, and wandered freely around the house, roof garden and garden, but one day, he just disappeared. Despite hunting everywhere for him, and putting up notices, etc., he just vanished into thin air, and we never saw him again. I can only surmise that perhaps a passerby saw him, and Malays in particular being very fond of cats, took him home with him. I hope so anyway. We then decided not to have any animals for a while, as we all got so upset when we lost them.

The bank had a holiday bungalow in Port Dickson in Negri Sembilan – an adjoining state to Selangor – for its officers, which was rotated round the officers. When it came to our turn, we would go there for a long weekend together with another family – say the Cunninghams – so that the children had someone to play with and the adults could have a bit of a break.

The bungalow had, I think, three bedrooms and a resident cookboy and amah, so you did not have to take lots of provisions with you. It was about an hour and a half from Klang – a hot and sweaty journey – as our cars were not air-conditioned in those days. The children enjoyed playing on the beach, but I remember the mosquitoes in the evening were large and vicious, so you had to ensure you took plenty of mosquito coils with you and smothered yourself with an insect spray called 'Peaceful Sleep' – a South African product, which was extremely effective. Oil of citronella is effective too, but as I discovered in the house, if you put it on your arms and then leant on the teak arms of the sitting room suite, it took the varnish right off the wood, so I can only wonder what that did to your skin! I am not a great beach person and was always glad to get home and get the sand out of everything.

One of the nicest things about living in Klang was that we often had unexpected visitors passing through, usually by ship from Port Swettenham. One evening, the captain of one of the Ben Line ships rang Jim up to say that he had a passenger who was a retired Chartered Bank banker, who was on his way to Hong Kong to celebrate his 90th birthday with his friend Bunon Tong, whom he had known in Shanghai since before the war. Bunon Tong was one of Hong Kong's wealthiest businessmen.

His passenger's name was Wynne Evans Thomas. Could we do anything for him? Jim immediately invited him to lunch. Wynne was a Chinese scholar and a renowned China expert, speaking quite a few Chinese languages, and during the war, had been on General Stilwell's staff. He was dropped behind the lines deep in China, where he stayed till the end of the war. When Ah Poon, who came from some small obscure Chinese province, came in to ask him what he would like to drink, Wynne took one look at him and started to talk to Ah Poon in his own language. Ah Poon was so astounded that he sat down next to him and started to have a conversation – I don't think he had heard his own language for years and years. They had a long talk.

Wynne told us he was getting four pensions – one from the bank, the British Government, the American Government and the army. In those days, the bank had a large sports club in London called 'The Wilderness', which every year held a sports day to which all staff, past and present, were invited. Wynne attended this every year. "Don't work too hard, m'boy," he said to Jim when he left. "Enjoy your pension. Every year I go to the sports day and walk past the directors' box, and I can hear them all thinking, 'Hasn't that old bugger died yet?'" He left us a copy of his book called *The*

Vanishing Face of China, which was an absorbing read. He died when he was ninety-six, so was still costing the bank money a good few years after we had met.

Our other most interesting visitors were another retired bank couple, whose names I cannot remember, who were on a cruise. They were also unexpected guests. She burst into tears when she came into our sitting room, as I had decorated the room with exactly the same colour scheme as she had done when they lived there. It had just been redecorated in a pale greyish-blue and white and looked very smart indeed.

They were the last couple in residence in Klang when the Japanese invaded Malaya. She left first for Singapore with the women and children and then was shipped to Australia, but somehow (I can't remember how), her boat was diverted to Ceylon, where she spent the rest of the war. He stayed behind to keep the bank open until the Japanese were nearly in Kuala Lumpur. He locked the bank safes and took the keys and ledgers with him. He had a large old American Dodge that he filled with aviation fuel from a nearby airport for the journey to Singapore, put all the bank ledgers and the keys in the boot and drove to Singapore, arriving just before the Japanese Army.

Evidence of the unsuccessful Japanese attempts to access the safes could still be seen on the Klang safe doors when we were there. He deposited the Klang books and keys in the Battery Road branch in Singapore's safe and was put to work in the accounts department. (Incidentally, this was the same department Jim had left to come to Klang, and Jim had seen the note written by him, saying that he could hear the Japanese planes flying overhead.) He worked there for about a fortnight before catching a ship to Australia. He was torpedoed, picked up, put on another vessel and torpedoed again. He was rescued once more and landed in Indonesia. He and several others walked across the island – Sumatra, I think – through virgin jungle to get to a rendezvous point to pick up the last Australia-bound ship, where he spent the rest of the war. Husband and wife were reunited in Australia after the war was over. What a story!

During the emergency in Malaya in the 1950s, many people had arms for protection against the terrorists – all the planters, every bank and agency house. With the Emergency long over, the police requested that all arms be handed in to them. Jim had quite a small arsenal at the bank – four shotguns, two Colt .45 revolvers and a pistol, plus ammunition. He also had four

Malay security guards who were armed with shotguns. He kept two of the shotguns for the guards but kept the ammunition separate as he did not fancy one of the guards letting off his shotgun in the crowded banking hall should there be a robbery. The police said they would allow the unwanted ammunition to be used on their rifle range, so Jim, Bill Cunningham and some of the men spent an enjoyable morning shooting at the police range.

We left Klang in 1968 at the end of our tour, bidding a sad farewell to Ah Poon, Ah Choo, Ah Lan and all our many friends, catching a ship from Port Swettenham and sailing to London via South Africa.

CHAPTER 5
SINGAPORE 2 (1968–1969)

After six months' leave in 1968, we were posted back to Singapore. To tell the truth, this was one place I did not wish to return to as I did not much enjoy our last tour there. However, this time Jim was seconded to the Eastern Bank. The Eastern Bank was owned by the Chartered Bank, and expatriate personnel moved freely between the two as and when the need arose. Jim was in charge of the bank's inward and outward bills departments, which meant he had a lot of contact with the bank's customers. This suited him much better than the last time he was here, when he was a 'backroom boy' in charge of accounts, with no dealings with customers.

When we were last in Singapore in 1965–66, it was a part of Malaysia from which it seceded whilst we were there. Not many people remember this episode in Singapore's history as it was so brief. Three years later, it was a well-established independent country, flourishing under the able and incorrupt government of Prime Minister Lee Kuan Yew and his cabinet.

During our sojourn, Singapore went from strength to strength, following various government initiatives, one of which was the 'Keep Singapore Clean' campaign. Before this campaign, Singapore was an average crowded Asian city, with the population generally unaware of litter in the streets, especially in the areas around the docks and in the slums in Chinatown. As well as media campaigns involving newspapers, TV and radio advertisements and jingles, initiatives in schools, etc., raising awareness of the necessity of cleanliness, the government ran a monthly competition, offering a prize for the cleanest street/shophouse in designated locations. Winner's names featured prominently in the media. However, side by side with this, the name of the dirtiest street/shophouse in the area was also headlined in the press – in bigger print than that of the winner. This caused great laughter and loss of face to those nominated, and the city was cleaned up in double-quick time.

Chewing gum was no longer spat out on the street, there was a proliferation of waste bins and littering was heavily fined – so much so that you could not flick ash from a cigarette on the street without a passer-by remonstrating with you. The Singapore River, once virtually an open sewer, was cleaned up and made attractive, all stagnant water drained away and the monster Singapore mosquitoes almost disappeared. The campaign was extremely successful, the city became scrupulously clean, and its citizens were very proud and aware of their surroundings.

New high-rise flats were built for the poorer inhabitants, and the slums were gradually cleared away. It was amazing how many slum areas caught fire, though no one ever got hurt. All Singapore citizens, whether Chinese, Malay, Indian or European had equal opportunities in government jobs and examinations, with posts going to the most able candidate. Singapore became an extremely efficient and pleasant place to live in – everything worked as it should, and its citizens were proud to say 'I am a Singaporean' rather than 'I am a Singapor/Chinese/Indian/Malay. This was in the middle of the hippie era, and in the eyes of officialdom, the word 'hippie' was synonymous with drugs. All incoming visitors to Singapore, therefore, had to be respectably dressed, and males have short hair. Those refusing to conform were either refused entry into the country or could have their hair cut upon arrival by the airport government barber before being allowed entry! It was their choice. Hippies were unwelcome. Drugs were prohibited, and possession and dealing were severely punished.

Expatriate parents of teenagers wrote warning letters to their offspring due on holiday, telling them to have a haircut before arrival – the few who did not heed the warning did indeed have a very short haircut at the airport before being allowed entry, regardless of how important their parents were – whether embassy staff or important businessmen.

As the population had grown considerably, family planning was a main issue. Singapore, therefore, offered free education to families consisting of two adults and two children. You were welcome to have more children if you wished, but you had to pay for them yourself. The population was told that the country could not afford to pay for any more.

We lived in an Eastern Bank flat at Cameron Court – I cannot remember the name of the road. There were two blocks of flats in the compound, and we were in the second block on the third floor. I cannot remember much about this flat, other than it was quite a good-sized two-bedroomed one. The compound had no garden as such, but a large lawn at the back of the flats, facing the main road, with car parking space in the front. I don't think we had a garage. The flats were smaller, and the compound was not as spacious or as nice as the gardens at the Chartered Bank flats in Shelford Road.

Not all the occupants of the flats were Eastern Bank staff; in fact, there was only one more Eastern Bank couple there, Alan and Helen Deverell, whom we had known in Calcutta before Jim and I were married. They had two little girls, Sandy, who was Roddy's age, and the other slightly older, whose name I cannot remember at the moment. Sandy and Roddy were great friends. They all went to Tanglin School, which was an excellent school for expatriate children, run on British curriculum lines, so that children going Home for schooling were able to fit in well at British schools. At two and a bit, Mhairi was, of course, still too young to go to school.

We also acquired a dog Susie the dachshund whom we looked after for about six months for a bank bachelor friend Billy Dawson who was on leave. Susie eventually flew off to join Billy at his new posting.

We had one 'black and white' Chinese amah, whose name I also cannot remember – though I can see her plainly in my mind's eye – she was efficient, tall, thin and middle-aged.

Jim thoroughly enjoyed working in the Eastern Bank. It was much smaller than the Chartered Bank in Battery Road and had a good mix of customers, including a large number of Indians. The bank staff were all extremely friendly, and we all often went out for dinner, which made for an enjoyable social life.

Every Friday, Jim and several of his Indian customers would lunch out at 'The Long Restaurant'. This eatery was a covered passageway near the bank, where you could get lunch – as much as you could eat – for one Singapore dollar. At the front of the restaurant, they served Malay food; in the middle, Chinese, and at the back, Indian. The conversation during the meal was conducted solely in Hindi, and anyone who relapsed into English had to pay the bill. Jim's Hindi improved by leaps and bounds!

One memorable evening, Jim returned to the flat with our friends from Klang Yeoh Tiong Lay and Yap Chin Leong who had come on business from Kuala Lumpur. "We've come to take Jim out for dinner," Chin Leong said to me.

"What about me?" I asked.

"No, no," he said. "You cannot come. We are going to a striptease show."

"But I don't mind going to a striptease show," I said.

"No!" he said firmly. "You can't come – it would not be fitting!" I must have looked very disappointed, because he added, "But we will come back and take you for dinner tomorrow evening." So that was okay.

The following evening, they arrived, and off we went to the Goodwood Park Hotel for the evening, where the cabaret starred the singer and dancer 'Cappuchine'. This turned out to be an extremely entertaining, slickly performed cabaret by a troupe of gorgeously gowned female impersonators, in the style of Danny La Rue, compered by a very witty pantomime dame compère, who called himself 'Les Lee'. In fact, the cast were so convincing that, though we were at one of the front tables, an American lady behind us got out a pair of opera glasses to ensure herself that they were indeed male. I thoroughly enjoyed the show. Later, I said to Chin Leong, "You wouldn't take me to see a striptease, but this was okay."

"Yes," said he, "because they are not real."

I was still singing, so I think either we must have had a piano at the flat or rented one. One day I saw an article in the *'Straits Times'*, which said a conductor was looking for local singers to do a performance of Handel's 'Messiah'. I auditioned and was offered the alto soloist part, which, of course, I accepted.

The conductor informed me that he was going to perform the oratorio in the original Handelian style, *à la* Colin Davis (who was very much in vogue then) and not in the Victorian style of Sir Malcolm Sergeant, with a pared-down orchestra and the soloists decorating the vocal line with ornaments, cadenzas, etc. "In that case," I said, "please may I sing the aria 'But Who May Abide' (which is usually either omitted or sung by the baritone), and the second part of 'He Was Despised' – 'He Gave His Back to the Smiters' – which is also usually omitted as it makes the aria very long."

"Yes," he replied. "I would be delighted if you would do that." I was also delighted. We had a very successful and satisfying concert (for me).

About November, the Eastern Bank manager in Kuala Lumpur went into hospital for an operation, and Jim was sent up to KL to sit in for him. The children and I remained in Singapore as Rod was still at school. Jim returned to spend Christmas with us on Christmas Eve, having travelled from KL on a flight that was absolutely bursting at the seams with Chinese returning to Singapore on holiday – they were sitting in the aisles, surrounded by all their packages.

Christmas came and went with the usual celebrations and staff parties. We were informed that all the staff were coming to visit us on Christmas Day, and as we were not keen on this, we decided to hold a staff Christmas party the weekend before instead. This we did; however, as it was 'traditional' for the staff to visit the officers on Christmas Day, they arrived to visit us anyway – so we had two staff parties, which were both very enjoyable if unexpected.

We were posted to Madras early in May and this time I left Singapore with a little more regret than I had in 1966.

CHAPTER 6
MADRAS (1969–1970)

India from the 1950s to the 1980s was known as a 'hardship posting' because of the extremely high income tax – unlike the foreign office, we always paid local taxes – many import restrictions and unpleasant and dangerous union problems coupled with much civil unrest.

We had loads of luggage and because of the strict customs regulations, Jim suggested that the children and I go to Madras by sea, accompanying the baggage. "No way," I said, unable to imagine anything worse than a six-day journey on a boat on my own with a five- and a two-year-old.

But he was very persuasive. "The last of the BI (British India) Line, the 'State of Madras', is still sailing – you can catch it at Port Swettenham and spend a few days with the Cunninghams (*Klang friends who lived on Midlands Rubber Estate*). I'm told it is an excellent ship. I will book you the deluxe cabin and put the luggage on board at Singapore so you won't have to deal with it until the ship docks at Madras, where the bank 'fixer' will clear it through customs for us." Accompanied baggage was apparently much easier to clear than unaccompanied baggage. He would fly direct to Madras because, as usual, the bank wanted him there yesterday. Against my better judgement, I eventually agreed to do this and arranged to spend a couple of days with Bill and Nancy. This turned out to be not the best idea Jim has ever had.

Rod, Mhairi and I flew to Kuala Lumpur on 11 May, 1969 where we were met by Bill, Nancy and the girls, Anne and Margaret, and we spent a happy two days together. On the last afternoon, Nancy and I took the children swimming at the Mariner's Club in Port Swettenham where we met a lot of friends, had a lovely swim, and, on the way back, called in at Peer Mohammed's store in Klang for some groceries. We were talking to Peer Mohammed when an Irish friend of ours, Kathy Davy, came in.

"You'd better get home quick," she said. "There are riots, and the Malays and Chinese are killing each other all along the Federal Highway."

Nancy and I looked at each other and shrugged our shoulders – we had seen no sign of trouble on our way into town at about two o'clock – it was now about five. Kathy must be exaggerating. We leisurely finished our shopping, bundled the children in the car and set off back down the highway.

Sure enough, Bill was waiting for us in his Land Rover at the bottom of the Midlands turning. "Where have you been?" he said. "Don't you know that there are communal riots in Kuala Lumpur, and Chinese and Malays are killing each other all along the Federal Highway? There's a curfew in force already!"

He escorted us up to the house and turned on the radio. We listened, aghast, to the news bulletins. Cars were being overturned, burnt and the occupants killed. Rioting had broken out all over Malaya between the Malays and Chinese, and the government imposed a country-wide twenty-four-hour curfew to try to control it.

Bill rang the police and arranged for a special curfew pass and police escort, allowing him to drive us to Port Swettenham that evening to catch the boat. We said goodbye to Nancy and the girls and set off in the Land Rover.

There being no traffic on the normally extremely busy highway, we got to Port Swettenham in record time. There was only one boat in the harbour – a rusty old tub, badly in need of a coat of paint, looking as if it could barely stay afloat. It had 'State of Madras' plainly written on the side. I couldn't believe my eyes. Was this what Jim had been told was 'the best BI ship and still very comfortable?' The ship was heaving with deck passengers, mainly Tamil rubber plantation workers returning to India on holiday. Bill collared the officer of the Watch at the foot of the gangway and asked him if the ship was leaving as scheduled. He was told that the sailing had been delayed for a day because of the riots. We looked at each other. "You'd better come back home with me till tomorrow," Bill said.

Back we went to Midlands. The next day, Bill got another escort, and off we set again. He saw us safely aboard and my heart sank as I saw his taillights disappearing in the distance. We were to be six long days on board.

I went into the cabin to get the luggage and children settled in. The deluxe cabin was on the top deck. It was a small four-berth with a bathroom attached. 'De luxe' I quickly discovered, meant that it only had cockroaches in the bathroom. They were huge!

It was very hot. I switched on the table fan sitting on the chest of drawers. The children were running round the deck and cabin exploring. I decided to remove my new contact lenses and laid everything out on the top of the chest of drawers. I had just acquired a pair of very expensive bright green hard micro corneal lenses in Singapore – they were the latest thing. As I took the first one out of my eye, the fan blew it off my finger. I searched everywhere for it without success and eventually rang for the cabin steward for assistance. He helped me look round the cabin, on the floor and under the bunk, amongst about six inches of compacted dust. I eventually found it lying on the bed. The steward was dispatched to get a broom to clean under the bunks – I think by the time I left the ship the cabin was cleaner than it had been for about twenty years.

I took the other lens out and repaired to the bathroom to clean them under the tap in the basin. I turned the tap on, and the water spat out at me. I leapt back, and the lens flew out of my grasp down the plughole. I called the steward once more. He sighed and sent for the plumber, who arrived and unscrewed the wastepipe. There, floating on the top of all the slime and gunge in the pipe, was my bright green lens – the same colour as everything else in the pipe.

I collected the children, and we stood at the rail and watched the people on the quayside. There were a couple of European men – hippies – standing beside a Land Rover on the dock. I wondered idly if they were going to join us, but to my regret, they drove off.

We watched the ship cast off and went down to dinner. It was an indifferent curry. I persuaded Mhairi to eat some rice and dhal, but Roddy would eat nothing – not even rice and tomato sauce as it wasn't Heinz and was slightly chilli hot. For the next six days, he existed on chocolate, some cardboard-like cornflakes, and an occasional banana sandwich.

The next day we arrived at Penang, and there on the quayside were the hippies again. Yes, they were joining us! Well, I thought, perhaps they would liven the trip up a bit. They did! They were English – I can't recall their names – and were doing the hippie trail by Land Rover – not an uncommon sight in the sixties. They were in a six-berth cabin, somewhere in the bowels of the ship, which they were sharing with four Indians. They had cockroaches everywhere and shared a shower. Unfortunately, a couple of their cabin-mates were extremely seasick for the whole journey, which made the hot, fetid atmosphere in the cabin most unpleasant and quite unbearable. They often slept in a deckchair all night, and I loaned them my cabin for a shower.

The deckchairs were dirty with greasy head marks on the canvas – I did not really care for sitting in them, but there was nothing else to sit on. I amused Mhairi for most of the day, and Rod tore round the decks with some other children he made friends with. Every time I saw him, he was a bit grimier than the time before. By the time we got to Madras, he was as thin as a rake, with great black rings under his eyes. Jim had a fit.

The hippies and I were invited to join the officers on their deck in the evening, which was very enjoyable. They had cane chairs to sit in and their deck was clean. The First Officer played an Indian-style harmonium, and we all sang some songs in English, and the officers sang us some songs in Tamil and some popular Bollywood ballads.

"Where's the captain?" I asked one evening.

"Oh, he's in his cabin composing an ode for his daughter's naming-day." I was told. The Captain's wife had given birth to a baby girl whilst he had been away.

"He should give it to Mrs Kemp," said one of the hippies. "She's a musician and will put it to music for him."

Sure enough, two nights before we docked, the Captain appeared with his ode, which he presented to me. I stared at it, aghast! It was about twenty verses of the most terrible doggerel. I put it to a simple calypso tune, and soon, everyone was happily singing it, to the accompaniment of the First Officer's harmonium. The Captain was thrilled and told me that he would sing it at the naming ceremony the next week in Madras and invited us all to come. Unfortunately, I could not go as I knew we would be occupied with welcoming/farewell parties, but I was very honoured to be asked.

All went well in the Customs at Madras. The Customs Officer was very intrigued by three boxes of wigs that I had brought with me. Wigs were high fashion in the late '60s.

"What is in there, madam?" he asked.

"Wigs," I replied.

"Wigs?" he asked, thunderstruck. "You are bringing wigs to Madras? This is the world capital of wig making, madam, why for you are importing wigs?"

I humbly said I had no idea Madras was the wig capital of the world. Still shaking his head, he chalked all our crates, whilst the bank fixer looked on in amazement.

Once through the Customs, I introduced Jim to my hippie friends, gave them our address and told them once they had got their Land Rover through the formalities, they could have a bed with us for a couple of days. They were very grateful as this meant they could also have a good bath and do their laundry.

We piled into the car and drove home. The bank house, known as the Mug House, was on Monteith Road in Egmore. This district is in the middle of Madras, just down the road from the museum. The Mug House was an old, circular, flat-roofed house shaped like an eight, near the Adyar River and divided into two very large semis. There was about an acre of garden, most of it brown lawn, as Madras was in its fifth year of drought. This got worse, and the government was talking of evacuating the whole of the city – about three million people at that time – how and where I do not know. Fortunately, the monsoon broke with a vengeance in June, and we then had floods. As all the sewers had become filled with rubbish, the city was soon shin-deep in floating sewage.

One side of the house was occupied by a junior bachelor, and we were in the other. The junior house was empty when we arrived, and we stayed in it whilst Jim was taking over the bank from Peter Rawlings. Peter and Dodo also had two children, slightly older than our two. As usual with the bank, we took over the house, lock, stock and servants. This arrangement almost always worked very well.

As the bank was Indianising their staff, they intended selling the house after we left, so the furniture and fittings were not up to the usual high standard. However, there was not much we could do about that, as the bank understandably did not wish to spend any money on it. Our lounge suite had definitely seen better days – its springs were coming through the settee covers. We did, however, have a grand piano, which kept me happy once it was tuned.

We mostly lived on the spacious veranda, which went right round the house. The bedrooms were upstairs and appeared pokey, as they were cluttered with 1930s chests of drawers and wardrobes. The downstairs veranda floor was an awful grey colour, and nothing seemed to clean it properly. Eventually, Jim got some oxalic acid with which to clean it, and we discovered that it was a lovely green terrazzo tiled floor.

Both children went to the small English school nearby. Roddy was five, and Mhairi was only two and a half but insisted on going because Rod was there. We had quite a retinue of servants: John the No 1 bearer, Balan the cook; two *malis* (gardeners) Kuchipin and Balarahman; Sandry the Christian *ayah*; a No 2 bearer; a sweeper and a *dhobi* or washerman. It was an expensive household to run.

John, the bearer, did not last long. He had been with the bank for seven years and thought he would run the house and everything in it – including me. He had several nice little rackets going. We got through an enormous amount of sugar, alcohol and soft drinks. He and I soon fell out, and I sent him packing, much to his astonishment – and mine – it is the only time I have ever sacked a servant. He was replaced by a Muslim bearer called Nathan. The other servants got a fright, the cookbook suddenly became much cheaper, things did not disappear quite so rapidly and the household settled down.

Before she left, Dodo took me along to join the British Women's Association (BWA) – known locally very unkindly and quite undeservedly as the 'Bitches and Witches'. Dodo was Chairman of the Entertainments Committee, and when she left, the Committee members asked me to take over. I protested that I knew nothing about the BWA or the Committee, but they said, "Never mind. We'll show you what we do every year, and you have an ideal house in which to hold our monthly meetings." So that was that!

Amongst the goods I had brought from Singapore was a little set of bottles of food colourings – I think there were about six of them, which you could mix and match. I gave these to Balan, the cook, and instructed him to make a cake for the ladies' monthly meeting. He was entranced with them, and what a ball he had, producing a beautifully decorated technicolour iced cake for our coffee every month. The question was what flavour it would be underneath the icing – lemon, chocolate or coffee. Before long, we were laying bets on what colour the cake being served at the meeting would be and what it would taste of this month.

The BWA did a lot of much-needed charity work. We had a special Charity Committee members of which did this. Every morning, a couple of members went down to a school for poor children, which we supported, where they supervised a 'milk run' for the children. They supervised the cow being milked by the cowman, bought the milk, poured it into paper cups and stood and watched the children drink it and eat the couple of glucose biscuits they were given, ensuring that the child actually got the milk, that it was unadulterated, and that they did not take it home to their mother.

I used to get fresh milk for the family and drove to the cowman's hut to collect it in my milk can every morning, then took it home to be boiled before we could use it. On one occasion, I complained to him that the milk tasted watery, intimating that he had watered it. "*Ah*, but *memsahib*," he replied. "It has been raining, and the cow has eaten the wet grass. That is why the milk is watery today." It was such a good answer that I could think of no reply. However, to support his claim, many years after we had retired, I was listening to a farming programme on the radio, after a bout of particularly rainy weather, and I heard the dairy farmer explain how his milk was not as creamy as usual as his cows had been eating a lot of very wet grass. I experienced a wry moment of déjà vu.

Every year, the BWA collected a lot of money for charity. Everyone – shopkeepers, businessmen and private people, gave us money, as they knew every penny would not only be accounted for, but that we would ensure the charities spent the money properly. We never actually gave anyone cash. The charity would come to us with a request for, say, a new roof, or to mosquito net in a veranda, or to paint a building or supply uniforms/books, etc., for school children – whatever it was they wanted. We would send one of our members to the charity to see if they really needed whatever they had requested, ask them to get three estimates, choose the most appropriate estimate (not necessarily the cheapest) and after the work was done, go and inspect that it had been done properly. This was an arduous, time-consuming task, very well performed by our hardworking welfare committee.

We ran an annual film premiere, with a huge raffle and prizes donated by various firms for our charities. I was informed that the *memsahib* always bought our servants a ticket each for this raffle and a seat for the premiere, so I duly did this. Balarahman, our gardener, won one of the star prizes – a huge hamper, which he duly presented to me back at the house. This was a dead loss, as, of course, nothing in the hamper was of interest to him, and I had to pay him for the value of the goodies therein. I later learned that this was about the third year running that one of our servants had won the star prize. I wonder how they fixed that!

We had been about three months in Madras when one of our neighbours, who worked for Macmillan the publishers was made redundant. They owned two wire-haired fox terriers, mother and daughter. As they were expecting a baby, they decided that they could not afford to take two dogs home with them and pay for the six months' quarantine and were going to have them put down. I was horrified, so we ended up with the mother, who was called Trichinopoly, and our friends the Stedmans had the daughter Brumas.

Trichinopoly, Trichy for short, was a beautiful animal. She was nine years old. When she arrived, she was rather pampered, wore a blue ribbon in her hair, liked to have a saucer of tea and was not used to children. I wondered how she would get on with our tribe. Within five minutes, her ribbon was off, she never ever had tea and Mhairi was steering her round the house by her short stubby tail. She was an ideal dog to have for children and loved to play ball – many was the cricket match she ruined, as she made off with the ball and refused to bring it back.

She would sit with me on the veranda at teatime, studying the flame tree just by our boundary wall. If she saw a lizard or a chameleon climbing up the tree, she would just take off, leaping down the three veranda steps and springing up the tree. It was beautiful to watch. If she caught the chameleon, as she usually did, she would toss it in the air, and you would hear a crack as its neck broke and it dropped to the ground. She would then turn her back on it and tiptoe away – in true terrier fashion, if it did not move, she was not interested in it. She came everywhere with me in the car, which she loved, and if for some reason you refused to take her, she sulked when you returned and refused to talk to you. She came on all our trips upcountry.

The educated South Indian is a very cultured person, and both eastern and western music, art, literature, drama and dance are very alive in Madras. Once a year, the world-renowned Kalakshetra School of Dancing performed a re-enactment of the Ramayana. The whole performance is spread over about five days, and we were invited one evening by our friends Uma and Karthik Narayan to see them performing the story of the abduction of Sita.

This is the story where Ravana the wicked demon kidnaps Sita and takes her to Lanka (Ceylon), and Rama and his brother Lakshman enlist the aid of Hanuman the monkey god and his monkeys. The monkeys build a monkey bridge over the sea from India to Ceylon, Rama and Lakshman cross the bridge, and, after many adventures, defeat Ravana and rescue Sita. Kalakshetra is one of the premier schools of dancing in India and teaches mainly Bharatnatyam, the dance style of Tamil Nadu, but also Manipuri, which comes from the northern state of Manipur and Kathakali, which comes from Cochin. We felt extremely privileged to have seen them – especially with such knowledgeable guides as Uma and Karthik.

I became a member of the Madras Musical Association, which had a choir under the conductorship of Handel Manuel – what a wonderfully apt name for an organist – a gifted musician and a very accomplished pianist and the organist at St George's Cathedral. Handel played everything from Bach to Boogie with equal relish and in any key and was also the Director of Western Music on All India Radio Madras. I was soon singing with him, and we gave a recital with a local guitarist for the Madras Musical Association, which was most successful.

He invited me to do a half-hour radio spot with him about once every couple of months. We would put together a varied programme of German Lieder, opera, modern English art and Hebridean songs that I would probably have been unable to put into a live recital programme. The programmes were recorded in the All India Radio studio, and for the first one I did, we had a sound technician. This young girl sat in a cubicle with a sound recorder, and it was her job to ensure that the machine's needle did not go into the red zone. As I have a powerful voice, I stood well back from the microphone. Despite explanations, she kept running over and putting it in front of my mouth. This happened several times before I started to sing. I gave up. Once I started to sing, however, the needle must have been well into the red zone, as she dived out and pulled the mike further back. In the end, Handel dispensed with her services.

We then recorded in three rooms, one each and one for the machine – and he said to me, "I shall switch the machine on, then run round to play the intro, and every time you hit a high note, just stand back!" So he would switch on, rush into his studio and off we would go. This worked well if I did not get too carried away with the power of the music and remembered to step back, but the high notes were usually at the climax of the aria, and if I forgot, you could hear a crackling and buzzing on the microphone. We eventually got this down to a fine art after a couple of goes.

I did several concerts for the MMA, and Handel asked me to go on tour with him to Goa. Unfortunately, I was unable to do so, as by that time I was expecting a baby. However, about ten days after Tom was born, I sang the alto in the 'Messiah' with Handel and the MMA choir. I have always regretted not going on tour with him.

We had many visitors in Madras. The British Council, who bring British artists out to foreign parts, brought the celebrated soprano, Isobel Baillie, who sang a lot with Kathleen Ferrier, out on a tour of India. She was by then an old lady of about eighty but gave us a wonderful lecture recital of her career, illustrated with some beautiful English art songs, which she sang superbly, new to me, but which I noted down and added to my repertoire. I was introduced to her, and next day she came and had lunch with me, gave me a singing lesson (accompanied by Handel) and was very complimentary, inviting me to visit her in St John's Wood to have some more lessons. Unfortunately, she died before I could do so.

Jim had a letter from a doctor friend of his in Hong Kong, asking if he would take care of his nephew John who was on the hippie trail, when he arrived in Madras. Of course, we said yes and promptly forgot about it. We heard no more, until one day, this scruffy, smelly youth arrived at the door – it was John. I took him inside, gave him a meal and hinted unsuccessfully that he could do with a wash. "Wouldn't you like a bath? We have plenty of bathrooms!" I kept asking him. Eventually, I got him to go for a bath, gave Nathan all his clothes to be immediately washed (perhaps he had fleas, as he had been sleeping God knows where) and gave him some of Jim's clothes to wear in the meantime.

Jim arrived home from the office to be confronted by a strange, bearded young man dressed in his shirt and trousers. As we were going out for dinner to the trade commissioner that evening, I phoned and asked if we could take our young guest with us. My hostess assured me she would be delighted, and off we set. I remember we had chicken casserole for dinner. There were twelve of us there, so there were twenty-four pieces of chicken and two left over (as they tell you to do in all the recipe books). Unfortunately, young John had a hearty appetite, and despite having had a good lunch, then tea at the Mug House, was hungry again when we ate at about nine o'clock.

When he was served, he had four chicken pieces – leaving Jim and the host with only one each. (Indian chickens are very small – more like pullets.) It was the same with the vegetables – young John had good helpings. I shall never forget the look of sheer consternation on our poor hostess's face, as she saw more and more food piling up on his plate. We all watched John in awe. I think Jim and the host, who were served last, only got a small spoon of mashed potatoes and a few peas between them. There was absolutely nothing left to give anyone a second helping. It taught me a lesson I have never forgotten, and to this day, I always over-cater.

North and South India are like two different countries. North Indians are Aryan with, generally speaking, fairish skin, and South Indians are Dravidian and much darker. Originally, the Dravidians inhabited the whole of the subcontinent, but various Aryan invaders from the 2nd millennium BC onwards pushed them farther down the peninsula into Southern India. South Indians also speak a group of different languages to North Indians, the main ones round Madras being Tamil, Telugu and Malayalam. Not many of the local older generation spoke Hindi in the late 1960s, and the Indian Government, which was trying to make Hindi the national language, met with a lot of resistance in Madras. There were riots, and buildings had slogans like 'This is India, not Hindia' painted on them.

Tamil Nadu is mainly a Hindu state, but there are also many Christians there of all denominations – not many Muslims, as the Moghul Empire did not stretch down into Madras. I never realised till I went to Madras how many castes, sub-castes and sub-sub-castes there are in the Hindu religion. The adverts in the marriage column always stated very specifically what was wanted, plus, of course, the educational standards required and 'must be fair' put in somewhere.

Madras, now called Chennai, is a very old, historic city. Originally, there were two fishing villages in the area, one called Chennapattinam and one called Madraspattinam, shortened by the Portuguese to Madras. In the seventeenth century, the British developed Madras into a major urban centre and naval base. Madras was where Robert Clive started his career as a writer or factor in the East India Company Civil Service, and the city was at the centre of the conflict in India between the English and French during the eighteenth century. One of the pleasures of being in Madras was that you were able to get out of it quite quickly, and there are many interesting places to visit in the surrounding countryside. I guess it takes longer to get out of Madras these days, as the city has grown extremely large.

The bank had a beach house at Covelong, one of the lovely beaches that fringe Madras. We often went there for a weekend with our friends the Stedmans and their two children Samantha and Michael. The Stedmans were strong swimmers, but we always took a tow rope with us, as the rip tide at the beach was treacherous. Not being a good swimmer, I only ever ventured in knee deep, but the Stedmans used to swim quite far out.

I remember being there one weekend with them and another couple of friends Fred and Roma Alberts. Fred, Roma and I were holding hands and paddling in the water when a large wave hit us, knocking Roma over before surging away, taking Roma's glasses with it. The tides were particularly strong and dangerous during the monsoons. There were quite a few drownings at the beach, mainly of local young girls who went paddling in the sea wearing saris – swimming costumes being seen as too revealing. If they got knocked over and carried out to sea by the wave, there was no way they would have been able to get back, especially with a sari wound round their legs – even if they had been strong swimmers. Hence our caution.

We went to Arcot, where Clive besieged and then later was himself besieged in the fort in 1751 by Chanda Sahib and his French allies led by Dupleix, then head of the French settlements in India, based in Pondicherry, which we also visited.

There is still a strong French influence in Pondicherry, mainly seen in its buildings and French is still spoken by its inhabitants. It was a French settlement until 1954. However, nowadays, it is mainly known for the Sri Aurobindo Ashram, whose town of Auroville lies about ten km outside the city. As far as I can gather, Sri Aurobindo, who lived in the early 1900s, wanted everyone to live in peace and love. When he died, his place was taken by his disciple called Mira Alfassa, also known as The Mother, who ran the ashram for many years.

There are many international disciples. The ashram does many charitable works and runs a craft centre, which makes handmade paper, among other things. Auroville was supposed to be a town built to promote human unity and peace, but when The Mother died, there was much internal squabbling, and building came to a standstill in the late '60s and early '70s. I think since then, some peace has been restored, and work is still going on to finish the town.

Many of Jim's customers were leather merchants, and he often went to the villages round Madras, inspecting their tanneries. One of them, called Mohammed Yusif, had a tannery near a place called Yiligiri, which was on a hill about three to four thousand feet above sea level. It is now a small 'hill station', but in 1969, there was nothing there but a *dak* bungalow.

A '*dak* bungalow' literally means 'post house' in Hindi. There are *dak* bungalows all over the sub-continent. They were built by the British, a day's horse ride away from each other, and were used not only by post riders but also by District Officers and other government officials, who stayed in them whilst touring their districts on government/company business. There were only a couple of thousand Indian civil servants running the whole of India, so a DO's district was huge! The *dak* bungalow was usually, a two-bedroomed en suite bungalow, with a large sitting-cum-dining room and kitchen out the back. It was staffed by a cook/bearer, a hamal or kitchen worker, a sweeper and perhaps a watchman. The servants kept the house clean and provided the DO with his meals, the first of which was always chicken curry, known as 'sudden death curry', as when the cook heard the officer coming, he would catch and kill a chicken, which you could hear squawking before it died. These bungalows are still in use, and anyone can book them in order to stay a day or two – many of them are now called 'government rest houses').

Mohammed Yusuf spent weeks persuading Jim to go to Yiligiri, and eventually they set a date, sometime in July, and his customer said he would 'fix everything – bedding and everything'. Jim, the two children, Trichy and I in our Triumph Herald, and Derek and Sheila Stedman with their two children, Samantha and Michael, Trichy's daughter Brumas, and their driver, in the Eastern Bank's Ambassador – a Morris Oxford – set off for Yiligiri – about two hundred and fifty-eight kilometres from Madras – which took about four and a half to five hours. Yiligiri is about three thousand feet above sea level, and the road from the plains to the top is steep, with fourteen hairpin bends.

Being the middle of the monsoon, it started to rain as we climbed the hill, and it was pouring cats and dogs when we arrived. When we got out of the car, we saw that there was an Indian family already in residence. Obviously, Mohammed Yusuf had got his wires crossed, as no one had ever heard of us.

Fortunately, there was a working telephone in the bungalow, and Jim contacted Mohammed Yusuf, who said not to worry; he would send up some palliases, plus bedding, so that we could stay both the nights, which he proceeded to do, but these took some time to arrive from the bottom of the hill.

The Indian family – there were about nine of them – kindly said they would share one bedroom and we could have the other. The Stedmans decided they would sleep on the dining room table, whilst Jim and I (who was very pregnant), all four children and the two dogs would take the other room.

By about ten o'clock, we had all settled down – the four children – two head to tail on the two beds, Jim and I on a palliase spread on the concrete bedroom floor with the dogs. The bedroom had a stable-style door, and though it was cold, damp and still raining, we left the top half open to get some air. About two a.m., I woke up freezing cold, with the damp rising from the concrete floor through the palliase and the baby complaining – woken by something coughing just outside the door. There were leopards in the area. "Jim, Jim, wake up," I hissed. "There's a leopard outside!" Jim woke up, and bleary-eyed, staggered to the door. Holding his *lunghi* in front of him to protect him from the leopard, he reached for the open door and slammed it shut.

By this time, of course, all the children and dogs had woken up. "Can we come and sleep with you?" asked Samantha, so we ended up with all four children, two dogs and ourselves sleeping on the palliase on the floor. The Stedmans never heard a thing. The 'leopard' turned out to be the local parish priest's dog, who had had his throat bitten by a leopard, and when it healed, it had left the dog with this cough, which sounded just like a leopard, so I wasn't far wrong.

Next morning was Sunday (still raining), and after breakfast, we asked the bearer where the Catholic church was. We knew there was one, as another of Jim's customers, a French priest, Father Guezo, who was also a stonemason, had built the church at Yiligiri, with his own hands. "Oh, yes," said the bearer, "the church is down the road, and the priest lives in a house nearby with his wives." Wives? Catholic priest and wives – plural! *This sounds interesting!* we thought. When we walked along to the church, we found that there was a convent next door to the church with about six nuns in residence – and they had a guest house, where we could have had a very comfortable bed. As the rain was still hurtling down, we decided to call it a day and returned to Madras early.

Jim was secretary of the Madras branch of the UKCA (United Kingdom Citizens Association), an India-wide association, spread all over the subcontinent, which takes care of and assists distressed British subjects and does a lot of other charitable work. Madras was the headquarter for the Association for South India, and his remit covered the Nilgiri Hills. 'Nilgiri' literally means 'Blue Hill', *neela* meaning blue in Hindi, and *giri* meaning hill. They are so called because they are covered by the blue *kurinji* flower, which blooms once every twelve years and turns the hillsides blue. We were lucky enough to be going to Kodai in a year when the *kurinji* was in full bloom. The honey from the I flower is a very dark brown, almost black in colour, and it has a very strong and distinctive taste. You must take care to get it from an accredited honey supplier, as it is often sold much adulterated.

The hill stations of Kodaikanal (known locally as 'Kodai') and Ootycamund (known as 'snooty Ooty', it being one of the main hill stations of the Raj) are both in the Nilgiris, and both had a number of retired Brits living there, who had decided to stay on after Independence. They were all now well into their seventies and eighties, and with the recent devaluation of the rupee, many were living in straitened circumstances – what had once been a handsome pension was now a pittance. Jim had spent nearly a year of his childhood in Kodai, as his father, who worked in Bombay, had a heart attack during the war and was sent to Kodaikanal to recuperate. He was keen to return to see how much it had changed. So, the first available chance we got, we packed our Triumph Herald with our luggage, including bedding, children and dog, and drove up to Kodai via Mahabalipuram with its seashore temples, and Madurai with its famous erotically sculptured Meenakshi Amman Temple complex.

The temples at Mahabalipuram date back two thousand years and, as it was on the main north-south Indian Highway, always attracted many devotees. The present temples were built in the seventh century by a king called Mamalla, and several of the seashore temples are now underwater. The remaining one has a retaining wall built round it to prevent further erosion. In typical Indian fashion, its next-door neighbour was a large atomic power station.

There is an enormous open-air bas-relief sculpture on two huge boulders at Mahabalipuram, called Arjuna's Penance, which is thirty-one metres long and nine metres high. There is much controversy as to the interpretation of the bas-relief. While some believe that it shows Arjuna, one of the five Pandava brothers in the Indian epic story the Mahabharatha, undertaking a penance to obtain a rare weapon against his enemies, others believe that it depicts Bhagiratha performing a penance to bring the River Ganges to Earth. The tale of the descent of the Ganges tells how Lord Shiva stood under the great river, allowing it to drop on his head and flow through his hair, so that it would descend gently onto the Earth beneath.

The Meenakshi Amman temple in Madurai is dedicated to Lord Shiva and his consort the Goddess Parvati in the form of Meenakshi. The complex houses fourteen magnificent towers or Gopurams, including two golden ones for the main gods, all of which are elaborately sculptured and painted.

Kodai is about three hundred miles from Madras, and we stayed at the English Club for five days. The journey took about eight hours. The last part of the journey was all uphill, rather like going up to Darjeeling, Kodai being about two thousand one hundred and thirty-three metres above sea level. The drive up was disappointing, lots of scrubland, whereas we were expecting to drive through the pine forests, which Jim had assured us were all around Kodai, but they were nowhere to be seen. We later learnt that the pines had all been cut down by Raleigh Cycles to make crates for their bicycles and had not been replanted. This played havoc with the wildlife and the weather, the monsoon now often failing.

The Nilgiris are both tea and coffee growing areas, with the coffee being of particularly good quality. South Indians are great coffee drinkers. Coffee needs shade, and originally this had been provided by rosewood trees – but these had also been felled and turned into furniture, so the shade was now provided by fast-growing banana trees. This did not work out particularly well, the coffee preferring the shade of the rosewood, and the quality of the coffee, I understand, suffered greatly. The bananas have more recently been supplanted by orange and lemon trees.

We stopped for a picnic at the Silver Cascade Falls. These spectacular falls are the overflow from the Kodai Lake and drop one hundred and eighty feet into a pool by the side of the ghat road. No sooner had we stopped the car than Trichy jumped right into the pool for a swim and then leapt into the back seat, soaking everything including the bedding on which the children were sitting. We were glad to turn into the English Club, where we had a huge en suite bedroom with a fire, which we lit. It was cold for us Madrasies.

The English Club was a real throwback to the Raj, with a sad air of better days, worn-out splendour and general seediness, large, overstuffed leather armchairs, and everything furnished in shades of brown – the white uniforms of the bearers and the linen tablecloths now a delicate shade of grey after the many ministrations of the *dhobi*, and some of the tablecloths darned in places.

That evening, we wandered up to the club bar, where there were only three other people propping up the bar: a couple of Englishmen in their late seventies whose sole topic of conversation was who had died last week, who had died today and who would be dying tomorrow – and a young man in his thirties. We introduced ourselves and Jim said he was the UKCA secretary from Madras. The young man called Edward had travelled from Britain to find his great aunt who was about ninety. His family had lost contact with her and did not even know whether she was alive or dead. He was horrified to find her, living in an old mausoleum of a house full of Chinese antiques. She was senile and bedridden, living in an upstairs bedroom and being looked after by the servants. The house and bed were filthy. She was a wealthy woman, and the bearer got her to sign blank cheques, which he cashed and used to keep her fed, and he was gradually selling the antiques in the bazaar.

Jim's contact in Kodai was an elderly clergyman the Reverend Bagshaw whom he introduced to Edward, and who took charge of the young man and his problems. The upshot was that Jim arranged for the Reverend to have a power of attorney over the aunt's funds and to visit her once a week, to see that she was being properly cared for and that the money was being used to buy her food and see to her comfort. Even that was not an ideal state of affairs, but better than nothing, and Edward was able to return to the UK with some peace of mind. Mind you, the Reverend Bagshaw was no spring chicken either, and we didn't know how long he would be able to supervise this, but I certainly don't think the aunt would have survived being transported back to England.

Quite a few people in similar circumstances came to see Jim in Madras, the most memorable being two ladies in their late seventies, who turned up at the bank one day, looking as if they had stepped out of the pages of a

1920s magazine, complete with hats and gloves. They explained to him that 'they had decided, dear, it was time for them to go Home'. Indeed, it transpired that they had not been Home since the 1920s. They had been married to two brothers who worked in the Indian Post and Telegraph Service and stayed on in Madras as widows after their husbands both died, on what was a good pension. However, they were now reduced to living in the garage of what was once their house, dependent on the kindness of their Sikh landlord.

Years passed, but now, "Things are so expensive, dear, we can no longer afford to live on our pension, and it is time to go Home," they said. Jim said he would see what he could do for them and contacted the High Commission, which said it was none of their business, and the UKCA would have to deal with it as best they could. Jim was livid.

He could get the old ladies Home, but what would happen to them then? Within a week, the Brigadier of the Salvation Army came to see him, saying he understood Jim had a problem. On learning what it was, the Brigadier said that if Jim could get the ladies Home, he would arrange for them to be met by the Army at Heathrow and taken to one of the Army's old folks' homes on the south coast, where they could stay for the rest of their lives. He also undertook to see that they received a small pension so that they would have some spending money. Jim contacted the manager of BOAC (as it was then), who arranged a couple of free plane tickets for the ladies. The Brigadier collected them in the Army lorry, and off they went to spend the rest of their lives 'at Home' – hopefully happily.

One day, Trichy and I went shopping at the market, and as I was buying the vegetables, I met a Gond an Indian tribal who had a grey squirrel on a string running all over his arms. "Look, *memsahib*, tame squirrel," he said. I bought it for a couple of rupees. Trichy nearly went mad in the car trying to catch it, but it hid under the front seat. Once we were home, I let it go and it ran up a tree. Not tame at all but drugged with a bit of opium. I never saw it again but don't think it survived very long, as the Gond had removed all its front teeth so it wouldn't bite.

We often saw the Little Sisters of the Poor at the market, begging for fruit and vegetables. They ran a Home for about one hundred destitute old folk in Madras – mainly Eurasians. The Little Sisters begged for all their food, and such is their reputation that not a single stallholder ever refused them. They never had to ask, just held out a gunny sack, and it would soon be filled with produce. "People are so good and kind, and our old folk never go without," they used to say to me.

At Christmas, I ran a BWA choir, and the old folks home was one of the places where we performed. I have never been anywhere that had such a moving atmosphere. We sang in their 'garden', which was just a beaten earth compound with a few bushes in it. All the old folk came out of dormitory-type buildings to listen and join in the singing. Many were infirm, but they all helped each other – those who could walk helping those who couldn't. It was extremely touching and brought a big lump to my throat – I conducted furiously, blinking away my tears – when I looked up, I saw that all my choir were singing with tears streaming down their cheeks. The nuns said to me humbly afterwards, "We see it every day, dear, and have got used to it. We had forgotten how moving it is." After our concert, a blind old man produced his mouth organ, and we all sang more carols together.

The Sisters had a small account at the bank and visited Jim about once a month. He would give them biscuits and a cup of coffee and sit and chat with them. One day, they told him that their roof was leaking and they badly needed it fixing before the monsoon. We used to go to a convent church in Madras that had a small expatriate congregation – mostly American, and Jim said he would see what he could do but warned them that he would be unable to collect anything like the sum needed to fix their roof. "Oh, it's all right, Mr Kemp," they said, "We will pray, and God will provide."

"I daresay He will," said Jim, "but sometimes He needs a little help."

"He will fix it, we will pray," they said.

Now, it so happened that Jim was having the bank refurbished, and he asked the contractor Mr Subramanium a real hard-headed businessman if he would go and see the nuns and cost the repair of their roof. Jim said he had only collected a few thousand rupees for them, but perhaps the money would repair the worst bits. About a month later, two beaming nuns arrived at the office. "Oh, thank you so much, Mr Kemp," they said. "You are such a kind and wonderful man!"

Jim looked bewildered. "What did I do?" he asked.

"You sent us that very kind Mr Subramanium, and do you know, he has not only repaired our roof, but he has repainted all the rooms in the home for us in different colours." Well! Jim was gobsmacked! "See," they said before they left. "We told you we would pray and look what has happened!"

When Jim next saw Subramanium, he said to him, "What happened?"

Subramanium shrugged his shoulders. "They asked," he said helplessly. "And who could refuse them!"

We had a low wall round the Mug House and could easily see people passing in the road beyond. One Sunday, Jim and I were walking in the garden, and a couple of men walking past with a basket shouted over the wall, "*Sahib, memsahib*, would you like us to catch all your snakes?" Now, we backed onto the old manager's house and garden – a huge place, now derelict, with the jungle growing up through it like something out of a Disney jungle lost city movie. It was a massive house, once owned by Skinner of Skinner's Horse, with a large ballroom on the first floor. The bank was unable to sell it, and as it was too expensive to knock down, it was just left to rot. We were separated from it by a wire fence, and though it was just the kind of place snakes love, we had never seen a snake in our compound.

"We have no snakes!" I said.

"But memsahib, if we catch any, will you give us five rupees per head for them?"

"All right," Jim said. "But we have none!"

"*Ha,* sahib," they said, "but will you pay?"

"*Accha*! Okay," said Jim.

So, over the cattle grid into the compound they came. All they had was a wicker basket, a couple of gunny sacks, a piece of sacking with a hole in it and a snake charmer's pipe. They wandered round the garden playing the pipe, and snakes appeared from everywhere. Some from a pile of old roof tiles stacked by the gate, a few from the fence by the old house and some from various bushes and trees in the garden. The whole household gathered to watch open-mouthed with amazement.

Altogether, they found thirty-five snakes, including several cobras, two of them kings and some kraits – which are more venomous than cobras – plus two nests full of babies, one in the pile of tiles and one in a hole in the flame tree, which Roddy loved to climb. As the snakes appeared, the man with the holey sacking would throw it over the snake's head, pick the squirming snake up behind the head, and put it into one of the sacks. Once the snakes stopped appearing, one turned to me and said, "*Memsahib, baba log sap ka hood decknae mangta?*" (Would the children like to see a cobra spread his hood?)

"Yes!" we said. He squatted, produced a small piece of wood, pulled one of the cobras out of the sack and teased it by flicking its tail with one hand. The cobra immediately sat up in striking position, hissed and spread its hood full out, really cross. The snakecatcher then held the small piece of wood just above the cobra's nose, and the snake folded its hood and cowered away from him. We had never seen anything like it. He then picked it up by its tail and put it back in the sack. Thirty-five snakes – this was going to cost a fortune!

"*Khalli doh ruppiah oh chotta batcha sap ka waste!*" I said, trying to bargain.

"*Only two rupees for the baby snakes.*" He looked at me.

"*Memsahib, burra ke chotta, joh sap baba koh kattaiga, baba murjaiga.*" (No matter if the snake be big or small, if it bites the child, he will die.)

We paid them in full!

The sequel to this episode was that the morning after they had left, I saw a huge cobra in the compound slithering towards the kitchen door. I screamed for Nathan, who killed it with the broom. In India, they say if you kill a snake, you must get rid of the body either by burying it, burning it or throwing it in the river, or its mate will come and get you. I reckon this cobra was looking for its mate.

I have never seen anything like this before and don't know how they really did it, though I know there are special villages in India whose villagers claim they are immune to snake venom and who collect and gather snakes, most of which they skin alive, selling the snakeskin to the tanneries to make into shoes and handbags for the fashion industry. The rest they sell to snake charmers or laboratories so they can milk the venom to turn into antidotes. The snake is skinned by holding it behind the head and holding the tail still with the toes. They then slit the skin up the middle of the belly to the head, like undoing a zip, put their hand inside the skin to pull the body out, then over the head, throwing the body aside. If the snake is dead, the skin will stick to the body and be spoilt.

We had an English friend called Harry who was a snake expert and wildlife photographer – he had just written a series of articles on the white python for *National Geographic* – whom we told about our snakecatcher visit. "It is a trick," he said. "But I've never been able to find out how they do it. Snakes are deaf, so they will not hear a pipe. They will have thrown them into the garden before they came. I know every snake on my estate, and yet they found about fifty!"

"But Harry," I said. "If they did throw them into the garden, snakes are not like dogs; they won't come just because you call them, so how do they appear just like that?"

"I don't know!" said Harry, sounding very frustrated.

One day, we went to Harry's farm to have lunch, and he took us to see his pet python called George. George lived in a concrete coal bunker at the entrance to Harry's drive. He was eight months old, so not fully grown, but already over nine feet long. Harry got him out and wrapped him round his neck to show us. "See," he said, holding him out, to me, "you have him, he is quite tame and feels quite warm, not cold like they say snakes are!"

"No, thanks!" I said firmly. Just then, George got a bit frisky, winding himself further round Harry, whose face started to get alarmingly red. It took Harry and his helper about ten minutes to unwind George and put him back in his bunker.

As I was driving home one day, I saw a crowd just outside our gate bending over a crippled boy about nine years old who was lying on the pavement. I stopped. "What's wrong?" I asked.

"*Memsahib,* he has fainted from hunger," they told me. "He has not eaten for forty-eight hours."

I told them to put him in the car and took him home, where, having established he was a vegetarian, I got Balan to give him some *dhal*, rice and egg, admonishing him to eat slowly or he would get sick. He had a withered foot. Now what was I going to do with him? I phoned Jim to ask if I could give him a job as a gardener's boy. "No!" he said firmly. "You know nothing about him. His parents might turn up and accuse you of kidnapping him. The other servants would be most resentful of him, and before you know it, things would start to go missing, and he would be blamed whether guilty or not." Feeling very guilty and responsible for him, I eventually sent him off with ten rupees which should have fed him for at least a week.

At Christmas, we had our usual lunch for anyone who was on their own, with Ian Kippen our manager who was a bachelor, and John McLeod the manager of I think Grindlays, joining us. They bought Mhairi a lovely little china doll's tea set. After lunch, we had coffee on the lawn, and I have a vivid picture of John and Ian, both big men in their late forties or early fifties, sitting cross-legged on the grass, solemnly drinking water out of the tiny cups and saying to Mhairi, "More tea, please, Missus. Do you take milk? And sugar?" and Mhairi, who was about three, carefully pouring the water into their cups.

We made some very good friends in Madras, and we needed them. Being the accountant, Jim was in charge of personnel, which meant dealing with the union. Indian unions are extremely difficult to deal with at the best of times, but the Madras union included the secretary of the All India Bankers' Union. The president of the local union was mentally unstable and used to fly into uncontrollable rages, literally frothing at the mouth. Both men were militant communists and out to cause as much trouble as possible. The rest of the staff were terrified of them, and they made life in the office hell for everyone.

There was much labour unrest in India in the late 1950s to '70s, particularly in the cities, Calcutta and Madras being the worst affected. One of labour's 'industrial actions' was to '*gherau*' management. In the bank, this meant that all five hundred staff would try to squeeze into Jim's office, which measured about eight feet by ten feet – the overflow standing outside, barricading him behind his desk and shouting slogans at him for an unspecified time – sometimes an hour, but usually four or five. During that time, he could not move out from behind his desk, either to go to the lavatory, or drink or eat.

He told me he would stand behind the desk and clench his fists tightly in his pockets, afraid if he took them out, he might hit someone – and that would be it – he would have been killed. He therefore just stood there, whilst they shouted slogans like 'Go home, white bastard, little white colonial monkey!' at him, sweating profusely, breathing curry and garlic all over him, occasionally spitting at him if they got very agitated, and generally trying to make him lose his temper. Once they had finished in his office, they would all troop into the manager's office next door, accompanied by Jim, where they would start all over again. Of course, being five hundred of them, they could come and go in relays and return refreshed.

Once before a holiday, the union came to him on a Friday afternoon, requesting that he allow them to have a loan for the pujas. He replied that, as they had had one before, he foresaw no difficulties, but he would have to get permission from the chief manager's office in Calcutta (which they knew), as it was beyond his remit to grant the loan. "*Ah*, so you do not wish to give us a loan," they said.

"No!" he replied and reiterated that he would have to contact Calcutta.

"Very well," they said. "If we have no reply by Monday morning, nine a.m., we will strike."

They were well aware that by now, the Calcutta office would have closed for the weekend. After much trouble – no mobile phones in those days, only some very unreliable telephone connections – Jim managed to contact the chief manager, who agreed to grant the loan. When the staff descended on his office on Monday, belligerently asking him if they could have the loan, Jim replied that yes, they could have one. Immediately, the secretary turned on him. "So, you just wanted us to beg," he said. "White imperialist monkey – we will not beg! We will not accept the loan!" He stormed out of the office, followed by the rest of the staff.

Whenever Jim met the staff afterwards, they would say, "It is nothing personal, sir!" But to us it was – *very personal!*

We were not the only ones with union troubles. Our friends, the Narayans, who owned the Standard Motor Company, were in the middle of a very vicious lockout. They had armed guards at the gatehouse of their house as the union was demonstrating outside the gates and threatening to kidnap the children.

One afternoon, the government family planning officer came to visit Jim at the bank. This lady wanted talk to the staff about family planning. "You mean you wish to speak to their wives about this? I shall have to ask the union," Jim said.

"No, no," she replied. "I wish to speak to the men – it has nothing to do with their wives."

"How many children do you think a family should have?" queried Jim.

"Oh, about five or six," was the reply.

At the time, the government was running a family planning campaign. The publicity poster showed a man and a woman with two children as the ideal family. As it was so expensive to sterilise a woman, the government was offering men who had the 'snip' a transistor radio each. However, this policy did not take into account the high infant mortality rate – maybe two children out of about five or six making it to adulthood. If neither of the two made it, who would look after the parents when they were old? Presuming the children were male, that is – daughters were assimilated into their husband's household. Also, an infertile male was the butt of all sorts of jokes from his mates. This was not a very popular policy. Jim told her not to bother.

The union invited Jim to the raising of the flag ceremony at the office on Independence Day – 15th August – and wanted him to raise the flag. Jim replied that he was honoured to be a guest and would gladly give a speech but he felt that, as a foreigner, he could not raise the flag. After much argument, they accepted this, but Jim expected some sort of trouble. So, he thought it might defuse the situation if the whole family went to take part in the ceremony. After the raising of the flag, they sang the national anthem. However, this being Tamil Nadu, and the anthem in Hindi, the only one who knew all the words was me, who had learnt it at school for the first Independence Day celebrations in the convent in Darjeeling in 1947. Nothing loath, I sang with the rest of them, and one by one, they gradually fizzled out until I was singing solo right on to the end. The silence was deafening when I stopped. Instead of a speech, Jim then read a poem by Tagore, all about freedom in Hindi – translated from the original Bengali. They were absolutely dumbfounded and went home quietly after the ceremony without any trouble. We were lucky.

We had some American friends who were building a fertiliser factory, under the American aid programme. There was a large American presence in Madras. They lived a totally different kind of life. All their food was imported – flour, butter, sugar, meat – everything and, of course, everything was so clean that it was almost sterile. The Americans were always sick because of this as they developed no natural immunity. They would go to a local house for dinner, e.g. mine, where nothing was imported – and of course they were always ill. On the other hand, they bought shellfish from an itinerant fisherwoman who went door to door selling fish. Her prawns were lovely, but they fed on untreated sewage at the mouths of sewers, and no matter how fresh, I always felt they were suspect and would never dream of buying them. Betty, one of the wives, was a first-class organist – she travelled with her organ and accompanied me for several concerts – so I had two wonderful accompanists. She played for the BWA choir.

Some of the Americans were Catholics, and went to Mass at our convent church, whose priest was a lovely old Englishman of about eighty. The Americans were very generous with their collections – they are always the most generous of people. One of the reasons the collection was so good was because the money went to the nuns who spent it on poor children. Soon the collection plate came to the attention of the bishop, who decreed that the collection should go to him, not to the convent, to dispense as he thought fit. The reply from the congregation was that if that was the case, the generous collections would cease. They did! After a couple of months of miserable collections, the bishop relented and the nuns got back their collections, which once again soared.

When Tom was a month old, he was christened at the church. The nuns really went to town – unbeknown to me – and when we got there, had decorated the font in a net drape, with blue ribbons all over it. It was beautiful. The old priest presided over a wonderful ceremony, and we all had christening cake made by Balan – all white this time – and sandwiches in the hall after the ceremony. We then adjourned back to the house, where Balan had made us a lovely curry lunch for about thirty, with another christening cake.

We were supposed to leave Madras about October 1970, but that was when the baby was due, so I would be unable to fly. We decided that I would have to take the children, fly Home on my own in August and have the baby in the UK. My in-laws made all the necessary arrangements for this, and we were booked on the last possible flight out of Madras. To say I was not looking forward to having a baby on my own in the UK was putting it mildly.

BOAC (in those days) had two planes a week flying direct from Madras to London – on Tuesdays and Thursdays. We were booked on the Thursday flight, and on the Tuesday, Jim got a telegram from London, which just said, 'Kemp to remain in Madras indefinitely'.

"Well, I am not going Home," I said to Jim. "I shall have the baby here." We undid all the arrangements – my long-suffering in-laws must have been highly annoyed with me, but they never said anything, bless them. Someone was looking after me though, because the Thursday flight was the first plane ever to be hijacked. It came down in the desert just outside Cairo, where it was held for a week. There was a pregnant woman on the flight, but I think she was let out quite early on – that could have been me.

I started to go into labour at about six o'clock in the evening of October 9th. Jim was still at the office, and the telephone was dead. We did not know whether that was a telephone company fault, or whether it was the union who had cut the line! Just as I thought I was going to have to get myself to the hospital, he appeared and off we went. He left me at the hospital, and Tom was born about five in the morning of October 10th. He was a very big baby. "Do you know how big that baby is?" asked Dr Madhuvan the obstetrician. "Ten pounds and four ounces!" "Shall I call your husband?" asked the nurse.

"No, let him sleep. He will be here at seven anyway," I replied, forgetting that the phone was out of order.

In those days, you stayed in hospital for five days after the birth. The day after Tom was born, Sheila Stedman came to see me. "It's very boring in here!" she said. "Shall I bring a couple of the girls in and we can have a game of mahjong?" I readily agreed. So, to the amusement of the nursing staff, three ladies appeared in my room with the mahjong set and table, and we played mahjong every morning till lunchtime.

Just before Christmas, the bank telexed Jim to say he could now depart on leave. We were afraid that if the union knew exactly when we were going, they would somehow stop us – either by contacting the tax man and stopping our tax clearance, without which you could not leave the country, or just making us miss the plane with a demonstration, so we told no one, not even our friends, exactly when we were leaving.

As Trichy was now eleven years old, we reluctantly decided she would probably not survive quarantine and found her a good home with a family who worked for National & Grindleys Bank and had two boys slightly older than Roddy. Trichy was very happy with them and eventually died, deaf and blind, a grand old lady of nineteen.

We got the packers in as all the luggage had to be sealed and signed off by the Customs Department at the house before it could be taken to a warehouse to be put on a ship. Of course, as the bank was selling the Mug House, not only did we have our own luggage to pack up, but also the bank crockery, cutlery and glassware, etc. It was quite a performance – especially as some things had to be left out to be used for our farewell parties. However, we got it done in time.

The Mug House was duly sold and is now a four-star hotel, called The Ambassador Pallava Hotel.

I returned to India in 1998 to attend the Silver Jubilee celebrations of INDUS, a ladies' society I was a member of in Bombay (now Mumbai).

The celebrations included a trip to South India and, of course, a visit to Madras (now Chennai). The city was so altered I could not find my way around at all. In fact, we went to the museum, which was just down the road from the Mug House, and I could not find Monteith Road. The road is now full of blocks of flats, instead of old colonial-style houses with large gardens, so no wonder I couldn't recognise it.

I rekindled my friendship with Uma Narayan during the two days we were there, and she took me to see the Ambassador Pallava Hotel. I don't know who the architect is, but the Mug House was not knocked down; it has been incorporated into the hotel and the whole thing has been done in a most beautiful and sympathetic manner. They have built a 'skyscraper' on to the back of the hotel containing the hotel rooms and the Mug House is now the entrance to the hotel; the veranda and downstairs are now the hotel foyer and a large function room – several walls have been knocked down, but the shape of the house is still quite clear and the upstairs bedroom floor is now dining rooms.

Uma and I went into the hotel, and as we stood in the foyer, I could clearly see that I was standing on my veranda (now walled in), looking into my house and the bedrooms above – though the floor is now grey and white marble and not green. But the veranda pillars are still there. It was very evocative, and I thoroughly approve of the improvements and modernisation. They even have a grand piano in the downstairs function room – I wonder if that is the same piano that I used to play in 1970 – quite possibly it is, as it has the same style of leg. The bank would have had no use for a grand piano and possibly it would have been thrown in with the real estate package. It would be lovely to think so, as it will now be used to entertain the hotel's customers. It was a good piano, so I hope so.

Departure day soon arrived, and we quietly left, looking forward to spending our first Christmas for nine years with our family in St Albans.

CHAPTER 7
SANDAKAN (1971–1974)

In 1971, Jim was appointed by the bank as Manager East Coast, Sabah, Malaysia, which meant he was in charge of three branches, Sandakan, Laha Datu and Tawau. We were based in Sandakan.

Roderick was now eight, Mhairi five and our youngest, Tom, nine months old. As there was no English-medium school in Sandakan, this meant Roddy had to go to boarding school. We could, of course, have taught him through a correspondence course, but we felt that, as we were going on a three-year tour, he would miss out by not having formal schooling and would probably find it much more difficult to fit into a school when he was older. I also felt that as this would be his sixth or seventh school, he having been at school when we were on Home leave, it would be altogether too many changes for him, all the schools having different methods of teaching.

Having looked around various prep schools whilst we were on leave, we decided to send him to Beechwood Park in Markyate, and my in-laws, who lived in nearby St Albans, would be his guardians whilst we were out of the country. We sent him to Beechwood as a day boy for a term before he became a boarder, which got him used to the school, and I stayed until after the next half-term, so he could get used to being a boarder, whilst Jim preceded me to Sandakan.

The bank had recently decreed that children could join their parents for every holiday, so we would be seeing him three times a year. This was a vast improvement on the previous terms of service, which paid for children to come out once a tour (i.e. once every three years). This was the norm for companies employing expatriates, so to jump from once every three years to three times a year was excellent news for us.

Sandakan is in Sabah (formerly known as British North Borneo) in East Malaysia. If you look at a map of Malaysia, you will see that Sabah, Brunei and Sarawak take up the top of the island of Borneo. The rest of the island, called Kalimantan, belongs to Indonesia. When we were in Sandakan,

Malaysia was having a long-running border dispute with Indonesia – called *Konfrontasi* (confrontation in Malay). Indonesia, of course, wanted the oil in Sabah, Brunei and Sarawak – especially Brunei.

The border is very long and impossible to police, as much of it goes through primary jungle. The jungle is so dense, you often don't know which country you are in, and wandering tribes come and go over the border, as they have always done. I think most of the interior of Borneo is still unexplored, though I am not up to date about that now. Logging will have cut down a lot of the jungle.

Everyone knows now where Sandakan is because of the Orangutan Rehabilitation Centre at Sepilok, but in 1971, nobody had ever heard of it – or Sabah. There were no direct flights. You flew to Singapore, which was a twenty-one hour journey from London, stayed overnight, changed planes and flew to Kota Kinabalu (previously known as Jesselton), the capital of Sabah, then changed planes again to get to Sandakan. It was a very long and tiring journey.

Mhairi, Tom and I flew to Singapore via Qantas. Mhairi was just five, and Tom was about nine months old. This was quite the worst flight I have ever had. We stopped once at Dubai. We had the bulkhead seat and were supplied with a cot, but Tom was a large baby, so his head bulged out at one end of the canvas cot, and his feet hung over the other. There was a man with a little boy of about four and a girl about seven sitting on the opposite side of the aisle to us. The little girl had both her legs up to the top of her thighs in calipers and spent most of her time with me, playing with Mhairi. I think the air hostesses thought we were all one family.

I had stupidly made up enough bottles of milk for Tom to last the flight. Fortunately, he was only on one bottle a day (at night) by that time. However, all the milk went sour. I asked the air hostess to clean the plastic bottles, but the smell of sour milk had permeated into the plastic. That was the only time the cabin crew made any attempt to come near either myself or the family across the way. I have noticed this on airlines. Normally, the only passengers who get any sort of individual attention from air hostesses are unattached males in the age range twenty to fifty. Women with children – especially those with tiny tots – are given a wide berth.

The children were all very good. The other family was emigrating to Sydney, which was God knows how many more hours away. I felt very sorry for their dad, who told me he had never been out of Britain before.

The plane touched down at Dubai, where we spent an exhausting couple of hours trailing round the airport concourse. There was nothing there to look at as far as I can remember, except a jeweller's shop, which sold very expensive ornate gold jewellery. We were very glad to get back on board the plane.

We touched down at Singapore at ten p.m. next evening, about three hours late. Fortunately, the bank had a very nice young representative called Christine who met all bank personnel going through Singapore, and she was there to meet us.

Christine relieved me of Tom, who was getting a bit crotchety by now – especially as he had not had his bottle. We waited and waited for our baggage, until it eventually became apparent that our cases were lost. Christine advised me to see the Qantas manager, who had now appeared and was surrounded by irate passengers complaining about lost baggage, and tell him that, as our baggage was lost, we had no clothes and were travelling to Kota Kinabalu the next morning, Qantas would have to do something about it. He gave me a voucher for ninety Singapore dollars – quite a lot of money in those days – but it had to be spent in Singapore. Christine loaded us all into the bank car, and off we went to Raffles Hotel.

It must have been past midnight when we arrived, and Tom was howling for his bottle. I asked room service to please sterilise the empty plastic bottle, but when they returned with it, it still smelt of sour milk. By this time, I was so tired, I just warmed up the baby's milk and gave it to him, deciding that I would risk him having a sore stomach! As soon as he had finished it, he fell fast asleep and I dropped into bed exhausted. He had no ill effects.

Next morning, Christine arrived early to pick us up and take us around Singapore so we could spend our voucher before catching the Sabah plane. It was about eight thirty in the morning and most of the shops were shut. If anyone had told me it would be so difficult to spend ninety dollars in Singapore, I would never have believed them. Eventually, we found a boutique that was open, and I bought a pale blue linen dress. It was a bad buy, did not fit well and I would never ordinarily have bought it – I think I wore it once. However, I had spent my voucher, vowing never to fly Qantas again. I haven't.

We caught the flight to Kota Kinabalu, where Jim met us, and I thankfully handed the children over. We changed planes yet again and flew to Sandakan. It took me about ten days to recover from this journey, plus the trauma of leaving Roddy behind. We all missed him terribly.

The house in Sandakan was built on the top of a hill or *tanjong*. The whole *tanjong* belonged to the bank and was about three miles out of the town. The two-storeyed house was large, airy and cool. Upstairs, there were three large air-conditioned en suite bedrooms, with a big walk-in linen cupboard on the landing.

Downstairs, there was a big sitting/dining room with a small study area in one corner, a pantry and kitchen at the side of the dining room, and a small bathroom at the bottom of the stairs. Best of all, in the corner of the lounge by the dining room, was a brand new, French-polished, tropicalised Yamaha upright piano, which Jim had bought for me from the Yamaha agent in town. I was ecstatic!

The sitting room area was surrounded by a veranda, divided from the lounge on two sides by wall-to-ceiling wooden shutter doors, which we closed at night and when it was stormy. The house was surrounded by a three-foot concrete strip, with an open drain in the middle of it to collect the rainwater from the roof. In front of the veranda, beyond the drain, the hill fell away steeply to a concrete retaining wall, a quarter of the way down the hillside. Behind the wall were about ten timber posts, up which grew ground Vanda orchids – both purple and white. We had about five acres of garden, three of which round the house was cleared and laid to grass to discourage snakes and other animals, and the rest was primary jungle.

It was Eid (Ramadan) when we arrived, which the Malays call '*Hari Raya*', and this year it coincided with Chinese New Year, which meant there was a five-day public holiday. Jim had invited our neighbours over to meet us over a cup of tea. There were about six of us sitting on the veranda. David Ashley one of our neighbours was playing with Tom – pretending to be a tiger, growling and lurching towards him. Tom was laughing with glee and stepping away backwards from him when he took a step too far and fell into the concrete drain, sustaining a deep cut just above his eyebrow. Of course, being just skin and bone there, the cut bled profusely, and we tried to find a doctor to put a stitch in it, without success. Eventually, we patched him up with sticking plaster, but he bears the scar to this day. We were lucky he had not fallen down the hillside and impaled himself on the wooden orchid stakes. 'Elf and Safety would have had a field day at our house.

The resident bank servants had retired when our predecessors left, and this would have been a real problem, had Jim not managed to get an excellent South Indian Tamil cookboy called Ramasamy and his wife Padma to work for us. They had been employed by one of Jim's customers who worked for Cadburys in a cocoa plantation upriver in the jungle – a helicopter ride away, at a place called Rumeidi.

The plantation was on Jim's books, and he had gone up the *ulu* (Malay for 'jungle') to inspect it. It really *was* carved out of the jungle. Jim was warned to watch where he put his hand as he opened doors in the bungalow, as the plantation was full of snakes, which often came indoors, where they liked to curl themselves round the door handles.

The family were returning to Britain, so Ramasamy and his family were looking for a new job. They were a delightful family. They had two boys, Nagarajah and Nanarajah and a little girl of about nine called Silly. That was not her real name, but one given her by the Rumeidi family's little girl, who, when they were playing one day, said to her, "You are a silly!" and Silly she remained.

Mhairi and Silly became great friends, and we kept in touch with her for years. She became a nurse in Kuala Lumpur. Tom was soon commandeered by Padma, and she carried him around on her hip whilst she was doing her housework. Whenever we came home from shopping, he would toddle into the house shouting, "Where my Padma, where my Padma!" and she would appear from the kitchen. Otherwise, she was very quiet and silent, and you never knew she was there. The boys were in their late teens and still at school but helped with the garden in the afternoons, though we also had a Malay *kebun* (gardener). Ramasamy was short, roly-poly and smiley.

When we first arrived, the jungle was much closer to the house, so Jim arranged for the Prison Department to bring round a gang of prisoners to cut back the *lallang* – long scrub grass that grows on the outskirts of jungle. They were happy to do so, and I think the prisoners enjoyed coming, as we saw to it that they and their warders were liberally supplied with squash, biscuits and cake, and they had a day out from the gaol. They were mainly political prisoners and no menace to anyone. Nor could they escape – because where would they go? They cut back the grass with *parangs*, a Malay knife supervised by the warders, who strolled about and sat around in the shade with their *lathis*, or large canes, which they used to keep order. Unused in our case!

We did have a petrol lawnmower and a large Flymo to cut the grass on the slope. This Nanarajah, Nagarajah and the *kebun* would lower down the bank on a rope and pull up again whilst it was cutting the grass. The grass on the level was cut by the petrol lawnmower by the *kebun*, who one day, unthinkingly, put his hand in the machine to rescue an oily rag he kept to wipe it. Fortunately, he did not lose his hand but badly cut his fingers. We wrapped his hand in a towel and drove him to the hospital, where there was a very able Egyptian surgeon who sewed his fingers back on. He was back at work in a week.

The whole hill belonged to the bank. There were several other houses built round the slopes of the hill which were leased from the bank. Saleh Sulong the Sabah Minister of Finance lived opposite us on his rare visits to Sandakan from Kota Kinabalu (known locally as KK), and further down the hill were three more houses occupied by Bunty and Simon Wallace who worked for Borneo Company, Norah and Ronnie Babanao who worked for the Royal Institute of the Blind and Maggie and Jim Seaton. Jim was the accountant at the bank.

Ronnie was blind – at least, he was partially sighted and could only see shadows. He had spent many years in the Indian Army, where he had lost his sight due to some peculiar virus, been invalided out of the army and sent back to Britain. There, he was trained by the Royal National Institute of the Blind in London. He was now in Sandakan, teaching local blind people how to farm. This he did very successfully. His pupils kept hens and grew vegetables, particularly tomatoes and spinach. They did this by growing the plants in rows of wooden boxes with string running down the row, so they could feel their way along the string and tend to the plants. Though he had a stick and wore Darth Vader-style glasses to protect his eyes, Ronnie moved around with such confidence that you forgot he was blind. This was brought home to me when I rearranged the lounge furniture one day and never thought to tell him. He got a lift into town every morning with Jim and, of course, bumped into the newly arranged furniture. He was not pleased and went round the room several times, familiarising himself with the new layout, muttering darkly under his breath all the while.

After we had been in Sandakan for a few months, Jim was able to get some of Ronnie's blind women a job with an oil palm nursery, pricking out palm oil seedlings into larger pots, where they were grown on before being planted out in the ground. It was found that their sensitive fingers were adept at handling the tiny plants, and many more seedlings survived to be successfully planted. This was an ideal job for these women and very lucrative. Ronnie was very pleased.

The last house on the hill was occupied by Jim's accountant Jim and Maggie Seaton. Jim was a Scot and Maggie was Hong Kong Chinese. They were great fun. Jim was trying to learn Cantonese, largely, I gathered, so that he could impress his mother-in-law. Now, Cantonese is a very difficult language to learn. There are nine tones, and the same word spoken in another tone can mean something quite different. When we went out for a meal, our Chinese friends always asked him to order 'bean curd', the Cantonese for which is '*tawfu*', but '*towfu*' in another tone means 'underpants'. Of course, Jim always ordered 'underpants', and the Chinese were always convulsed with laughter. Similarly, '*mah*' means 'mother', but '*maah*' means 'horse' (or vice versa – I cannot remember now which is which). When Maggie's mother visited Sandakan, she did not appreciate him continually calling her a horse.

There being no English-medium school in Sandakan, we were extremely fortunate that Bunty Wallace an ex-teacher started a small kindergarten. The Wallaces had two little girls, Mary who was Mhairi's age, and Linda who was nine and had just started boarding school. Bunty ran the school in the mornings from eight to twelve. This was very convenient for us, as Mhairi walked down the hill to school every morning accompanied by Padma and Tom and returned at midday. The Wallaces' house was built Malay style – on stilts.

The school was held under the house, in what was the carport. Plenty of room, cool and out of the rain. Bunty had a class of nine – just enough children for her to be able to produce '*Snow White and the Seven Dwarfs*' at the end of one term, with Mhairi being Snow White! It was a delightful performance and quite an achievement for Bunty, as all the children were word perfect and sang the Walt Disney Snow White songs very sweetly. Mhairi was there for two years until the Wallaces' went on leave and were then unfortunately posted elsewhere. Mhairi then joined another small school run by Padma De Silva, the Agricultural Officer's wife.

Life in Sandakan was what you made of it, as there was not really all that much to do. I remember Bunty's mother, who had had a similar life when she was young and was on holiday with Bunty, saying to me one day, "Life abroad is what you make of it, my dear, but always remember, never read before luncheon!" How true that is!

We started collecting orchids, particularly species, and soon had a large collection. All our hybrid plants came from other local collectors, there being no nurseries in Sandakan. We all swapped *anaks* (small plants), and as a result, we had some quite rare and expensive plants – our Rothschild/Sanderiana crosses, for example. In return, we were able to give our friends some of the specie orchids Jim's loggers brought him.

By the time we left, we had over three hundred plants, which we divided amongst three of our orchid friends. Jim built me a small orchid house at the back of the house, where we kept our non-flowering plants. Those in bloom, we hung on hooks round the outside of the house. The white *phalaeonopsis* or 'butterfly' orchid is indigenous to Borneo, and we had many with differently coloured throats, plus one or two pink hybrids. Some of the orchids were spectacular, but others, mainly the species, were quite insignificant. We had one which only flowered once every seven years (no flowers whilst we had it). And another with a dark red, black and white striped flower that looked like a parrot's claw.

Once Jim's logging customers knew we were interested in orchids, they would bring him ones they had found at the top of the trees they had felled. As it is so dark in a primary jungle – the sun does not penetrate much through the leaf canopy – there is not enough light for flowers to grow at ground level; plants found on the jungle floor consist mainly of green leaves. Most of the blossom on the trees and the orchids grow at the top of the jungle canopy; some trees grow to two hundred feet high. The best way to see the flowering jungle is to fly low over the canopy by helicopter, which can be a bit hairy sometimes.

Our neighbour David Ashley was a helicopter pilot and took Mhairi, Tom and me on one of his flights. Just before we landed, the engine cut out and it was wholly due to David's skill as a pilot that we did not crash. A Chinese friend of ours Ngui Tet Ming was not so lucky. His helicopter crashed in the jungle, and all aboard lost their lives.

I also grew bougainvillea and swapped cuttings with my friends. I ended up with about thirty varieties, both single and double-flowered, ranging in colour from dark purple and pale lilac, through all the reds and pinks to oranges, yellows and white. One of my prized plants had both white and purple flowers on the same plant. Most of these plants were in pots, and again, those in flower were brought to the front of the house. I also put some of the flowering pots on the retaining wall in front of the vandas.

Whilst I was pruning these one day, I put my hand out to cut what I thought was a dead branch, only to find two little eyes looking at me. It was a thin black snake. I screamed for Nagarajah, who killed it and, of course, told me it was very poisonous. As bougainvillea only flowers on new shoots, you can keep it in almost perpetual flower by continually pruning the branches that have finished flowering. A Malay friend told me that if I cut round the soil in the pot about an inch away from the rim, thus cutting all the hair roots, the plants would send out more flowers and new shoots – this worked a treat.

The rest of our gardening was done in wooden boxes round the back of the house, *à la* Ronnie Babanao. Here we grew tomatoes, winged beans and 'everlasting' spinach in burnt and sterilised soil. Unsterilised soil was always full of *poochies* (insects) or some variety of fungus, virus or mildew. Winged beans were a new vegetable for us. The beans were cooked in the normal way, and you could also eat the leaves (only once, as far as we were concerned). The rest of the plant could be used as a good source of manure. None of the plant went to waste.

At the entrance of our drive were two large Borneo cannons. These came off pirate vessels in the late 1800s and early 1900s. Pirates still sailed in the waters around the island. We had another two cannons by the front door. In front of the house, by the drive, was a huge red flame tree covered with white pigeon orchids. When both were in bloom, this was a spectacular sight. Alongside the front door of the house, the *kebun* (gardener) dug a huge flower bed, into which we piled old airmail copies of *'The Times'* – it apparently had to be *'The Times'* – and then planted canna lilies. They love the potash in the newsprint, and these bloomed well. One of the pleasures of gardening in the tropics is that things grow so quickly – almost whilst you are looking at them in some cases.

The rest of the garden had the usual mixture of tropical shrubs and trees dotted all over the lawn. There were various hibiscus, ixora ranging from orange to pale yellow and petrea with its lovely two shades of blue flowers. The heavily scented frangipani stood out, as did the silver and pink congea. There were also Bunga Raja, which has a large, heavily scented, white night-blooming flower with leaves like a climbing cactus and flowers for one night only. Rose of Sharon was another bush a rather straggly plant. If you were having a dinner party, the large white flower of the Rose of Sharon could be cut in the morning, kept all day in the fridge and put on the dining table in the evening. As you dined, the flower would turn pink, which led newcomers to think that they had had rather too many pink gins.

Down the hill at the back of the house, a chunk had been cut out of the hill and made into a large flat plateau. Nestling into the side of the hill were the spacious servants' quarters – I think there were about a dozen rooms for Ramasamy, his family and the laundry. Jim eventually got permission from London to build a swimming pool here, but we left before it was built. However, in anticipation of this, we planted coffee and tea bushes and some lime and lemon trees around the perimeter of the plateau. These would take about three years to mature and fruit, so our successors would reap the rewards.

The coast around Sandakan consists of mangrove flats – unlike Kota Kinabalu, which has spectacular sandy beaches. In 1971, there were six streets, a market and harbour full of sea-going *kungpits* – a sort of large, long canoe with an outboard engine – and four large wooden trawlers, belonging to the Sandakan Prawn Factory. The population was just over three thousand, ten per cent of which were millionaires. The main business of the town was logging, hence the millionaires, and logging concessions were bought from the government by Chinese timber *towkays* (merchants). At that time, no attempt was made to reforest the jungle. The only reforestation was done by a British firm North Borneo Timber Company that replanted areas they logged with softwood albizia for papermaking and oil palm.

Many of Jim's customers were loggers, and as he (i.e. the bank) loaned them millions of dollars, he used to helicopter over the jungle to inspect their concessions. The first time he did this, he was horrified to see the destruction caused by one of the foreign-owned logging companies. They chose a strip of jungle, parked a line of tractors chained together along it and moved the machines slowly forward, ploughing down all the trees along the line, leaving a sea of mud and destruction behind them – this was painfully visible from the air. Fortunately, none of the other loggers logged in this way.

The first time Jim met the minister, he spoke to him about this and asked what was going to be done to preserve the jungle for future generations. The minister shrugged his shoulders and said that his family were all right, and anyway, he had a large farm in Australia. So much for conservation!

There was much barter trade between Chinese merchants and Suluk/Filipino *kungpit*owners, thus avoiding both Filipino and Malaysian import duties and the banned trade with Indonesia caused by *Konfrontasi*; the import of American cigarettes into Sabah being one of the main items traded, whilst the Chinese exported rice and white goods.

The expatriate community in Sandakan numbered approximately one hundred. Businessmen, traders and loggers were mainly Chinese, whilst the Malays were fishermen who lived in houses on stilts in a kampong or village on the seashore. The indigenous population consisted of Land Dyaks, most of whom lived in longhouses on river banks in the jungle, Ibans, Muruts, Kayans and Kedazan-Dusuns.

The majority of people in Sabah and Sarawak were not Muslims. The Dyaks were mainly animists, that is, they worshipped the animal and tree spirits of the jungle, and the Kedazans and Kayans were mainly Christians. When Sabah and Sarawak joined Malaysia, the non-Muslim majority's main fear was that they would be overrun by Malays from the mainland and Islam imposed on them – particularly if they wished to succeed in their businesses, and especially if they were employed as government servants. This is exactly what happened.

The financial clout was in the hands of the main Chinese families; though, of course, government officials and ministers did very well out of the country's prosperity. The Chief Minister Tun Mustapha who decamped to mainland Malaya was a billionaire with an estate in England. He used to replenish his funds when he visited Sandakan, by playing cards with the timber *towkays* (businessmen), who agreed between themselves beforehand how much money each was prepared to lose. His successor was Donald Stephens, whose brother Ben was the resident in Sandakan. The Stephens were a Catholic Kedazan family, but Donald converted to Islam to further his political career. He was killed in a tragic accident just before we left Sandakan.

What happened was that Donald and the whole of the Sabah cabinet were at a conference in Kuala Lumpur. They had done a lot of shopping in KL, so they chartered a small plane for their return, but the luggage was apparently incorrectly stowed, much of it being stashed in the aisle.

Donald's sixteen-year-old son was learning to fly, and it is understood, though not confirmed, that he was piloting the plane when it was coming in to land at Kota Kinabalu. The unconfined luggage swept forwards, and the plane nosedived into the ocean. All passengers and every member of the cabinet were killed.

Many wealthy Chinese became Muslims to further their businesses, as non-Muslims were rarely given timber concessions. Concessions cost an arm and a leg in bribes. These were paid in James Bond-style briefcases, each of which, when full, held a million Malay dollars – transactions frequently took place in Jim's office.

A meeting would be arranged between the logger, the government representative, usually a sidekick of one of the ministers and the Japanese timber buyers. The logger arrived carrying the required number of briefcases, as did the government 'rep'. They would leave their briefcases in two different parts of the room. Business would then be discussed, and the two parties concerned would leave, each carrying the other's identical briefcase. No money changed hands, only briefcases. Empty briefcases for full, just like Abanazar's 'new lamps for old' in *Aladdin*.

Not all Jim's customers were loggers. One of his favourite customers was a pig farmer. This enterprising Chinese farmer kept pigs, which he fed by collecting all the hotels' food waste. He piled this into a concrete mixer, made it into slurry and then fed to the pigs. This was cheap and had spectacular results. He applied to Jim for a loan in order to import a couple of breeding pigs to enhance his stock – he bred Chinese pigs, which were very fatty and wished to import some 'big whites' from Australia, which were leaner. This he did with great success. We went to a dinner party at the piggery, where we had our meal in a room just beyond the piggery, to celebrate his first piglets. Years later, we were pleased to learn that his enterprise had gone from strength to strength, and he was now a large exporter of pigs to Singapore, Hong Kong, China and other Southeast Asian markets. This was the sort of business that gave my husband a great feeling of achievement and much personal job satisfaction, rather than lending millions of dollars to vast conglomerates.

Sandakan had a yacht club, two hotels and a pharmacy. There was a general store aimed at the expatriate community and wealthy young Chinese, owned by the Yong family. and a number of smaller stores catering to locals and the timber/oil palm concerns. The town boasted three banks (to cope with all the millionaires) and a hairdresser, which was very important for the ladies. Other amenities included an airport and two ice cream parlours, which were very popular with our children. A few miles out of town was the Orangutan Rehabilitation Centre at Sepilok. At the time, it was in its infancy but is now world-famous.

There were two cold storages in the *kedai* (town), but as you had no idea how often the frozen food had been defrosted and refrozen, or how long it had been left on the quayside in the sun upon arrival, we had a six-monthly shipment of frozen food sent from Singapore. There was a very large chest deep freeze in the larder. When it was emptied, Ramasamy, who was a little, fat, jolly man, used to climb inside it in his bare feet to mop up the last of the melted ice, as his arms were not long enough to reach the bottom. I don't know how he could stand the icy water; his feet must have been as tough as old boots.

I have never been a fan of large chest freezers, as they are difficult to manage. Things you do not really care for invariably slip to the bottom. Before we left, we discovered a large turkey in ours, which we had had for two years. We defrosted it and had it for a supper party. No one suffered any ill effects.

Apart from collecting orchids, we collected butterflies. All the children loved doing this – our own, and any others who happened to be visiting – and it was not unusual to see six or seven children and a couple of adults with butterfly nets rushing all over the lawn. We originally had a 'killing bottle' (a large Nescafè jar) with a bit of cotton wool soaked in chloroform in the bottom of it, but the children soon became adept at killing the butterflies as they caught them, by squeezing their 'neck' – the join between their thorax and abdomen. Death was painless, instantaneous and safer than carrying around the jar. Any imperfect specimen was discarded from the net and allowed to fly away.

Early mornings are best for butterfly catching. The butterflies have just hatched, and their wings are perfect. As the day progresses, wings are often shredded by flying through dense vegetation. We soon learnt which shrubs the butterflies lived on. The large yellow Birdwings, for instance, which are the size of a small bluetit, love lantana, and you would often see a cloud of newly hatched butterflies winging their way out of a lantana bush. The green and black, iridescent, equally large Rajah Brooke's fly high in the trees and are difficult to catch.

In addition to these two spectacular species, there is a proliferation of others, all shapes and sizes. Among them are some very interesting enormous moths, particularly the Atlas moth, as well as various interesting species of beetles – stag beetles, ghost beetles and fiddler beetles – to name just a few. We asked the British museum to send us some exhibit boxes and amassed a large collection. Most of these we donated to the Bournemouth Natural Science Society after our retirement, where I assume they remain. There are over eight hundred species of butterfly in Malaya, and I daresay are a lot more in Borneo!

We had a Japanese entomologist friend who was butterfly hunting with Roddy one day. Rod caught a Birdwing, and on examination, the entomologist said he thought it was a new species. He sent the butterfly to Tokyo for identification. The museum said he was correct and named it after Roderick, who was thrilled. It is, of course, now illegal to collect butterflies like this.

We saw a lot of unusual wildlife in Sandakan. There was a family of large monitor lizards who lived halfway down our hill and used to walk across the road twice a day, holding up the traffic until they passed. A wild boar lived in the jungle in front of the veranda, and we occasionally saw him on the edge of the *lallang*.

About once or twice a year, we would have a plague of flying ants for an evening or two. A huge swarm of winged ants would suddenly appear after dark, out of nowhere, and invade the house. They were attracted to the lights, so we would switch on a veranda light and rush round closing all the windows and wooden shutters – usually too late, as they could get in the slightest crack – and they would fly around the room. They didn't bite or do any harm but flew into your eyes, hair, mouth, down your neck and crawled over your skin, shedding their wings on the way. We would normally retire to the air-conditioned bedroom for the evening – that having normally been shut up at dusk to keep out the mosquitoes – running into the darkened room, trying to race the ants for it before they could alight and creep onto your bed and between the sheets. By next morning, they had all disappeared, leaving behind a carpet of wings and crunchy bodies for Ramasamy and Padma to vacuum up.

David Attenborough visited Sandakan to make his first Borneo film whilst we were there, and Tony Lamb, who worked for the Rubber Research Station at Ulu Dusun, collected many animals for him to photograph. We visited Tony one Sunday for lunch to see an orchid which only flowered every twelve years, and which was in full bloom in the jungle by his house. Tony lived in a wooden bungalow covered in flowering creepers – bougainvillea, white night-scented jasmine and Dutchman's pipe – a sort of pitcher plant creeper.

We all got ready to walk through the jungle to see the orchid. Not far from the jungle's edge, Tony said, "Watch out, there's a large pit viper sitting on that leaf, but don't worry, it won't harm you, as it has just had its dinner and won't move for a couple of days." Sure enough, curled up on a huge leaf, slept a large bright green snake with a lump in its middle – doubtless the luckless mouse it was slowly digesting. Mhairi flatly refused to go any further, so she, Tom and I were left looking at the snake whilst Tony and Jim went to see the orchid. I was very disappointed, but Jim tells me it was a ground orchid growing on a large rotting tree stump with four-foot-long sprays of small pinkish-purple flowers.

Tony had a variety of bugs and small animals to show us, the most fascinating of which was a leaf frog, which he kept in a shoebox full of leaves. You had to look very carefully into the box to see the frog, as it was so well camouflaged and even Tony had difficulty finding it. He eventually took it out to show us. It was shaped like an assortment of maple leaves, one large leaf for its back, the stem for its tail and two of the three prongs of the leaf coming over and shading its eyes. Each leg was made of two smaller leaves – one went from his shoulder to elbow, and the other from elbow to end of foot, the prongs extending over his toes. Once he replaced it in the box, and we blinked, it had gone and we never managed to glimpse it again.

He also had a green flying snake, which we had seen captured at the Hong Kong bank house. The children and I went for a swim at their pool one day, and as we drove in, there was a tree across the drive. The gardener had caught the snake in the tree and put it in a bag for Tony to give to Attenborough. Flying snakes are not that common and, of course, don't have wings; they have a pair of floating ribs and some spare skin, which they inflate and use currents of air to fly from tree to tree. To film the snake flying, one of the Ibans put it down a blowpipe and then blew it out. They managed to recapture and film it twice before it flew off into the blue. Everyone knew that Attenborough was coming – particularly the animals. Tony said that when he went filming with him, animals just appeared out of nowhere and he saw things he had been looking for without success for years.

We took all our visitors to see the orangutans at Sepilok. 'Orangutan' in Malay means 'man of the forest'. The centre was very small. In a clearing in the jungle stood about half a dozen cages for the orangutans, a wooden hut for the staff and a wooden bench for visitors to sit on. About a dozen orangutans would be wandering around, ranging from three-year-olds to adults. They wandered in and out of their open cages, with no fear of visitors. Some would be walking on the fringes of the jungle, and you could take them by the hand and go for a walk round the clearing.

One of the females called Mary had a small baby. You were warned not to go near her or the baby, as she was very protective. They are big. An adult male is my size or bigger, and a lot stronger. Six- or seven-year-olds are comparable in size to a child of that age. All the orangutans had been rescued from captivity, and the centre staff taught them how to fend for themselves in the jungle – what fruit they could eat, where to find it and how to make their beds for the night – orangutans make themselves a sleeping platform of interwoven branches high in the trees. We went to the centre at least once every holiday with the children.

When I returned to St Albans and went to Rod's prep school on a PTA evening, I asked his science master, how Rod was doing. "Quite well," he replied, "but he does have some very peculiar ideas."

"What do you mean?" I asked.

"Well," he said, "we were having a lesson about animals, and he asked me whether on his next visit to Borneo, I would like him to bring me an orangutan."

"Well, yes," I replied and told him about the centre, and how you could take the animals for a walk and sit by them on the bench. "Well, yes, Mrs Kemp," he replied. "But take it on the plane sitting beside him."

"Yes," I said patiently and repeated myself, adding that a nine-year-old would not know about quarantine regulations.

"But, Mrs Kemp," he said, exasperated, "sitting beside him in the plane! How would it go to the toilet?"

At which point I gave up, as it was obvious to me that he had no idea of how these 'foreign' children lived. In fact, no one at the school had. Rod would come on holiday with a project to do on some topic like 'Medieval English Villages'. Now, not even the British Council in Kota Kinabalu had much information on this subject. Eventually, I said to him, "Why not do a project on orangutans instead?" This he did with great success.

Roddy and Linda Wallace were great friends. On his first trip, my sister-in-law told me that at Heathrow, Rod was crying and reluctant to board the plane on his own – despite having a BOAC Auntie.

As they were standing at the barrier, a little girl came up to him and said, "Are you Roddy Kemp?"

"Yes!" he said tearfully.

"Well," she said, "I'm Linda Wallace – come with me." And she took his hand and off they went.

Bunty and I tried to organise it so that they both flew out together, but this was not always possible. When they did fly together, they stayed overnight in adjoining rooms at the same hotel. On one memorable trip, Linda said to Bunty, "That Roddy Kemp is so embarrassing! He knocked on my door in the hotel last night and said, 'I'm lonely, can I come beside you?' I said, 'Yes,' but the next morning he could not find his wallet and passport. Everyone was looking all over the place for it and guess where they found it – under my bed."

Linda was ten. The pair of them spent a lot of time playing board games on our dining table – Monopoly and Totopoly were firm favourites. They were both terrible cheats! Mhairi and Mary were often roped in to play, but Mhairi exasperated everyone by buying as much property in Monopoly as she could and then refusing to sell anything, bringing the game to a grinding halt. "You must sell something," Rod would shout at her.

"No, I won't," she would say firmly, and that was that!

Every now and then, the Wallace children, our children and Silly all went to the 'Snowy' ice cream parlour with our friend Judy Cockburn for an ice cream. We would drive into town in my little Datsun 1100 – Judy and I in front and all five children in the back. Judy was a local Chinese girl and had not long got married to Peter an English forestry officer. At Snowy's, we would all order a large fancy ice cream, sitting on benches in the shop – our favourite was a banana split, but Judy favoured a ginormous Rainbow Snowy Ice Cream Special – I don't know where she put it. Judy was great fun, and she and I used to play mahjong (English style), together with another couple of wives every week at the bank house.

As it cost as much to fly from Sandakan to Singapore as it did to fly from Singapore to London – Malaysian Airlines having the monopoly on that route – we could only afford for me to either collect Roddy on arrival or to go with him to Singapore on his return journey. I chose to do the latter and spent an extra couple of days in Singapore staying with friends and shopping.

After my first trip, when I stayed in a hotel, our friends Sheila and Derek Stedman were posted to Singapore, where they lived in the bank Shelford Road flats, and I stayed with them, which was far nicer. I would see Roddy off on the first evening and then spend a couple of days shopping. I did all my Christmas shopping in September. The first September, I remember buying a Fischer-Price boat with little people in it for Mhairi. This Tom commandeered on Christmas Day, and I still have it – it has given countless children endless hours of fun – and the next year, I bought Mhairi a Barbie doll's house. This house had a lift in it which went up and down with a pulley sort of contraption, and Mhairi, Tom, Mary and Silly spent hours playing with it. Unfortunately, it was not very robust and did not survive past Sandakan.

We had no dogs in Sandakan. During our time in the bank, we spent an absolute fortune taking dogs from posting to posting, and being in between animals before we got to Sandakan, we decided we would have no more pets. But Bunty told me that Mhairi was desperate to have a cat, and I thought, *well, cats are not the same as dogs: you can pass them on with the house. No need to carry them around with you – is there?*

It so happened that a couple from Sime Darby were returning to Britain and looking for a home for their Siamese cat, so we said we would take him. Tao was a large, beautiful neutered male Siamese. He was half-wild and liked to spend most of his time in the jungle. We knew nothing about cats, never having owned anything but dogs, but as advised when we got him, we put butter on his paws and shut him in the bedroom for ten days, then let him explore the house before we let him out. As soon as we opened the door, he was off into the jungle. We called and called but he wouldn't return, so we got hold of his old Chinese cookboy, Ah Tam, who came to the house and called Tao, who returned for him. This happened three times, and the fourth evening, he disappeared.

We said to a tearful Mhairi that perhaps Tao did not want to live with us. It was about five in the evening and getting dark. At that moment, the heavens opened and there was a tremendous thunderstorm such as you can only get in Borneo. The rain lashed down, bolts of lightning flashed across the sky and thunderclaps crashed overhead. We ran to close the veranda doors, leaving just a bit at the side open in case Tao came back. After about ten minutes, we heard a plaintive '*miaow*', and a little head appeared round the door. A bedraggled, soaking wet Tao stalked in, shaking his feet. He took a look round the room, focused on Mhairi and jumped up into her lap, where he stayed.

From then on, he was definitely Mhairi's cat. Every morning, he followed her down the drive to see her off to school, then turned and stalked off into the jungle. At five to twelve, he would appear by the front door and sit in the carport, waiting for her to return. As he saw her coming up the hill at the end of the drive, he would run out to meet her, then return to the jungle till evening, when he would reappear and spend the night lying on her bed. He was more like a dog than a cat.

We built Mhairi a small Malay house at the side of the garden, and Mhairi, Silly, Mary and Tom, accompanied by Tao, spent a lot of time playing there in the afternoons. Mhairi, Tom and I returned to Britain before Jim, and Tao pined. Jim did not know what to do with him, as he sat at Mhairi's bedroom door, miaowing continuously and would not eat. He got very thin and Jim thought we would lose him. Eventually, Jim sat on the top step hand-feeding him bits of chicken, trying to tempt him to eat. This went on for about ten days. Of course, we could not possibly leave Tao and took him with us to our next posting in Kuala Lumpur.

Jim was a member of several committees, – it went with the job. He was a Rotarian, Treasurer of the Red Cross, Chairman of the RNIB and Treasurer of the Leper Society. Donald Stephens asked him to become Treasurer of the latter, as Donald had had leprosy during the war. There was a small leper colony just by Ulu Dusun, and all they wanted was to have some visitors. The Chinese will have nothing to do with something like leprosy and remain unconvinced that anyone can be cured of the disease, but of course, these days they can.

As I have said before, you made your own entertainment in Sandakan. Jim became Commodore of the yacht club, which was rebuilt during his tenure, courtesy of his timber customers who donated all the lumber for the rebuilding. Every three months or so we would have a dinner dance, and I would produce a revue-style cabaret with skits, musical skits and music hall numbers. One of our 'cabarets' also included a short melodrama which went down very well, with the audience hissing and booing with gusto.

We even had a Barbershop Quartet, 'The Sim Sim Singers', comprised of Robert Yong, who had a beautiful Italianate high tenor voice, was a complete novice and had never sung in parts before. Nor did he read music, but after tediously hammering out his part for him on the piano, he was able to hold simple harmonies as long as he had the tune. I ensured he did. Nigel Lever one of the local doctors was the second tenor. Joseph Ng, headmaster of the Chinese school, professional singer, guitarist and music teacher (trained in Taiwan) was the baritone. Guy Nickalls, who worked for Harrison & Crosfield, was the bass. 'Sim Sim' was the place where the yacht club was built.

I love Barbershop and had a large selection of songs for us to choose from, their favourite being 'By the Old Mill Stream' and 'Lida Rose' from the 'Music Man', with me singing 'Dream' on top of them. We had striped aprons made for them in the *kedai*, and I made four boaters out of cardboard and cartridge paper with a stripey ribbon around the rim. They looked and sounded really good. Our local Chinese audience, who had never heard Barbershop before, were astounded and very appreciative. They were very popular and the stars of the show whenever they appeared.

As I had a piano at our first Christmas, I was asked if I would like to produce a choir to sing some carols. There was a young Australian missionary at the Anglican church Steven Howse who played piano and organ, who accompanied us, and whose wife Robyn had a very sweet soprano voice. About thirty people came to the first rehearsal. I think they expected to be singing 'Come All Ye Faithful' and general carols, but this is not my style. I photocopied (courtesy of the bank's photocopier) some lesser-known carols from the *Oxford Book of Carols* for them to sing – in four parts. Our programme included 'The Zither Carol', The Cowboy Carol', 'The Boar's Head Carol', as well as community carols.

From September till Christmas, we rehearsed once a week on Tuesday evenings – women twice a week, once on a Thursday morning. This ensured the men got special attention on a Tuesday and did not get bored listening to the women learning their parts – I didn't bother about the women getting bored listening to the men – they generally have a bit more patience. We had the concert the week before Christmas in our lounge; everyone was welcome and we served drinks and mincepies after an hour's performance. This was very popular with everybody, and we repeated the format (with different carols) every Christmas during the three years we were there.

We had a pantomime in January every year at the yacht club, written and produced by ourselves and Nigel Lever, the doctor, who was a keen Amdram man and had spent some of his medical student days in London earning an extra penny or two, being 'First Roman on the left' at Covent Garden. The script for the panto always had to be sent to the government censor office for vetting, which meant you had to ensure there was nothing objectionable in the script, i.e. beware of political jokes. I often wondered what the local censor made of it all. We became adept in circumventing this censorship.

Our first production was '*Aladdin*', and we called the villain Mustapha Beah (pronounced 'Must Have a Beer'). Since the chief minister was called Mustapha, I was doubtful we would get away with this, but we did and a lot worse besides. The audience loved our shows – particularly the Chinese, who love slapstick. They often stopped us in the street to say how much they had enjoyed the show, and would we do it again? The next year we did 'Dick Whittington', which being set in London was not as easy to write as the more locally set '*Aladdin*'.

We also celebrated St Andrew's Night. There were four Scots in Sandakan – just enough to make a St Andrew's Society. We had been in Sandakan a year when Ian MacGregor who worked for Sime Darby decided we should have a St Andrew's Night – and we all thought that this would be a good thing.

We had just enough members for a Chieftain, Ian Macgregor; Treasurer, Bunty Wallace; Secretary, me and one other committee member, Sandy Guy. Once a week from about September, I taught Scottish Country Dancing to tapes in our lounge – enough room for four sets when the furniture was set back against the walls. Approximately, one hundred people came to the evening, including many of our Chinese friends and British Airways flew us heather and haggis, which I was detailed to cook.

The first year this happened, small haggis for about one hundred people arrived. As neither Ramasamy nor I had ever cooked haggis before, I looked up the recipe in Mrs Beaton's and said to Ramasamy, "We just have to boil it." This we did, putting all the haggis in a large pot. But we did not realise, nor did Mrs B. tell us, that you have to prick the haggis first.

Next thing we knew, the haggis all burst, and we had a sort of dirty grey sludge floating around in the bottom of the pot. Disaster! Ramasamy and I looked at each other and I said to Ramasamy, "Well, just strain it all and shape it into big lumps for about six, and by the time we pour the whisky all over it, no one will know any different."

This we did, and they didn't, apart from Ian, who gave me a strange look when he had to slay the haggis with his skean dubh after reciting Burns' 'To a haggis'. It was already looking very dead. By the time our guests had had a couple of glasses of my homemade Atholl brose (whisky, honey and lemon – it was too hot to bother about oatmeal and my old traditional recipe said it was 'optional'!) and got to the haggis after the Scotch broth, they were feeling no pain.

"What is haggis?" our Chinese friends asked. By the time we had told them about it being a bird which flies backwards so you have to shoot it over your shoulder, and how it has one leg shorter than the other to enable it to go up and down the hills more quickly, they just looked thoroughly confused. The dancing was a great success, and it was amazing that no one was thrown down onto our orchid poles during particularly enthusiastic and energetic Eightsome Reels and Dashing White Sergeants.

Most people left at about two a.m., barring Don Williamson a forestry officer friend of ours who stayed and finished a whole bottle of Parfait d'Amour all on his own. This is a liqueur which I think we inherited, made of essence of violets. It is a beautiful deep purple in colour and sickly sweet. I don't know how he managed to drink it all.

Eventually, at about four a.m., he left and wove his way to the bottom of the drive to get into his car. We heard him start the engine and went off to bed exhausted. We woke the next morning, came downstairs and saw to our horror a car balancing on the edge of the hillside, two wheels over the edge of the khud hanging in mid-air. We rushed out to find Don fast asleep on the back seat. We gingerly woke him up and got him out, then Ramasamy, his two boys, Jim and Don gently pushed the car back onto the road.

Celebrations for Chinese New Year lasted a week. The first day, traditionally, was a day of gambling. All the Chinese *towkeys* (businessmen) played mahjong for big money. Some of them gambled away their businesses, houses and timber concessions, fortunes often being made and lost overnight. A prominent businessman committed suicide one year, and the police then clamped down on the gambling for a bit – it was supposed to be illegal anyway.

On Chinese New Year's Day, it was customary for Jim to visit all his Chinese customers. He took the whole family with him, as this meant he did not have to drink quite so much. The children loved Chinese New Year. It is a Chinese custom to give all children and unmarried people a present of money in a red envelope. The amount of money can be anything from one dollar to as much as you like. It must be in odd numbers and in new notes. Jim got a supply of envelopes from the bank, which he filled with new one-dollar notes. At every house you went to, the children would dance around and shout at the adults, "*Li sze dao la, li sze dao la!*" – 'Give me some money, give us some money'.

We set out at eight in the morning after a hearty breakfast. Our first stop was always Ban Seng and his daughter Mary, one of Jim's customers who did a lot of barter trade. His shop was a veritable Aladdin's cave full of dried birds' nests, mushrooms, ginseng, octopus, sea horses and other Chinese specialities hanging all round the shop. He once gave me two large stuffed turtles, which I hung on our sitting room wall until I discovered the stuffing was full of insects. He also gave me two Chinese geese, on the hoof, as he was sure we suffered terribly from snakes in the garden (apart from the snake on the bougainvillea, I never saw a snake), and the geese would keep them away. Snakes hate the smell of goose droppings. Me too!

These two ghastly, belligerent geese took up residence in our garden, where they chased everyone and made a terrible mess on the lawns. However, they were terrific watchmen and honked loudly as soon as anyone came near the house. They were quite friendly towards Mhairi, but one day when she bent to pet them, one of them bit her, just missing her eye. That was enough for me! Off with their heads and into the pot. Ramasamy casseroled them, but they were as tough as old boots, so we gave most of them to him for a curry.

Ban Seng imported birds' nests and, at Chinese New Year, always served us birds' nests pudding instead of a soup – very sweet, expensive and horrible. Jim got brandy to drink, and I had Babycham. At eight in the morning!

I do not drink but once made the mistake of having one Babycham at one of his dinners, so every year he brought in a crate of Babycham especially for me. After staying about an hour, we went on to our next customer, trying to end up at the Yongs for a late lunch, which no one could eat.

It took us until about four o'clock to get round all the customers. I drove, as poor Jim had to have at least one drink per household. Even the children were so full of pop, they could hardly move by the time we got home.

I decided that Mhairi should learn to play the piano and asked around for a teacher. A friend of mine, Ngui Su Ket, recommended Joseph Ng, a teacher at the Chinese school who was teaching her daughter Susu, so Joseph came along to the house. He was a first-class musician – not only did he teach piano but was a superb guitarist, lovely baritone and a very nice man. He was a graduate of the music college in Taiwan. We became firm friends.

Jim decided he wanted to learn to play the guitar. I already had one, which I had tried unsuccessfully to teach myself to play in Klang. But Joseph found a lovely one for Jim, made in the Philippines, with a gorgeous ringing tone. It was big with a fat belly… I sat listening to the two of them playing for a while, and it wasn't long before I, too, wanted to learn. I, of course, had an advantage, because not only did I read music, but I quickly discovered I could apply all the theory of music I had spent years learning to the instrument.

We enjoyed our lessons tremendously, and Joseph taught us some Chinese and Malay songs as well as Burl Ives and country and western. It is amazing how many songs you can play with just three chords and three keys. He also taught us various guitar rhythms, so we could play the same song as a samba, rhumba, an offbeat *chacha*, foxtrot, pluck the strings or just strum. I am ashamed to say it has been over thirty years since I played my guitar.

Most Saturday mornings, during the school holidays, a party of wives and children would board Harrison & Crosfield's launch and speed off to Berhala, the nearest island to Sandakan with a good beach. It was uninhabited, but during the Japanese occupation, the island contained one of the most terrible of their prison camps – the men were encamped on one side of the island and the women and children on the other.

Many people lost their lives there, as illustrated in the book *And Three Came Home*, which is all about life in one of these camps written by Agnes Keith, an American married to a British government officer in Sandakan. She wrote the draft for this book in the prison camp on old can labels and in the margins of old newspapers. Old Sandakan hands told me she was loathed by the local expat community, who said she collaborated with the Japanese. I later found out that she apparently did so to get medicine for her sick child, which she would not share with any of the other women. Don't know what I would do in the same position – guess you never really know until it happens to you. There was nothing much to see at Berhala, just a large, very unsheltered beach. No birds sang in Berhala. It was much more interesting to go to the Turtle Islands at Selingan.

Selingan was much further away than Berhala – it took about three hours to get there by kungpit. It was a protected island, and you had to be invited by the agricultural officer in charge of the turtles to go there. Fortunately, Stanley D'Silva was a friend of ours. We went for the weekend. You took all your own food with you. There was a very basic wooden guest house on the island. The outside loo was a deep hole in the ground, with a plain wooden seat cover – a long drop. There was a bucket of lime beside it with a trowel, and you threw a trowelful of lime down the hole after use – having first made sure there were no scorpions, snakes or other undesirable creepy crawlies in residence when you visited it. There was also a turtle hatchery.

Visitors were not really welcome, as they disturbed the turtles. The island had beautiful golden sandy beaches. The water was crystal clear around all the islands and you could see twenty feet down to the bottom. So clear, that Jim got off the boat into what he thought was three feet of water and sank about seven feet, holding his camera above his head to try to keep it dry. He was unsuccessful.

The turtles come up late at night to lay their eggs. We waited patiently for them to arrive, and at last, at about ten o'clock, they came. The rangers motioned us to wait until the turtles had started laying before we went to see them. It was pitch black, the only light being that of the moon and the beam of the ranger's torch as he showed us where to go.

The female turtle comes up the beach and digs a nest in the sand, just below the vegetation line, with her flippers. This takes her some time. If she is disturbed, she will leave and not return. Once she has made her nest, she starts laying her eggs. She lays about fifty eggs. She groans loudly whilst she is laying them and cries. You can see the tears rolling down her cheeks. Once she has started laying, she will not move till she has finished. After all the eggs are laid, she covers them up with sand and then makes her way slowly back to the sea. You can disturb her then if you like – the children went for a ride on her back.

The rangers mark her nest, come back later, dig up the eggs and take them to the hatchery, where they are dug back into the sand and left to hatch. Each cache of eggs is surrounded by a small circle of chicken wire, to stop predators from digging them up. Every morning, the rangers go out with a bucket and collect any small hatchlings, which they take and put into the sea.

The journey from nest to sea is when the hatchlings are at their most vulnerable – a delicious morsel for marauding gulls and other predators. Once at sea, they still have many enemies, but if they survive and grow, they will make their way back to the place where they were laid. Turtle eggs are a great delicacy, and we had a couple for breakfast – it takes half an hour to boil a turtle egg.

On Roddy's last holiday before we left Sandakan, my cousin Grace, who was an artist, came to visit us. She had just retired. We met them at KK, and Rod was livid and not speaking to her. She was wearing a name tag, and had been escorted by the BA auntie. Of course, Rod was now a seasoned traveller, and this was frightfully infra dig. We took them straight up Mt Kinabalu, where we stayed at one of the national park huts for the weekend. Jim borrowed a Land Rover so we could get up the mountain. It was a red laterite road, and by the time we got to the hut, we were all covered in red dust.

It rained most of the weekend, and we did not attempt to go to the top of the mountain, the children being too young. We went halfway up the slope and a bit into the jungle, until Mhairi discovered a couple of leeches on her leg, screamed her head off and would go no further.

Here we saw the world's largest flower, the Rafflesia, named after Sir Stamford Raffles the founder of Singapore. The flower was about six feet in diameter and weighed about fifteen pounds. Its fleshy petals have a carcass-like appearance with red spots. There is no stalk – it blooms on the ground and smells like decaying flesh, sometimes emitting heat, much like a recently killed animal. These traits help the flower attract the carrion flies that pollinate it. It has a bud the size of a football. It is quite rare to see one.

At the bottom of our garden, on the plateau by Ramasamy's house, grew a huge albizia tree, whose fifteen-foot branches hung over the road to the top of the hill. Albizias are trees with very brittle branches which often break off. We had already had a couple fall on the road, bringing down the telephone wires, and Jim thought that unless something was done about the tree, someone could well get hurt. He contacted Peter Cockburn at the forestry department to come and see it.

Peter recommended that we take it down, so he arrived with about a dozen forestry workers to do so. We watched them from Grace's bedroom window. The tree was about fifty feet tall, with a girth of about twelve feet. Peter's workers fastened guy ropes round the tree so that they could guide its fall, and started sawing the trunk so it would fall onto the *padang*. They had cut three-quarters of the way through the trunk and were pulling on the ropes when suddenly the tree spun on its axis and crashed in the opposite direction bringing down all the electricity and telephone lines and smashing the large water pipe leading to the houses on the hill.

Jim, Peter and a couple of his men escaped with their lives by leaping into the large monsoon ditch full of muddy water as the tree fell. Some of the branches fell right over the ditch, and we were relieved to see them clambering out unhurt once the tree had landed. They soon sawed the tree up and cleared the road, but we were a week without a telephone and forty-eight hours without electricity and water. We thought we would all have to decamp to the nearby Sabah Hotel, as life without access to water, especially in the tropics, is impossible.

Jim flew to Lahadatu, Sempoorna and Tawau to inspect his branches about once every three months. Sempoorna was a real Wild West frontier-style town, plagued with Suluk (a tribe from the Philippines) smugglers/pirates who, when in harbour, swaggered through town in their check shirts, jeans and stetsons, pushing the terrified locals off the pavement. Many of them were armed with *parangs* and very old rifles left over from the Japanese occupation.

On one occasion, a group tried to rob the bank. The Chinese manager resisted and was badly beaten up before the police arrived. There were just not enough police to control the area, which is pockmarked with little bays into which the smugglers could sail and hide. At the time, there was considerable unrest in parts of the Philippines, and Suluks came over in their dozens and set up camp on the outskirts of Lahadatu, and sometimes Sandakan before they were rounded up and sent on their way by the police.

The family was invited by Robert Yong, a director of Sabah Pearl, to visit the Pearl Island off Lahadatu, where they produce cultured pearls. We flew to the island in a small plane. Living conditions there were fairly primitive, but the water in the bay was crystal clear. Roddy, much to his delight, was taken off by one of the Japanese and caught a large fish, much bigger than him. We spent the day on the beach there and flew back to Sandakan in the evening.

Robert's boss and owner of the Pearl Island Junior Kwan who lived in Hong Kong, occasionally visited Sandakan, but was politically persona non grata in Malaysia. When Malaysia was originally formed, he was a founding member of the Chinese People's Party (non-communist) in Sabah, in direct opposition to the pro-Malay party headed by the then Chief Minister Tun Mustapha. Junior made no secret of his belief that Mustapha was a crook and hurriedly left Sabah for Hong Kong to avoid being jailed in Ipoh, where most of the political prisoners (i.e. anyone vocally opposed to Malay hegemony) were 'rehabilitated'. However, his family were too rich and powerful for the government to make any trouble when he visited Sabah on the odd occasion.

He had a wonderful wine cellar but was no wine expert. We went to dinner one evening, and he produced a case of Château Rothschild, which at that time was worth about forty pounds a bottle. "Look at this wine," he said to Jim, vigorously shaking a bottle. "It is no good, look at all the bits floating in it!"

"Stop shaking it and give it to me," said Jim. "I'll take it home and decant it for you."

"Well, you can keep it; I don't want it," said Junior. Jim was delighted, took the case home, stored it correctly in the linen cupboard and decanted each bottle carefully just before he drank it. It was exquisite, and no bits.

Queen Elizabeth and Prince Philip visited KK in their yacht 'Britannia' whilst we were in Sandakan, and as Jim was the Honorary British Consul for East Coast Sabah and his boss in KK Arthur Norrie Honorary Consul for Sabah, we were invited to go and meet them at a garden party. Arthur flew the biggest Union Jack anyone had ever seen from the bank flagpole – so large that government house requested that he run up a smaller flag, as it was larger than theirs. In order to display the different tribes in Sabah, the hosts had got together a whole lot of Dyaks who lived in the town and lined them up in native dress complete with blowpipes. True to form, Prince Philip asked one of them to blow a dart out of his pipe. The dart barely made it out of the pipe and nosedived into the ground at Philip's feet. "*Humph*," he said. "I can see you haven't done that too often."

The timber market was booming, and Jim made a lot of money for his customers – whilst he was in Sandakan, the branch's profits quadrupled. When Jim left, one of his customers gave him a little present for me. I had already left for the UK, and unfortunately for me, Jim opened the box whilst still in Sandakan. It contained a large solitaire diamond ring. He immediately returned it, but his customer could not really see why he would not accept the gift. He said Jim had made him a millionaire, and the value of the ring was insignificant compared to the amount of money Jim had made him over the period he was in town.

I left Sandakan before Jim. The bank had said we would return, so we left our household unpacked for the use of our temporary replacement.

We had a spate of farewell parties before we left, the most memorable of which was a dinner at the Sabah Hotel given to us by the Yongs. There were about fifty people there, and the hosts were serving cocktails called 'Around the World in Eighty Seconds' – a lethal blend of brandy and about five liqueurs. The drink was placed on the lazy Susan in the centre of the table which was spun round, and whoever it stopped in front of had to '*Yam Seng*' it – that is, drink it all in one go. They ensured the drink kept landing opposite Jim. By the end of the evening, he could hardly see.

After dinner, we went to Edmund Yuen's the local architect for coffee. Jim left our car at the hotel and went in one of the Yongs' cars, whilst I went with Doreen and Edmund. As Edmund had also had several of these drinks, we had a terrifying drive down the wrong side of the dual carriageway up to their house. "Edmund, you *do* know you are driving on the wrong side of the road," I said.

"Oh, yes, never mind!" he replied. I took a deep breath and shut my eyes. Fortunately, it was late at night, there was no other traffic and we arrived safely at their bungalow.

When we departed Grace, the children and I left Sandakan sadly – Ramasamy and his family were at the end of the drive with tears running down his face. "We'll be back soon!" we shouted.

Not long after I left Sandakan, Jim started getting death threats on the telephone. Both Ben Stephens the Resident and Joe Muett the Police Chief were extremely worried about this, as firearms were easily obtainable. They put a tap on his telephone, and though the caller had a recognisably Malay voice, none of them could think of any reason why he was threatening Jim. Jim was very popular with his staff, whose union he had helped considerably, and he could think of no Malay customer to whom he had refused an overdraft. For his last couple of weeks, he had a police guard shadowing him in the bank, two officers shadowing him at home and one sleeping in the house at night. This somewhat marred his last few weeks in Sandakan.

Halfway through our leave, the bank changed its mind and we were posted to Kuala Lumpur. Maggie Seaton packed up the house for us as best as she could and sent everything, plus Tao, on to KL.

CHAPTER 8
KUALA LUMPUR (1975–1976)

Jim's new job in Kuala Lumpur was as Manager Administration, Malaysia. His brief included taking charge of all the bank properties in Malaysia, including a large building programme for new bank houses in Kuala Lumpur.

I was particularly delighted with this posting. It meant not only could we keep Mhairi, who was now eight, with us for another three years, as there was an excellent school for expatriate children in KL, I also knew from our posting in Klang that KL had many opportunities for music making.

Jim left for KL early in 1975, and Mhairi, Tom and I joined him after half-term. We stayed in the bank house at Kenny Hill – an attractive three-bedroomed house with a lovely medium-sized garden. Our predecessors, Peter and Dodo Rawlings, whom we had taken over from before in Madras, had left for their next posting by the time the children and I arrived.

I remember that there was a triple row of Diefenbaker plants lining the steps into the house. These plants have highly ornamental leaves – green with splodges of other shades of green, ranging from dark green to a creamy colour on them and are popular house plants all over the East. However, they are also poisonous, and I am extremely allergic to them. I was not in the house half an hour before I had succumbed to a massive dose of hay fever, with a runny nose and eyes almost shut. When this happens, the first thing we do is eliminate all the house plants. All the Diefenbakers were therefore relegated to the bottom of the garden under a tree – far enough away from me that they could do no harm. My hay fever cleared up nearly as swiftly as it had arrived.

As well as the house, we took over the Rawlings' servants – two young Chinese amahs Ah Lan and Ah Ying. Ah Lan was the cook and head amah, and Ah Ying the wash amah. They were not 'black-and-white' amahs – that is, they did not wear a black and white uniform. They were young and modern – so I asked them what they would like to wear. They decided on a yellow and red batik trouser suit. They chose the material themselves, had it tailored in the *kedai* (bazaar) and I paid for three suits each. They were very pleased with this. They were both very pleasant and efficient, and Ah Lan was an accomplished cook, who made a scrumptious lemon meringue pie.

We also had an elderly South Indian lady *kebun* (gardener) who had green fingers. She spent her time taking cuttings of all our ferns and potting them on for the new house. By the time we moved, we had a huge collection of various types of ferns. I also had the use of Jim's driver Meor – a lovely young Malay man in his twenties, though I normally drove myself.

Our Sandakan luggage and Tao the cat had all arrived in good order. We were also looking after the redoubtable Gulliver, a basset hound, whilst his owners, another bank couple, the Browns, were on leave. I have never had a dog quite like Gulliver before or since. He was a great character. Bassets are large dogs on short legs – and heavy. Gulliver commandeered the space under the staircase as his kennel, where it was cool and from where he could see the whole of the downstairs of the house and part of the garden. This was fine, except, like all hounds, he did smell rather, and when he was in residence under the stairs, the whole house smelt of dog. Gulliver was heavier than he should have been.

This was largely because he was such an accomplished thief. He could stand on his hind legs and reach the top of the dining table. It was impossible to leave any food on the table unattended – not even the butter, as he would be up there scoffing the lot. On one memorable occasion, I was having some ladies for tea, and Ah Lan made a lovely chocolate cake – big enough for about eight people. Mhairi opened the fridge door to get a drink, and quick as lightning, Gulliver sneaked in behind her, grabbed the chocolate cake in his mouth and fled to the bottom of the garden, where he devoured the lot in double-quick time before anyone had realised what had happened. At that time, I don't think anyone realised how lethal chocolate is to dogs, but it did not seem to do Gulliver any harm whatsoever, as he wasn't even sick. Poor Ah Lan had to make another cake.

We had a cane bar on the veranda, with bar stools and a foot rail round the bottom of it. We would usually have tea on the veranda coffee table, but Ah Lan had to put the tea tray on top of the bar, as an anti-Gulliver plan. This only just worked, as I came in one day to find Gulliver standing with his hind legs on the bar rail and stretching up to the tea tray on top of the bar. Unfortunately for him, he was about an inch too short and could not quite reach the plate of biscuits on the tray. Full marks to him, though, for effort and ingenuity. We had Gulliver for about six months, and then shipped him to Bangkok, where he safely rejoined his own family.

Both Tom (now five) and Mhairi (eight) were at school at the 'Alice Smith', where they settled in very happily. School hours were eight to twelve, and there were all sorts of extracurricular activities they could join during the afternoons.

My main occupation during the first half of our stay in KL was furnishing the new house. Four new houses were being built on the site of the old Chartered Bank manager's house. This lovely old colonial house was built on the top of a hill with extensive grounds, taking up the whole hill. The old house (which, I understand, contained a sprung ballroom) needed major renovation and the upkeep was horrendously expensive. With the formation of Malaysia, the bank restructured the business into suitable divisions with the headquarters in KL and now required more housing for its senior executive officers. The new house on the top of the hill was for the Chief Manager, Malaysia, and the other three, which were built on sites carved into the hillside, were for the Manager, Kuala Lumpur, the Manager, East Coast Malaya and the Manager of Administration, Malaysia (Jim).

These four mammoth houses – known locally as 'the palaces on the hill' – were completely air-conditioned and looked like something straight out of *Homes and Gardens*. I really cannot understand why the bank did not employ a professional interior designer to furnish the houses but left that to the four wives who just happened to be posted there at the time.

The most furnishing I, for one, had ever done was to purchase a new lounge suite and a couple of sitting room carpets in a couple of previous postings. I was completely inexperienced and found the task quite daunting, particularly as the budget, which had already been agreed before Jim took over, seemed to be rather haphazard at times – for instance, no budget was made for the lighting, which somehow had been forgotten about. It had originally been suggested that the 'Kenny Hill' house furnishings could be used in the new house, but this was inappropriate as most of the furnishings were too small.

We did keep the beds, coffee tables and a sitting room suite, which I had recovered and put upstairs in the family room. Despite teething problems, all four houses turned out spectacularly well, each having a totally different interior atmosphere.

The Chief Manager's house was on the top of the hill and had a tennis court. The road went past this down to the next house, which was for the Manager Kuala Lumpur then down again to our house which was for the Manager Administration, and down yet again to the house for the Manager, Kuala Lumpur.

There was a visitors' car park further up the hill by the Chief Manager's house, and the drive then went past the Manager KL's house on to ours. It bellied out in front of our house and the large double garage – everything about these houses was large except the drive. There was just enough room in front of the garages for cars to turn. We had a Volvo which is quite a large car.

All the houses were built of red sandstone fair-faced brick. This was the first time this had been used in KL and posed quite a few problems for the contractor. There was a covered 'carport', for want of a better word, which led down some stairs to the entrance. On the top right-hand side of the house were the bedrooms, and on the left a sort of half-dome affair that housed the staircase. Jim called it 'our phallic symbol'.

On either side of the 'sunken entrance' were two large flowerbed spaces, which I filled with pots of various types of ferns (courtesy of our green-fingered lady *kebun*) and anthuriums. The carved meranti front door led into a spacious entrance hall that in turn led into a corridor, which passed the dining room and the lounge and ended up at the foot of the grand stairway. Meranti is a type of Southeast Asian hardwood, which is often used in buildings in the area.

Downstairs was open plan, so you could see over the top of the corridor wall into a sunken lounge, which was separated from the dining room by large carved meranti sliding doors.

Between us, Jim and I designed two throne-like chairs for the hall and the 'Spanish ranch' style dining room suite. The dining room carpet came from the Kenny Hill house, and the celadon green sitting room carpet was new. Both carpets were 9ft x 12ft. The door at the back of the dining room ran into the kitchen.

The built-in kitchen was very spacious and beyond that were the servants' quarters-cum-laundry room – no hot water. This room was not air-conditioned, but if the kitchen door was left open, the air-conditioning easily cooled this area. The air-conditioning unit had a room to itself at the back of the house. It took us some time to get used to the central air-conditioning. It was freezing inside the house, but if you turned the cooling unit down beyond a certain temperature, the air did not circulate properly, and you could hardly breathe. If you turned the air-conditioning off and opened the windows, the walls 'perspired' and ran with water. So, to get some fresh air, I sometimes opened all the windows for an hour or two, with the air-conditioning on full blast and then shut them again.

When I put the sitting room carpet down, my neighbour Tessa Smallwood came round to have a look. "Now," she said, "where are you going to put the suite? (ordered but not yet arrived). Will it be round the carpet, or on the carpet?" I hadn't a clue – thinking I would just play around with it when it arrived – which I did. Tessa had furnished a big flat in Hong Kong, so she was much more knowledgeable than I was. I designed some glass/chrome tables for the lounge, which I was very pleased with. The floors in all the houses were of Italian marble – a choice of either brown or grey – I chose grey. As marble is porous, this was specially treated with an impervious coat of varnish, so that anything spilt on it was not absorbed.

The veranda ran round the back of the house beyond the living/dining room, and there were three steps down to the 'garden'. Our garden was just the steep hill leading down to Maxwell Road, partially cleared of the existing jungle. Jim tried to get the bank to terrace it, so that we could make a garden and preserve the hillside so that it would not be swept away by the torrential Malayan monsoon rains. Permission was refused. I understand that a couple of years after we had left, that is exactly what happened and the foundations of the house were exposed, necessitating expensive repair work.

We had breakfast on the bit of the veranda nearest the kitchen, but otherwise did not use it much because it was so close to the remaining jungle; it was alive with mosquitoes. It also had a brick floor, which was so uneven that it was impossible to run a trolley over it.

Once the furniture had arrived, it barely filled about half of the sitting room. "What are we going to do with the other half?" I asked Jim.

"I know," he said. "I shall hire you a grand piano." And he did. The full-size grand filled up a corner of the room. At the side of the piano were the lovely meranti doors separating the lounge from the dining room.

As it would have taken many yards of material to curtain the windows and the curtains would never be fully closed, I hung velvet drapes at the side of the windows with a white tulle net curtaining in between. These opened and shut, so that the French doors onto the veranda could be opened. It looked very effective. I would have loved to have had some leather ranchero-style armchairs and settee, but our budget did not stretch to these.

At our housewarming party, the wife of one of Jim's staff officers, who collected and sold Chinese porcelain sourced from old graves on the east coast of Malaya, (Kelantan, I think) looked at the wall between the corridor and the sitting room and said, "I have just the right plates to go there – I will bring them to you."

When Jim told me, I said, "I don't want any more plates – we have enough ornaments as it is." However, when she turned up a couple of days later with the most beautiful pair of large Japanese Amari plates, I fell in love with them and quickly changed my mind! She sold them to us for a song, and I still have them.

The corridor curved past the living area, up to a grand '*Gone with the Wind*'-style staircase that swept up to the first floor. At the back of the lounge was a golf store (we did not play golf, but it was a very useful storage area) and a 'ladies' loo and a 'gents' loo, complete with urinal. I had never seen a urinal before. Both toilets were spacious. The ladies' room had two toilets, plus a sitting area in front with wash basins and mirrors, so you could redo your make-up – rather like the 'ladies' cloakrooms in Harrods.

Upstairs, there were four en suite bedrooms and the family room. The master bedroom had a dressing area, but only one cupboard had a hanging rail high enough to hold an evening dress for me – and I'm not tall. There were loads of deep cupboards under the windows that reached way under the eaves. You had to crawl in to get anything. All the bathrooms were equipped with showers, a bath, his and her basins, a toilet and a bidet. We were given a choice of about six different ceramic tiles in three or four colours to choose from, for the bathrooms and the kitchen.

I chose curtains with a sort of Mondrian design on them for two of the bedrooms – red, black and white for the master suite, brown and green for Tom's bedroom, a floral pink and blue design for Mhairi's room and another modern design for the guest-cum-Roddy's room. In Rod's room, I hung two large Kelantan kites on the wall, which looked quite spectacular.

There was a special room at the end of the house that held the central air-conditioning unit. The electricity bill was extremely high, but fortunately, the bank paid it. We could not have afforded to live in the house had we had to pay it ourselves.

The ceilings were very high, so once a month, we employed a firm of commercial cleaners to clean the light fittings and the marble floors. There was no way I was going to let my *amahs* climb steep ladders to clean the light fittings in case they fell, and it was a big house to clean.

There was no garden to speak of – just a bit behind and at the side of the garage. I grew some orchids and had some beans and a passionflower vine in boxes. A Chinese friend of ours Dr Lam gave us two mangosteen tree stumps on which we grew some hanging orchids – mainly dendrobiums – which we 'planted' on the hillside outside our front door. Orchids apparently love mangosteen tree stumps. This was very effective.

While in KL, we attended the Roman Catholic St John the Evangelist Cathedral. They had a youth choir accompanied by several guitars and a pair of bongo drums. They sang the then relatively 'new' church music, which was a mixture of folk and 'beat' music, that is supposedly easy for congregations to sing and appeals to the youth. We sang similar music very successfully in the church in Singapore during our tour there. However, at St John's, they sang the 'new' music in the old style – namely 'slowly is holy' – with the guitars playing what is called 'the continuous beat', i.e. no rhythm. This removed all the soul out of it.

I complained vociferously about this to Jim for a couple of weeks, until he got irritated with me and said, "Well, why don't you do something about it!"

"Okay, I will!" I said. After mass, I introduced myself to the members of the choir, the leader of whom appeared to be the drummer, Leslie Fernandez, and one of the guitarists called Doray. We chatted for a while, and Leslie informed me they had just lost their choirmaster, so I offered my services and was welcomed with open arms.

There were about thirty members, aged from about eight to thirty. As with all church choirs, this fluctuated from week to week. There was anything from two to eight guitarists and Leslie on his bongos. They were all very keen and rehearsed for half an hour before mass, so they could teach the congregation the new music. "And Mrs Kemp," said Leslie, "we rehearse three afternoons a week." Rather more than I had bargained for.

They could do this, as most of the older members seemed to be jobless, and the school-aged children either went to morning or afternoon school. "All right," I said.

We started off with a hymn they knew and me saying to Leslie and the guitarists, "Now, this has got to be faster – see – it's a Viennese waltz – *one*, two, three, *one*, two, three, *strong*, weak, weak, *strong*, weak, weak. Try and dance to it!" They looked shocked. "And it's happy – listen to the words!" Though I was no guitarist, I could play a little, having had some lessons in Sandakan with Joseph Ng, a gifted teacher. Joseph taught me how to play various rhythms in a couple of keys, so I could demonstrate.

Doray was very talented. He could not read music, but all you had to do was sing what you wanted him to play, and he would copy you. Soon all I had to say to him was, 'This is a foxtrot' or 'quickstep' or 'rhumba', 'samba', 'calypso', 'rock', 'off-beat chacha' – and they were away. We sang all sorts of music – the only thing I banned was the 'continuous beat'. Now and then, I would throw in an old hymn slightly jazzed up – we did a very nice slightly jazzed-up 'Regina Coeli' for Easter, and 'Personent Hodie' (not jazzed up) for Christmas, both in Latin and both sung extremely fast.

Half an hour before mass on a Sunday, I would go into the pulpit and run through the hymns with the congregation at the new speed. They all joined in and sang heartily. I thought we might have some complaints about the new tempos, but we didn't – at least *I* didn't!

When we moved to the new house, they came up to Maxwell Road for rehearsals, which they enjoyed, as it was cool. Ah Lan used to put a couple of jugs of orange squash and some biscuits on the trolley for them to have at half-time, whilst we rehearsed.

Just before Christmas, Leslie said to me, "Mrs Kemp, every Christmas we go carol singing. We hire a lorry for four days before and visit every member's house, singing. Whoever's house it is gets to choose the carols."

"Oh dear!" I groaned to Jim later, "I shall die of a surfeit of 'Drummer Boy' and 'Little Donkey'". I could not have been more wrong. To my astonishment and huge delight, the most requested carol by a long chalk was 'Personent Hodie'.

It was not easy in Malaysia to get a good job, especially for ethnic minorities, so Jim helped Doray to get a job as a messenger with the bank. After we left, we heard that he did very well indeed, becoming first a clerk and then an assistant officer. He must have worked extremely hard in a very competitive field. I do hope he kept up his guitar playing.

After mass, we would often take the children to the Equatorial Hotel for Sunday lunch. This was mainly because there was a trio of Filipino guitarists playing during lunchtime. There was a kind of syllabub on the dessert menu, which we always ordered. This was made at the table, with a lot of accompanying razzmatazz.

First, the head waiter appeared bearing a large silver bowl with the ingredients in it – mainly egg whites and cream and then waiters with egg whisks. The band would come over playing their guitars, and the head waiter would whisk the mixture up in the bowl, in time to the music. First very slowly, and then the music would go faster and faster, and faster and faster and *faster and faster*. Still, he would whisk in tempo until eventually, whisking and music would build up to a molto vivace crescendo. Sometimes, the performance would last five minutes or a bit more when they saw how much we all enjoyed it.

The head waiter would then pour the mixture into a serving dish lying in smoking dry ice and serve it. As far as I remember, the pudding did not actually taste all that good, being very frothy and rather like eating cotton wool – but the whole experience was well worth the outrageous price charged. We all loved watching this.

Early in our stay, I contacted the School of Music and did a few concerts for them and the British Council, one of chamber music, one with the Philharmonic Society of Selangor and a very enjoyable 'Christmas from Dickens' programme, which was a mixture of skits, monologues, readings and parlour songs that you would have heard in Victorian/Edwardian Britain. I sang a couple of lieder, as well as 'Father, Dear Father, Come Home to Me Now' a parlour song and 'The Honeysuckle & the Bee', a music hall song – so quite a variety. It was a most successful evening.

'Father, Dear Father, Come Home to Me Now' is a very lugubrious song about an alcoholic father, who spends his money at the pub instead of on his starving family. His little boy is sent to stand outside the pub – children not being allowed entrance into the pubs in those days – and plead with his father to 'Come home', where his brother is sick and dying. A popular, tuneful song of its day, it was basically a social commentary on life in Victorian Britain – a genre of song that, in modern times, is generally lampooned, but which, sung straight, can, and did 'bring a tear to the eye'.

Through the Music School, I found a lovely singing teacher, the wife of the Austrian trade commissioner, with whom I had a most enjoyable hourly lesson every week. She introduced me to the songs of Mahler, Richard Strauss and Robert Stolz, the latter the composer of many lovely waltzes, and the musical 'White Horse Inn'. I had sung in the chorus of 'White Horse Inn', staged by the Arbroath Operatic Society one year when my parents were on leave. It is a very tuneful musical, with 'every song a smash hit', as they say in the adverts.

My last concert in May 1976 was with Helga and five other KL singers: Patricia Wood, mezzo, whom I had sung with when we were in Klang in 1966; soprano Gerda Revenger; Eddy Chin, a popular KL light baritone and tenor Leow Siak Fah, accompanied by Ling Ai Ee, Siak Fah's wife. She was a wonderful accompanist who was also a medical doctor. How talented can you get! The concert was called 'A Night of Romance' and made up of extracts from 'New Moon', 'Perchance to Dream', 'The Merry Widow', 'Show Boat', 'The Bat', a tribute to Robert Stoltz and some romantic Malay songs, which are very tuneful and a bit Hawaiian in character. The concert was held to raise funds for the Assunta Hospital in KL. We played to a full house and made a lot of money.

Once a week, I played 'Scrabble' with three other friends: Winnie Brown, Elizabeth Taylor the UK trade commissioner's wife and another friend. Elizabeth was a great scrabbler. Everything that was in the Chambers Dictionary was allowed. This included words like "Jo—"

"Not a word!" I said.

"Oh yes, it is!" she replied triumphantly. "It's Scots for 'darling' as in the song 'John Anderson, Ma Jo John' (Rabbie Burns). You should know that!" says she to Winnie and me.

We sat abashed! And 'zo', which is a cross between a yak and something else and which you can spell 'zo', 'dzo' or 'dzho' – so a very useful word – and 'ai', which is a two-toed sloth. We felt highly educated by the time we had finished. When it was my turn to host the game, I would say to the ladies, "Don't forget to bring your cardies!" as it was freezing inside my palace with the central air conditioning, though it would be about ninety degrees plus outside.

We had quite a few 'visiting firemen' from London, notably one from the then bank chairman Lord Barber, accompanied by Lady Barber. The general manager of the hotel he was staying at was quite overcome at having a real live 'Lord' at his hotel, and when he welcomed him, 'Lorded' him all the time he was speaking to him. We had him saying, "Welcome, Lord... oh Lord... My Lord... Good Lord..." which had us all smiling. I don't know how Lord Barber kept a straight face.

It is quite easy to get out of KL, and we made the most of trips out of it with visits to Port Dickson, Ipoh (where, unknown to us, our hotel just happened to be the local brothel and we were kept awake all night with clients walking up and down the corridor outside the room), and a weekend at Fraser's Hill, where the bank had a lovely holiday bungalow for the use of its staff.

The latter trip was very memorable. We set off with our family and our friends Winnie and Bill Brown from our Klang days and their two girls, Wendy and Shona. We stopped for a picnic halfway by a waterfall, and the children were climbing up and down it, chasing butterflies. Roddy suddenly missed his footing and went tumbling down the waterfall. Fortunately, the next ledge was not far down and broke his fall. He was unhurt, but ever afterwards has suffered from vertigo and can't abide heights. Had he fallen to the bottom of the waterfall, he would doubtless be dead.

Having said we would be in KL for three years, in about June 1976, the bank posted Jim to Japan, where he took over from the manager, Tokyo, for six months whilst the incumbent went on sick leave. After that, and Jim's leave, we were to go to the Seychelles. To say that I was extremely annoyed would be putting it mildly. This meant that we would lose Mhairi to boarding school, the family would be unable to accompany Jim to Tokyo, (which I would very much have liked to do), as I would have to return to St Albans to find a suitable boarding school for her to go to, none of which I wanted to do.

We had only just settled into our new palace, were reconnecting with all our old Klang friends like the Yeoh Tiong Lays, and my singing had taken off. This always takes time in a new place. However, we had no choice – we went where and when we were told. We packed up very regretfully. I said a tearful goodbye to my choir, who gave us a lovely farewell party, presenting me with a Selangor pewter clock, which I still have. We made our way back to St Albans – or, in this case, to Harpenden, where my in-laws had found us a rented house, our own house being let out to tenants.

CHAPTER 9
SEYCHELLES (1977)

In January 1977, we went to the Seychelles. Whilst we were in KL the Bank had merged with the Standard Bank of South Africa, so we were now known as The Standard Chartered Bank.

Paradise on earth! Beautiful islands, wonderful golden sandy beaches bordered with swaying palm trees, sea, sun and sand. You get the picture. What more could anyone ask?

The Seychelles is a group of one hundred and fifteen islands, most of which are uninhabited, the largest inhabited islands being Mahe and Praslin and La Digue.

First discovered by the British in 1609 all the islands were then uninhabited, but apart from reporting the discovery to London, Britain took no further interest in the place. From then until 1720, pirates are believed to have used the excellent harbours to repair their ships and store supplies, and rumours of buried treasure abound. In 1756, Captain Nicholas Morphey claimed the islands for France, and they were put under the rule of the governors of Mauritius. The French planted vanilla and cinnamon plantations and brought in African slaves to work them.

During the Napoleonic Wars, the Seychelles changed hands several times between the British and French culminating in the islands becoming a British colony. They in turn brought over some Indians, Malays and Chinese to help work the plantations. In 1807, Britain made slavery illegal although it was still possible to own slaves. Full emancipation came in 1839, and slave owners were paid compensation for the slaves they lost.

Despite being British, Seychelles had the typical social structure of an ex-French colony. Rich planters, or the 'Grand Blanc', usually of French origin, enjoyed most of the wealth, while those of African descent scraped a living from the sea or small vegetable gardens. Those of mixed parentage, or the 'Blanc Koko' (the not-so-well-off whites), fell in between the two levels.

In June 1976, Seychelles became an independent republic in the Commonwealth. The story goes that when Seychelles went to the United Nations to ask for independence from Britain, the Secretary-General asked the Seychelles representative what it was that the islands wanted. "For the islands to be returned to their original inhabitants," he replied. The British ambassador to the UN replied drily that indeed Britain would be glad to return the islands to their original inhabitants, which was the giant tortoise. The flamboyant Jimmy Mancham became president, and Albert Rene became prime minister. This was the status quo when we arrived in Mahe in January 1977.

So as a people, the Seychellois have a short history. They came from diverse backgrounds, some from France in search of their fortunes, others Creoles, born in the colonies. Much of the population were voiceless slaves from Africa and Madagascar. This is reflected in the Creole language, which, though based largely on French, includes African, Malagasy, Arab and English words. Added to this melting pot were the descendants of the South Indian, Malay and Chinese workers brought to the colony by the British.

In a large Seychellois family, say, with ten children, you will find the racial characteristics of many races. A dark negroid child at one end of the scale, ending up with a redhead at the other, with a typical redhead's pale skin, blue/green eyes and freckles, and every shade of colour in between. Many of the islanders are inter-related, so you must take care about what you say about people, as they are liable to say, "He/she is my cousin!"

Most Seychellois are devout Catholics. This does not stop them having loose family ties, with frequent partner changes or cohabiting couples choosing not to get married until fairly late in life. It is a matriarchal society, with the children being named after their mother, e.g. *Jean ap Marie* (John, son of Mary). This is because the woman may well have had several lovers, any one of whom could be the father of the child. If this is the case, then all the men involved chip in to help support the child – that is, supposing they have any money in the first place. Seychellois men are not noted for their industry.

It was quite disconcerting to be introduced to a couple, and to meet them several times socially, under the impression that they were married, and then one day to find the man with a completely different woman on his arm, and to be reintroduced – "Oh, Noreen, this is Raoul Poole and his wife

Janette!" The other lady was his mistress – or *bulldoo*, as she was called. A '*bulldoo*' in Seychellois is a sort of sticky currant bun with honey in the middle.

Under this thin veneer of Catholicism lurks traces of voodoo, known as grigri and practiced by sorcerers. A good sorcerer can cast a spell on someone to influence his judgement, create a love potion, deal with a troublesome zombie or harm someone.

There are three main kinds of Seychellois music: one of African origin, a slow and very sensual dance, which at one time was forbidden by the church as lewd; the lively *sega*, which is the most popular dance of the islands and tourists – I thought this was akin to the dance of the hornbill, which we saw in Borneo, done by the Dayaks, albeit much faster and more suggestive than the slow and stately hornbill dance; and the *kanmtole* which sounds like Scottish country dancing, the music for which is played on violins, accordions and drums and I guess was brought to the islands by visiting sailors.

When I was writing this chapter, I went to the library and looked at a guide to the Seychelles, printed in 1994. How it has developed since the 1970s! There are umpteen hotels, things to do and places to see – all at a shocking price, I expect – the Seychelles has always been very expensive, both to visit and to live in.

But in the 1970s, tourism was in its youth. There were two jumbos a day, three large and some smaller hotels and assorted B&Bs. There was one large hotel on Praslin, a smaller one on La Digue and a sort of rest house on Bird Island. Today hotels abound! Water sports are all available, there are tours to various islands and a couple of national parks. When I read the brochure, I said to Jim, "Is this the same place that we lived in for nine long months?" I did not recognise it.

We arrived in January 1977, were met by our predecessors, the Wilkinsons and taken to our pensione, the Bougainville, a lovely old Seychellois house, with deep verandas and a thatched roof. Here we stayed very happily for a fortnight whilst Jim took over the bank.

As usual in a bank handover, we were royally wined and dined by customers and the Wilkinsons introduced us to all their friends. The chatelaine of the Bougainville very kindly used to babysit Tom, our young son, for us every evening. Tom was the only one of our three children now with us. He was six. The other two were at boarding school and joined us for all their school holidays.

When we arrived, Mahe was in the grip of a serious dengue fever epidemic. Seychelles had never had dengue fever before, and a plane must have brought the dengue mosquito into the islands. All planes were sprayed on arrival to get rid of any mosquitoes and any other unwanted passengers, but as the doors were opened to let the mosquito sprayers in, any self-respecting mosquito would have had time to beat a hasty retreat out into the lovely sunshine beyond the plane. This must have been what happened. As the locals had no immunity to dengue, the fever spread like wildfire throughout the island, and those infected were very ill indeed. About half the population was in bed with the fever – the staff at the bank was at half strength and Lianne's three maids were all ill.

Lianne, therefore, asked our landlady one evening if she would babysit her little girl Shona with Tom. She agreed, and Peter, Lianne, Jim and I happily set out for dinner. We returned to find the landlady tearing her hair out. Apparently, both children, having been put to bed before we left, had appeared in the bar in their pyjamas demanding a drink. They got a lemonade and ostensibly returned to bed. When Ghislaine went to the room to check on them, she found the place a total wreck. The children had put the plug in the bath and filled it with water. It had overflowed all over the floor. They then swung on the shower curtains, which had collapsed in a heap on the floor and were skating around the bathroom in the flood, which was just going to go into the bedroom.

Never having had any trouble with Tom before, I asked what on earth he had been playing at. 'It was Shona, Mummy', he said. "Shona didn't want to sleep!" I then discovered that young Shona had a reputation as a bit of a terror. Fortunately, the Wilkinsons left the next day, as we had now lost our lovely babysitter, who swore she would never babysit for us again.

We saw the Wilkinsons onto the plane the next day. Lianne collected shells. I have never ever seen anyone get on the plane with so many plastic bags – all full of shells collected from the beach, some of them apparently quite valuable! Lianne told me that the rarest shells are not usually the large conch varieties you normally see, but often the very tiny ones.

We returned to the Bougainville to pick up our luggage and move to the house. I can honestly say I have never lived in a more inappropriate house all the years we were in the bank.

It was a brand new house about a year old, halfway up Sans Souci, the highest mountain in the Seychelles. The architects had designed the house to sit into the mountain at the back of the building plot, so that you drove off the road into your garage, had your lounge, dining room and kitchen on the top floor, and your four bedrooms underneath. The rest of the plot was in front of the house and would have been the garden.

However, building in the Seychelles is not cheap, and once the house had been costed, the bank decided it was far too expensive to build. So, instead of redesigning it, the architects just halved the proportions and pushed the house forward to the front of the plot. This posed grave problems for the occupants.

You now drove down a long, steep drive with a hairpin bend halfway down. It was edged by cinnamon trees on both sides, which shed their leaves all year round, all over the drive, making it extremely slippery when wet. You had to go up in first gear. We always warned our visitors of this, particularly after they had been for dinner and were on their way home having had a good meal and several glasses of wine and other assorted drinks. Our parting words would be, 'Don't forget to go all the way up in first gear!'

But halfway up, they would think, *Oh, it's not so bad*, and change into second. This would be followed by the shriek of tyres as they spun on the tarmac and we waited anxiously until we heard them change down again, hoping they would not go over the side of the hill. I'm glad to say no one ever did.

There was no garden that you could sit in, as the house was now in front of the plot with a hill behind, with no view of anything but a bit of jungle at the side, the maid's little house and a sheer drop down the hill in front. We did clear a bit of jungle at the side of the house, stepped it and grew some vegetables – tomatoes, cucumbers and aubergines – the biggest aubergines I have ever seen, a deep rich purple colour. There were some bananas growing at the edge of the jungle. However, we did not get too many of the vegetables, as if you left them on the plant to ripen, they disappeared. So the gardener would cut the hand of bananas before they were ready and let them ripen in the garage, and the tomatoes, cucumber and aubergine would go on the coffee table in the veranda. The back of the site was a bit claustrophobic, with the hill towering behind you.

The garage was now underneath the kitchen. The front door led onto a small hall, off which lay the master bedroom. Down a corridor to the left were the other three bedrooms. As is normal out east, all the bedrooms were en suite. However, the corridor was only two feet six inches wide, which meant that two largeish adults could only just pass each other.

All the bedrooms had French doors, which led outside to a cleared strip of ground before it fell away down the hillside into some more jungle. These were all kept firmly locked. However, I found out later, that the doors were insecure. You could lift them out of their runners and open them quite easily. This only came to light at the end of our stay in Seychelles.

On her first holiday, Mhairi said to me the day after she arrived, "Mummy, someone was in my room last night!"

"Nonsense," I replied. "You must have been dreaming. No one can get in here!" She never said anything else. However, I did notice that her French doors were often open. As the bedrooms were air-conditioned, I was always saying to her, "What is the point of putting the air conditioning on if you leave the doors wide open!" I never thought anything more of it.

However, at the end of our stay, we had a friend's daughter Sara staying with us – she was about nineteen. The second night she was there, she said to me, "Noreen, there was a little boy in my room last night! Actually, he was there the night I arrived. I woke up in the middle of the night and saw him standing at the foot of my bed, but thought I must have been dreaming and suffering from jet lag. But last night, I woke up and there he was again, shaking my big toe through the bedclothes. When I sat up and put on the light, he ran off through the open French doors!" This turned out to be Louisa, the maid's little boy. I was horrified! We, of course, immediately put stoppers and new locks on all the doors to stop it happening again.

You went up the staircase in the hall into the lounge – a nice large room, then into the dining room and finally into the kitchen. The house was surrounded on two sides by a veranda. The view from the veranda was one of the most spectacular in the Seychelles. You looked out over the wooded hillside down onto Victoria, which is the capital, out onto the beach and the sea with La Digue floating on one side, and way out to Praslin in the centre. You could only see Praslin faintly on a very clear day. The sea was three shades of blue darkening as the water deepened.

Unfortunately, the veranda was so narrow that you could only put your chairs in a straight line to look out at the view. There was just room for a small table in front of the chairs.

The eaves of the roof stopped above the railings of the veranda. The architects had also forgotten (or never knew) that Seychelles has two monsoons. So, for one monsoon, you could not sit on half of the veranda, as you were washed out – the rain came in horizontally, and for the other monsoon, you could not sit in the other half of the veranda for the same reason. All my visitors used to look over the veranda and gasp in wonder at the view, but unfortunately, you can't live on a view.

As I have said before, all houses provided by the bank were fully furnished and usually extremely well kitted out. This included linen, china (usually Doulton, Wedgwood or something similar), silver cutlery, kitchen pots and pans, crystal and everything you could wish for in a house. As the choice of furniture and furnishings was extremely limited in Seychelles, someone in London had been assigned to buy the furnishings for the house. They had gone to Waring & Gillows, where they had bought expensive but entirely inappropriate furniture for the tropics.

We had a soft upholstered, brown dralon-covered three-piece suite, which was extremely hot to sit in and fully lined brown brocade curtains. Brown is not a suitable colour for the tropics. The curtains required dry cleaning, and the mud wasps loved them. Most mornings, I would pull a mud wasp nest off the curtains. I never drew them, as I think they were pitted with little holes. There were no dry cleaners in the Seychelles.

The Regency-style dining room suite was made of veneered chipboard – very nice to look at. However, in the hot, steamy climate, the veneer lifted off the chipboard sideboard and curled up at the edges This was the second lot of furniture, which the bank had sent out to Mahe, as the first lot had had some sort of accident on one of the lighters and had arrived in pieces.

There were no backdoor or backstairs, so all rubbish from the kitchen had to be taken out of the house through the reception rooms and down the main (indeed, the only) staircase. I often wondered what would have happened in the event of a fire – no fire escape!

There was no rubbish collection in Mahe. You put your bin in the car and drove to an open concrete bunker bin at the side of the main road going down the hill, into which you dumped your rubbish. The bunker was covered in flies, full of mangy dogs and cats picking over the rubbish, and rats at night. Almost directly opposite it, was a large sign saying, 'Keep Seychelles Beautiful'.

As it was illegal to have a bonfire in the garden because of pollution, we decided we would incinerate some of the perishable rubbish and Jim ordered a couple of metal bin incinerators from a friend who had a small wrought iron factory. Nine months later, they still had not arrived.

Further round the circular island road was 'smelly corner', so called as all the rubbish from the open bin bunkers around Mahe was collected by the rubbish trucks and dumped in a small bay. It stank to high heaven. Further round the road was a bay of great beauty where the scuba diving and sea life were amongst the most magnificent in the islands. Hopefully, the government has now dealt with this problem.

The roof of the house was shaped like a V, with the V being in the centre of the roof with a large drain in it. This was so that the house would look like a bird in flight – if you looked at it from the sea, that is. As the sea was so far away, you could not actually see it from the sea! All the water and debris from the roof collected in this V and soon came pouring in through the ceiling in places. It was difficult to clear the downpipes at each end of the V without special ladders and nearly impossible to find someone to do it. Workmen were at a premium on the islands.

The whole house was made of porous granite, and the outer walls in the veranda and by the garage wept when it rained. The upstairs windows leaked. I used to roll up a thick candlewick bedspread and lay it under the window at the top of the stairs to try to stop the water pouring down them. Despite trying, we were unable to get this problem fixed satisfactorily.

I looked with envy at my friends in Barclays Bank, who had an old Seychellois plantation-style house by the sea, with their own patch of rocks and an old boat for their boys to mess around in, cane furniture and washable cotton curtains.

As I said before, we arrived in the middle of a dengue epidemic. We inherited three maids – one who did the washing and ironing, a cook Marie, and Louisa who did the cleaning. They all had dengue, and one never returned. I hired another in her place – a young girl called Jacqueline.

I discovered that they all arrived at eight in the morning and left at three p.m. As Jim was in the office by eight, this meant that Marie only cooked lunch, and I cooked breakfast and supper. I tried to stagger their working hours – this was a major operation – and eventually managed to do so. As Louisa stayed on the premises, she arrived at seven to give us breakfast and worked until eleven, then returned at four and stayed till eight to give us supper. Marie came at eight and left at three, and Jacqueline came at ten and left at five after she had finished the ironing. If we had guests, they all stayed on longer and either Jim or one of the guests, took Marie and Jacqueline home after the party. This was very necessary, as it was not safe for women to walk home alone after dark. They got paid extra for the party.

A lot of my day was spent in the car. I sometimes felt like a glorified chauffeur. The day started early. Tom was at school and Jim in the office by eight, so I drove them down the hill and then returned.

When we arrived, I asked Lianne when she went to the market. She said about two p.m. – but there was never anything to buy, and I thought, *No wonder if you don't get there until two o'clock.* Everywhere I have been in the East and Africa, you must be at the market early – say from seven a.m. to nine a.m. if you want to buy the best produce. The first day I took Jim to the bank, off I went to do my marketing. The market was not even open. Indeed, there was no point in going there at all except on a Saturday morning – at about eleven o'clock – as there was hardly anything in it. A few tomatoes and onions, a few limes – very sweet, you can almost eat them with no sugar at all, bananas, bigarade – a type of very small orange about the size of a lime, which makes fantastic juice and marmalade – and that would be it. Not even any fish. No shops opened until about nine thirty, so I would drop everyone off and return home. Back to the shops at about ten thirty to see what could be had. Not much some days!

The main supermarket was an Indian store called Teemooljees. If you met an acquaintance on the street, they would say, "Hi! Teemooljees has got some tomatoes this morning!" And off you would chase to see if you could get any. I found this way of living tedious to say the least. Almost everything was imported, which is why living in the islands was so expensive.

By the time we left, the agricultural department had set up an experimental farm on one of the islands, and on a Friday their boat would come in with fresh produce – lettuce, tomatoes, aubergines and cauliflower, etc. There was a great demand for this, and you had to be on the quay side early (that is, at noon when the boat arrived) if you wanted the pick of the produce.

Back I would go up the hill, returning at twelve thirty to pick up Tom and Jim for lunch. Back down the hill at two with Jim and then take Tom off to the beach or to play with friends. Back again at five to collect Jim. I eventually got a morning job with a firm of architects who had their office next door to the bank. This halved our petrol bill and saved me from going bonkers.

Most weekends, we would go to the beach or sometimes on a special trip. All the children loved the Seychelles! There was a deep-sea diving school with an Australian instructor called Brownie at the Coral Strand Hotel, and Jim learned to scuba dive.

There are no snakes or sharks in the Seychelles – of the animal variety, that is! However, never go on the rocks without some sort of shoe – flip-flops won't do, as there are many other things which sting and bite, including some extremely vicious sandflies. Only Beau Vallon beach was sprayed against these – I expect this has now been extended to other beaches. Insect spray was essential.

A sea urchin spine in your foot is extremely painful – and stonefish. These evil-looking creatures look just like a rock – hence the name. They are sometimes quite large. But when you examine them, you can see an eye and a thin, mean-looking mouth staring at you. A bite from a stonefish is lethal. There was no antidote, and my Seychellois friends told me, "You die from ze pin."

One should always have a healthy respect for the sea and things therein. When Jim was diving, they were told never to touch anything. Fire coral can bring you out in a terrible rash, and moray eels can give you a nasty bite. So the golden rule is, do not touch!

There are also some bad rip tides. Whilst we were there, the British Trade Commissioner drowned. He and his family went for a picnic at a beach called Police Bay. I can't think why they went there, as there was a notice saying it was unsafe for swimming, and the beach is down a steep hill a long way from the road.

The whole family, father, mother, daughter and a girlfriend, had a picnic on the beach and the two girls went swimming. The friend got into trouble, and the daughter ran back to tell her father. He was not a strong swimmer but went in to help her. The friend made it to the shore, but the father was swept away by the current. His wife could not swim.

Apparently, if he had gone with the flow of the current, he would have been swept round the bay and up the other side, but unfortunately, he did not know this. I would not have known it either. His wife ran for help, and a passing Seychellois man dived into the sea and rescued the father. However, he had swallowed a vast amount of seawater and sand from being pulled under the surf. By the time the ambulance arrived and got him to hospital, he was dead, as some of the sand had lodged in his lungs. It was very tragic.

When the children came out for holidays, we did our best to go on some trips. I would love to have taken them to Bird Island, where you spent the night in an open-sided sort of shed place. The terns apparently lay their eggs all over the place – on the ground, on the rafters – you must be really careful when you are walking around not to tread on them, and the place is full of baby birds. However, this trip, on a six-seater plane, cost one hundred pounds each. This was in the days when one hundred pounds was a lot of money, and we just did not have five hundred pounds spare to spend on it, so we did not go. I have always regretted being unable to take this trip, as I think it would be fantastic.

We did, however, sail to Praslin Island, in Teemooljee's launch, which took a couple of hours. There was only one hotel there at the time – I think we were just about the only guests. The beaches are superb. As we went along the beach for an evening walk, two very well-endowed completely naked Italian women tourists came bouncing towards us round the corner of the island. Rod was fourteen at the time, his mouth dropped open and his eyes nearly popped out of his head. He could not believe what he was seeing! I guess this would now be commonplace.

Praslin contains the fabled Vallée de Mai, where the black parrot lives and the coco de mer grows. This is a large coconut palm, whose enormous fruit is shaped like a female's pudenda and is known as the 'love apple'. It is a favourite souvenir for the Seychelles tourist.

The Vallée was lush and green with giant ferns and coconut palms, and eerily silent and dark when you walked down it. Once in it, it sort of closed in on you and I thought it was quite spooky – a bit like one of those science fiction films you see, where people walk in a valley with huge vegetation growing on either side, completely dwarfing them. You really did feel like a puny human. We, unfortunately, did not see the black parrot – I don't think many people do as it is a very shy bird. The Vallée is now part of a nature reserve.

We were lucky enough to have a friend Harry Savvy who had a deep-sea fishing vessel. He used to hire the boat out to tourists – especially rich Americans. They would go out to fish for marlin, sailfish and other large game fish. Harry bought a new engine for his boat and invited us to go along with him one Sunday to test the engine before he hired it out to clients.

Jim and I, the three children with their friends, the two Heatheringtons, another child, Richard, whose parents had an ocean-going yacht, Harry and two Seychellois boatmen, set out. I went under protest as I am a terrible sailor. The rest of the family love sailing and are always trying to persuade me to go along with them, but I rarely do, as I am so ill. However, this day they prevailed, and against my better judgement, I went.

It was the last day of a three-day fishing competition run by the local Rotary Club. The boat that caught the most fish during the three days won the prize. There was also a prize for the largest fish.

I started off very well. The sea was as smooth as glass, deep blue and very calm. Harry strapped me in one of the two fishermen's chairs, and I caught the first fish – a large dorado. I was thrilled! There was a huge icebox on the deck, and my fish was duly deposited in it. About five minutes later, we ran into a small swell. That was the end of me – I retired to the cabin, where I was very ill indeed!

The Seychellois lads knew all the fishing grounds in the area, and it was not long before we ran into a large shoal of tuna. Tom, who was six, took my place in the chair and caught the next fish. It was huge – bigger than he was. Harry leant over the chair and helped him to reel it in. Tom was so excited. I could hear him shout, "I can do it, I can do it myself!" as he pushed Harry away. Of course, he couldn't, and they eventually reeled it in.

After that, it was just a case of putting the line overboard and hooking up a fish. All the children were going crazy. The Seychellois boys, Harry and Jim, darted back and forth helping them to haul in the fish.

It was not long before the icebox was full, and there were fish lying all over the deck. We caught tuna, dorado, and bourgeois – red snapper, which is delicious cooked the Seychellois way. The fish are cleaned, the skin cut and stuffed with a mixture of tomatoes and onions and then wrapped in foil and baked in an oven or on a barbecue. The swell worsened, and most of the children joined me in the cabin. After about half a day, Harry and Jim got a bit worried about me, as they thought I had become very dehydrated, so they turned around and sped back to Mahe. I was very glad to get back on dry land.

The fish were all unloaded. We caught three hundred and eighty-two pounds of fish and won third prize in the three-day event. The competition organisers could not believe we had caught so many in half a day. All due to Harry's boatmen, of course.

Tom got second prize for the largest fish, and we have a photograph of him standing next to the fish, which is hooked up to the scale. It weighed about seventy pounds. We all filled our freezers full, and the extra was given to the convent, who looked after a motley crew of orphans and other abandoned children in the islands. There were many very poor people in the Seychelles.

We often went sailing on a friend's catamaran. One Sunday, whilst out in one of the bays, the catamaran hit a wave and somersaulted. Rod and a couple of our friends who were on board fell into the sea, and Rod's leg got entangled in a stay. Fortunately, one of the others saw what had happened and cut him free, but his thigh muscle was badly dented and bruised. A passing launch picked him up and took him to the beach.

He could not walk, and we feared he had broken his leg, so we put him in the car and drove to the hospital. It was dirty and horrible, and there was only an orderly on duty. We asked for an X-ray but were told he would have to wait till Monday, as there was no radiographer on duty on Sunday. Meantime, his leg had eased up considerably, and he was able to limp about, so we knew it was not broken and took him home. He had the indentation on his thigh for a good three to four years.

I would not have liked to be hospitalised in the Seychelles. There were a couple of good doctors, but I am not sure what the nursing would have been like and though they had some equipment, I am unsure about how well they could use it. I know that they now have a dialysis machine, as the husband of a friend of mine who required dialysis raised enough money to buy one for the hospital.

Jim found working in the Seychelles very frustrating. Sometimes, members of his staff did not turn up, and when asked next time they arrived where they had been, they would say, 'I am not a slave! I did not feel like working, so I did not come'. No point sacking them, as their replacement would have been just the same. They would, however, have had something to say if you had cut their wages by the number of working days they did not attend the office. Hard work equalled slavery in their eyes! It was extremely hard running a hotel, as if half your staff felt like taking a day off, they just took it – you had no idea how many were going to turn up on a daily basis. My maids were the same.

Jim's customers were just as bad – both indigenous and expatriate. He met a couple of Englishmen who started a smokery and were turning out some lovely smoked kingfish, sailfish, and dorado. He put them in touch with Selfridges and Harrods in London. They got a contract with Harrods to deliver a certain amount of fish per week.

After about a month or so, Jim got a telegram from Harrods, who were going spare, asking what had happened to their weekly delivery of smoked fish. They had had none for a fortnight. He went round to the smokery to find that the owners had taken off round the islands on a month's fishing trip (holiday) and the smokery was shut. Ofcourse they lost their contract, but it did not seem to bother them in the slightest, and they were, in fact, quite irate with the store.

I had a Seychellois friend whose husband had started a pig and dairy farm – he had great trouble finding anyone to help him look after the pigs and cows. We used to get our milk twice a week from him. His wife Jenny would come up to the house and deliver it when she went shopping. One day she said to me, "You know, Noreen, the Seychelles grows the best copra in the world, and do you know why? Because we never pick the coconuts. We always wait for them to fall from the tree."

I duly relayed this story to Jim, who gave me a withering look and said cuttingly, "Don't be so stupid! They don't pick the coconuts because they can't be bothered to climb the trees!"

He had another customer who ran a guesthouse on the beach. We went there for lunch one day, and she had the most gigantic avocado tree growing with absolutely enormous, beautiful purple fruit. The ground underneath it was covered with avocados. Avocados, if you could get them in the market, were very expensive – at least five rupees each. Jim looked at these and said to her, "What do you do with all these avocados, Mimi?"

"Oh," she said. "Just help yourself – I have plenty!"

"Yes," said he, "I can see that! You could get a truck and sell them in the market – you would make quite a bit of money doing that!"

"*Ach*," she said. "It is too much trouble! I just sweep them into the sea!" That just about summed up the Seychellois' attitude to business.

Mind you, that did not mean that they did not want what you had worked hard to get – they just did not see why they should work for it. If, for instance, you had a dozen shirts hanging in your wardrobe, but only wore the red one rarely as you did not like it very much, you would find, one day, that it had vanished. If you asked the maid what had happened to the red shirt, she would say to you, "Oh, you never wore it, so I took it. I shall bring it back tomorrow!" But you would not want it back, as you never knew where it had been by then!

Venereal disease was rife in the Seychelles when we were there. One afternoon, I arrived home to find the health department van at the door. "What can I do for you?" I asked.

"Madame," they said. "We have come to see Jacqueline (one of my maids)."

"She is not here today," I replied. "Why do you want to see her?"

"Well, madame," they said, "we have a boyfriend of hers in hospital with gonorrhoea, and we know that she is a carrier as she has had it before!"

I was aghast. "Is it catching?" I asked, not being very well up in sexually transmitted diseases, and thinking of Jacqueline doing all our laundry and babysitting Tom. They assured me my family was quite safe! Jacqueline was nineteen and had been treated for gonorrhoea three times already.

There was no piano in the Seychelles house, so Jim bought me a very nice keyboard, which we brought with us. But I pined for some live music. There was not much call for classical music. I used to sing in the church choir. In fact, I often was the church choir. I sang solo, with one of the nuns from the convent playing a little electric keyboard for the service. Or, if she couldn't make it sometimes, I would sing unaccompanied. I don't really know whether this was acceptable or not, but no one (including the lovely French priest) ever commented or complained, so I just carried on singing. And sometimes during communion, I would sing a couple of Latin motets if the mood took me – *Anima Christi*, perhaps, or *Ecce Panis*, *O Salutaris*, etc. I was therefore really pleased to find that the Yacht Club had a folk evening every Friday night – though I did not know very much about folk singing, other than that done in the concert-platform style.

There was quite a big yacht club in Victoria, and a large drifting yachting community, known as Yachties. Ocean-going yachts would come in on their way from Africa to Australia, their crews delivering a boat for various owners and would often stop at Mahe for several months, reconditioning the vessels, provisioning and doing some sightseeing round the islands.

The organiser of the Friday Folk Evening was a Scots architect called Bill Smith. Bill was one of the founding members of the Scottish folk group The Corries who, when they originally started out, were a trio known as the Corrie Trio. Bill left them to return to his career as an architect. He was a superb guitarist, with a huge repertoire of folk songs. It was not long before I joined him and used to sing with him every Friday night – about three to six songs, depending on how many other performers were there.

As I have a powerful operatic voice, I felt somewhat like a bull in a china shop and totally ruined my voice by trying to sound like a folk singer. I tried never to repeat a song – apart from ones for which there was a special request. At the end of about eight months, I suddenly realised that I had sung over one hundred different songs. I even accompanied myself on the guitar sometimes – a painful procedure as I am not the world's best guitarist.

As a sop to me, Bill (who couldn't read music) and I even sang some Handel (*Ombra mai fu* – popular), *Where E're You Walk*, Lascio ch'io pianga, etc. It was amazing how many classical songs could be adapted for guitar accompaniment – especially the seventeenth- and eighteenth-century composers – and, of course, the two arias from 'Carmen', which were very popular. I also sang some Burl Ives numbers and a couple of Malay and Chinese songs.

Friday evenings at the Yacht Club continued throughout our stay in Seychelles until one night during a particularly nasty storm, the corrugated iron roof flew off! Thereafter, we repaired to the Coral Strand Hotel for our weekly sessions.

In the first half of 1977, Jimmy Mancham was the president of the Seychelles. He was a bachelor playboy and much in demand with the international jet set. He did not appear to be in Mahe very often. One Saturday night in June – the 5th, I think it was – we were invited by Air India to their annual birthday cocktail party at the Beau Vallon Hotel. We were also invited to dinner by some South African friends and decided to dine with the Johanssens instead of going to the Air India do, which we knew would be attended by everybody. We did not think we would be missed.

We went to a popular local restaurant and had a good dinner. It was very quiet. There was nobody else there. Usually, the place was hopping and full of the top Seychelles society set, including several ministers – especially later in the evening. I remarked to Gus Johansson how quiet it was, but as it was before midnight when we left, I thought it was still early by jet set standards. We went home to bed and thought no more about it.

At six a.m. on Sunday morning, Jim received a phone call from his accountant Roland Tester to say that Albert Rene had taken over the government and ousted Mancham as president. Mancham was abroad in the UK at the time attending the Commonwealth ministers' conference. The island was under curfew, and no one was allowed out of their house.

Later in the day Jim phoned Albert Rene to ask if on Monday he would be allowed to go into the bank to check the telegrams, etc. "Yes," said Rene, but he would be the only one allowed to do so, and the government would need to be able to get some cash with which to pay the Tanzanian mercenaries. Tanzanian mercenaries? – what Tanzanian mercenaries? – we knew nothing about Tanzanian merceneries! Jim phoned Roland to let him know what had happened, and we turned the radio on to the local station.

All the ministers involved had gone straight from the Air India cocktail party to broadcasting house, where they had taken over the radio station, the police headquarters and stations and various key government offices. To aid them, they had brought in mercenaries from Tanzania. There had been no resistance. Their biggest coup had been keeping the whole thing quiet. Seychelles, like most small places, is a hotbed of gossip and all sorts of rumour.

No one suspected a thing, though many people were involved in the rebellion, including our gardener, who was a cousin of Rene's. No wonder our restaurant had been deserted the evening before.

The rebels had planned their takeover well. Not only was Mancham abroad, but the commissioner of police – an Englishman – was also in the UK on annual leave. There were another three or four British police officers on Mahe, in charge of various divisions of the police.

After breakfast, we went out into the garden and heard a great rustling in the bushes. A couple of Seychellois maids appeared, running out of the jungle. "What is the matter? What are you doing here? Don't you know there is a curfew?" we asked.

They were the maids from the police inspector's house just below us. "*M'sieur*, madame, we are very frightened," they said. "Some armed Tanzanians came to the house, and they have taken *M'sieur* away. Madame is crying, and we don't know what to do!" Sure enough, every UK police officer had been gathered up by the rebels and taken to police headquarters.

The next day, they were put on a plane to London, together with their families. The women were given no information as to what had happened to their husbands but were told to pack one suitcase only to take with them on the plane. When they got on the plane, they were joined by their husbands. I and some other wives went to the police bungalows later in the week and packed up the policemen's houses for them to be sent on to London in due course. It was not pleasant.

The press descended on Mahe like a flock of vultures and propped up the bar in the Pirate Arms Hotel, collecting their news.

Things were tense, and the UK businessmen met with the ambassador to see what could be done in case there was an emergency, and the community had to be airlifted out of Mahe. They were informed that 'HMG were not responsible for the community, and they would have to make their own arrangements for that eventuality'. They were not pleased. The British Airways manager arranged for all UK citizens to be airlifted off the islands should that be necessary, and the ambassador was most disconcerted to find that his staff were not included in the arrangement.

Curfew was lifted, and the shops and offices reopened by the end of the week. It was a more or less bloodless coup. There were only three fatalities, all three on the rifle range where the Tanzanians were practicing. One was a stray shot that hit a passing cyclist after missing the target and another was from a rifle that one of the Tanzanians was leaning on. He had the rifle nozzle down between his feet and was leaning on the butt when the rifle went off and killed him. I can't remember what the third was, but it was also an accident.

The Tanzanians were very careless with their firearms. We followed a jeepload of them down the hill one day. They were sitting in the back with their rifles across their knees, barrels pointed towards us. "For God's sake, let them go!" I said to Jim. "Who knows whether or not they have a bullet up the spout!"

The first day the bank opened, one of the ministers, accompanied by some Tanzanians, came in. "Mistah Kemp, Mistah Kemp," shouted one of his female counter clerks from one end of the office to the other. "The gorillas are coming! The gorillas are coming!"

The minister swaggered into Jim's office. He was wearing a gun belt with a couple of revolvers stuck in it. Jim, playing the fool, dived below his desk with his hands in the air, shouting, "Don't shoot, don't shoot!" The minister shrugged his shoulders and lifted his hands in the air. "*Ach*," he said.

I understand the minister for health made his rounds in the hospital with a brace of revolvers strapped to his thighs, accompanied by his daughter, who was designated as his bodyguard, carrying an AK-47. I cannot think this contributed much to the recuperative powers of his patients.

Life altered after the coup. People became suspicious of each other, and there were a couple of very nasty murders. A prominent, wealthy, anti-government Indian businessman vanished one day. His car was found abandoned on the edge of a cliff, and his body has never been found. According to his family and friends, there was no reason why he should have disappeared or committed suicide. All sorts of rumours abounded – he had been kidnapped by government officials and been shaken down for his money. When he refused to hand anything over, he had been killed and his body thrown over the edge of the cliff. He had been asked to meet someone on the cliff top and been kidnapped, and/or thrown off the cliff… No one knows what happened to him. I don't know if the mystery has ever been solved.

The other brutal murder was that of a British retired businessman. We knew him slightly, as his brother Harry worked for the bank, and we were posted with him in Singapore. George loved the Seychelles and had retired there after a very successful career as managing director of a big international company. He had a large yacht and was building a house.

One evening, there was a bit of a storm blowing, and he told his wife he was going to see that the yacht was properly secured. It was before the days of mobile phones, and as the weather grew worse, she thought nothing of it when he did not return, thinking he had decided to spend the night on the yacht and make certain it was all right.

When he did not return in the morning, she went to the mooring to see what had happened. The yacht had disappeared. She alerted the police, who went out to investigate. They found the yacht about four days later, drifting in the ocean. When they boarded it, there was no one on board and the dinghy was missing. There were several bullet holes in the decks and vast quantities of blood everywhere, but no bodies. They sailed the yacht back to Mahe.

About a week later, they found the drifting dinghy with the decomposing body of George lying inside. The police reckoned that when George had boarded the yacht that evening, there had been a couple of Seychellois men aboard – how they knew this, I don't know. The men had forced George at gunpoint to take the yacht out of the harbour – why or where they wanted him to go, no one knows. Had they come aboard to steal the boat? Obviously, things had gone very wrong, shots were fired and George killed or badly wounded and put into the painter, which was then cut free of the yacht and left to drift. But what had happened to the Seychellois? No one knows, and that murder has also never been solved.

Jim had some questionable customers. There was the charming Italian, who lived further up Sans Souci than we did, in a beautiful house floored with Italian marble set amidst the swirling mountain mists by the tea plantation. We often lunched with him. It was rumoured that he was the front man for the mafia and in charge of money laundering operations for them with funds coming from Ciasaou.

One day, Jim had a visit from the French *Surete*, with a letter of authority from the Seychelles government, enquiring about one of his accounts. It transpired that one of his customers had been involved in a large bank robbery in Paris some years previously and was hiding in the Seychelles – fortunately, his account was well in credit. He was apprehended and taken back to Paris for trial. There were quite a few dubious characters of the same ilk wandering around in the Seychelles! They obviously felt they would be safe in the islands – rather like the marauding pirates of an earlier era.

One day in late September, Jim received a telex (it was before the days of emails) from London, which said, *'Need you soonest in Bombay. How long will it take you to relocate?'* He telexed back, *'Forty-eight hours!'* Back came the reply, *'Don't be facetious!'* It was actually a fortnight before we got away.

We had a farewell party at an Italian restaurant on the beach called *'La Tartaruga Felici'* – 'The Happy Tortoise' in English. There was a glittering guest list! All the government ministers were to be there, including President Albert Rene and his wife, prominent members of the business community, etc. We took over the restaurant for the night and ordered a sumptuous dinner. Guests were due at seven thirty. At five thirty, Jim and I went to the restaurant to see that all the arrangements were going according to plan. We arrived at the same time as special branch, half a dozen plainclothes policemen and a couple of government officials. The policemen were placing marksmen on the roof of the restaurant, and special branch was looking under all the tablecloths.

"What were they looking for?" I whispered to Jim.

"Bugs!" he replied.

"Bugs? There are no bugs here."

"Not that sort of bug!" he replied. "Listening devices! And presumably bombs!"

We were supposed to be meeting the government protocol officer. Jim had said he would get me to do a seating plan for the dinner but was told no, they had a special officer who had just come back off a protocol course in London, and she would do the seating plan. Okay. By six thirty, she still had not arrived. We were getting a bit agitated, and eventually said we would have to go home to get changed in order to return to meet the guests.

We dashed home, collected young Sarah our house guest and returned to the 'Tarturaga'. Yes, the protocol officer had been and done the seating. We went to check what she had done and were aghast! She had all the government ministers sitting in a line on one side of the table, facing all the bank officials on the other side – regardless of seniority. Sarah was sitting next to Rene – and the British ambassador was at the bottom of the table. He would not take kindly to that, being a man who stood very much on his dignity.

We quickly swapped cards, putting Rene and his wife between Jim and me and trying to arrange the other ministers and hosts in some semblance of correct seating, so no one would be offended. But there was not really time to do much before the first guests arrived. Special branch was still looking for bugs under the tables – no bugs but plenty mosquitoes as it was right by the sea. The rooftop was now crammed with security men with machine guns. No one, however, was looking out to sea, so presumably, you could have raided the restaurant with an armed vessel.

I wickedly left the ambassador at the end of the table. When I saw him later, I apologised profusely for the seating, saying it was none of our doing, but the government protocol officer's.

"Bizarre!" he said, very annoyed. "Extremely bizarre!"

I said perhaps he should have a word with London about their protocol course!

"Yes, yes," he replied. "I certainly will!" Despite this, the dinner was a huge success, and on our last evening, we were invited to dine with Rene.

I was not keen to do this, as when we got home that evening, Jacqueline, who was babysitting, informed me that there had been some Seychellois lads trying to get into the house. "To rape me, madame," she said. She had barricaded herself in and gone up to the lounge – leaving Tom asleep in his bedroom downstairs, which I was not too happy about. After some name-calling and shouting, they had left.

I said I would not leave Tom alone again. So, Jim rang up Rene, who said, no, we must come, and that he would send the police to take care of the house whilst we were at dinner. True to his word, he did, and we had armed police patrolling round the house until we returned that evening. I was still unhappy about it all!

There are no packers in the Seychelles, but we managed to pack up the house in double quick time and catch the plane to Bombay. The current joke in the islands when we first arrived was, 'First prize in the lottery is a week holiday in the Seychelles – second prize, two weeks'. In retrospect, would I wish to return for a holiday? Probably not! If I wished to have a beach holiday, I would rather return to the equally dazzling beaches, flora, fauna and people of Sabah or Sarawak in North Borneo.

CHAPTER 10
BOMBAY (1977–1980)

Jim, Tom and I arrived in Bombay from the Seychelles in October 1977 where we took over from the Goulds. Terry moved up to become the manager, Bombay, and Jim succeeded him as deputy manager. We cleared customs, got into the bank ambassador and drove down the dreadful road from Santa Cruz Airport to Bombay.

Jim was born in a district of Bombay called Colaba. His father was the managing director of Greaves Cotton Crompton Parkinson, a managing agency, and Jim spent the first twelve years of his life during the war, in Bombay, so it was a kind of homecoming for him. As my parents also worked in India from the 1930s to the late 1950s, I also was no stranger to India. But my memories of Bombay were limited to passing through the city when my parents were going on Home leave from Calcutta, and a trip with Jim on the way Home from Madras in 1970. India did not appear to have changed very much since then.

I love Bombay! This dirty, overcrowded, bustling, stinking, vibrant, poverty-stricken city teeming with people dreaming that the potholed pavements would one day be paved for them with gold. Sometimes, they are right. But more often not. I know it is now called 'Mumbai', but in the 1970s, it was 'Bombay'. The Portuguese named it 'Bom Baiee' – 'Good Bay' or good harbour – and that is what it will always be to me.

The journey from the airport is horrific and passes through some of the worst slums of Bombay. Miles of *jodh-jodhpatties* – huts made of wood, mud, bricks, with roofs of tiles, plastic sheets, wooden crates – anything the inhabitants can put their hands on.

There was electricity in some places, and in others, lighting was by oil lamps. Only one water standpipe per approximately fifty people, and water turned on for about a couple of hours or so a day – usually early in the morning, about four thirty to seven a.m. Little or no sanitation, but plenty of TV aerials and lots of phone wires. Not all the slum inhabitants are destitute – just most of them. The pavement dwellers have nothing at all.

We travelled up Warden Road, past Breach Candy and up Malabar Hill – known as 'Nob's Hill' – where the elite of Bombay live. We passed the Towers of Silence, the Hanging Gardens and stopped outside a compound with newish flats forming three sides of a square. This was Mayfair Gardens. Tacked onto the end of the square was an older, smaller five-storey block. This was Mayfair House, where the bank had had a flat for many years. The paint was peeling off the exterior walls, and the whole building looked sad and tatty. Unless newly built, the outside of most buildings in India werelike this. A lick of paint and a smart building invited a visit from the tax department to the landlord to see where the money had come from to do such repairs. Besides which, like all the rest of the Mayfair House inhabitants, the bank were sitting tenants.

Most tenants who had rented flats for many years in Bombay were sitting tenants and paid the landlord a very small rent in comparison to the astronomical rents paid by new tenants. This is because, once in, tenants could not be ousted, it being against the law. If their rents increased to reflect market prices, most tenants would just refuse to pay and there was nothing the landlord could do about it.

The driver stopped the car and we alighted, entering the hall. At the foot of the staircase in the centre of the hall was a large stone statue of Ganesh, the elephant god – god of youth and good fortune and the most popular god in Bombay. We were ushered into the 1920s lift with the steel mesh sliding doors. It creaked and groaned its way up to the third floor. The lift only went up to the third floor – the flat was on the fifth – so we had to climb the remaining two flights of stairs. I suppose this was good for your figure – especially in the hot weather – as it ensured you arrived in the flat sweating profusely, having lost a couple of pounds on the way up.

Once inside, the flat was large, old-fashioned and cool, with high ceilings and terrazzo floors – far preferable to the small-roomed, low-ceilinged, hot, pokey modern flats made for air conditioning, which, owing to electricity problems, was often not working. We had air conditioning in our bedrooms only, which ensured we got a good night's sleep. Accommodation has always been at a premium in the crowded city of Bombay.

The front door led into a small hall, which opened out into a large L-shaped room. One arm of the L formed the sitting room, with a couple of steps up to the dining room in the other arm of the L. At the bottom of the steps, in the corner of the sitting room, was a large Bechstein grand piano. I gasped in delight! This had been regularly tuned and had a good tone, though the key action was a bit stiff, as it had not been regularly played. The piano improved vastly whilst we were in residence, as it was in constant use.

A door from the dining room led out to the pantry, kitchen and servants' room and bathroom at the back. Beyond the sitting room was a veranda, onto which opened the door to the main bedroom and bathroom. Off the back of the sitting room was the second bedroom and bathroom. A large passageway joined the two bedrooms. The Goulds, who, like us, had two sons and a daughter, had turned this passageway into a small third bedroom, which shared the main bedroom's en-suite bathroom. This we designated Mhairi's bedroom, while Tom and Rod shared the other bedroom and bathroom, the latter containing an old-fashioned twin-tub washing machine.

The flat was furnished throughout with heavy, old-fashioned solid teak furniture – all of it very hard-wearing and of the type that would never wear out.

The bedrooms were air-conditioned and equipped with large old teak *almeirahs* (wardrobes) and a couple of chests of drawers (circa 1920s) for your clothes.

The sitting room suite was covered in white covers, sitting on the marble floor around a mustard-gold carpet. It was not long before I recovered the suite in a gold-and-brown-striped material, as the white covers spent more time in the washing machine than on the chairs, and they shrank. At the side of the sitting room under the window was an alcove, with a matching gold carpet, on which sat a coffee table. We had a floor-to-ceiling wooden shelving unit built in here and turned the alcove into a library.

We were very happy in Bombay: Jim, because he met friends he had not seen since his schooldays at the Cathedral School, most of whom were now very successful businessmen at the top of their careers; I, because there was a thriving music world, and I could indulge in my singing as much as I wanted; Tom, although only seven, because he found Bombay a fascinating place, which left a lasting impression on him. Our other two children were at boarding school but joined us for every holiday. It did not take us very long to settle in.

As was normal in the bank, we fell heir to the staff who went with the flat: three male servants – a Goanese cook called Manuel, a Gujarati bearer called Bauji and a Maharashtrian *hamal*/second bearer called Poona. This was a lot of servants in Bombay, where most people only had one, plus a shared sweeper. All three lived in a pokey servants' room behind the kitchen, by the backstairs. It was appalling. There were two bunk beds and another bed in it, a small barred window and a table fan.

It was like a coffin. They kept their belongings in tin trunks under the beds. I have never before or after seen such terrible servants' quarters in the bank – three people in a small room like a prison cell. All living on top of one another, with absolutely no privacy. It was murder in the hot weather. The servants would take their mattresses up to the flat roof to try to get some breeze and some sleep. We had a ceiling fan installed for them, but unfortunately, couldn't enlarge the room. However, they were lucky to have accommodation at all in Bombay.

The backstairs were filthy and smelt of lavatory. There were three large dogs in the flat diagonally below: an incontinent Great Dane and two black Labradors, none of whom got much exercise or were taken out often enough. The smell would waft up to the backstairs and into the sitting room. This crisis came to a head when Jim was descending in the lift one morning to go to work, and the Great Dane lifted his leg on the floor above, causing a huge stream of urine to descend cascading into the lift, all over Jim's suit.

The outcome was that we arranged to pay the building sweeper extra a month to clean both front and back staircases every day. Previously, he had cleaned them twice a week. We tried hard to get the other tenants to contribute to this payment, but only we and our neighbours below, the Moolgaokars, agreed to do so. It was a paltry sum – something like one hundred rupees extra per month – which worked out at about ten rupees per flat. There were ten flats in the building. All the residents could well have afforded that – especially the people with the incontinent dogs.

My servants were all men of about forty to fifty. Manuel and Bauji had each worked for the bank for about twenty-five years. Poona was a newcomer whom Maureen Gould had hired for me, as she had taken the resident bearer with her to the manager's flat, which was above the main branch of the bank in Mahatma Gandhi Road. Bauji, who had been second bearer/*hamal* for all those years, now got a well-deserved 'promotion'.

I soon discovered that my staff's salaries had not kept up with inflation, and this we rectified immediately. They were very pleased. They were paid monthly and put ten rupees in a savings account towards a pension, with us paying in the same amount. Now their salary had almost doubled. I asked if they could afford to put in twenty rupees a month, which I would match. They happily agreed.

When we left three years later, I gave them each three months' salary, according to custom. I did not give them the cash, explaining that I would put it into their savings account, knowing that if I gave them such a large amount of cash, they would probably immediately spend it. Of course, they could withdraw anything they liked at any time from their savings account. This Bauji and Poona understood and happily agreed to – but Manuel had great difficulty understanding this. First, I explained, without success; then the other two tried – also no success – until Bauji, thoroughly exasperated, eventually told him he was being a stupid old goat and just to look at his savings account book. At last, the penny dropped, and he left happy.

Manuel was an excellent old-style Goanese cook, who liked to have a drink on his day off. He cooked extremely good European food, with all the old British Raj dishes – beef chops, aloo chops, chicken *à la* everything, steak and kidney pudding and pie. He also made all the spectacular puddings of my youth – caramel custard, various steam puddings, lemon meringue pie, mango fool, maize pudding (a cream sponge cake decorated to look like an ear of maize) and fruit in a candy basket pudding, to name but a few. Every Sunday, he went to his cooks' club for the day – he was, of course, a good Catholic. His wife and family lived in Goa, where he went once a year for six weeks when we went on Home leave.

Bauji had a piece of land somewhere in Gujarat and returned there annually when we went on leave. This he had to do, so that he could retain his rights to the land. His wife lived there with the rest of his family. According to Indian law, landowners must return once a year to their piece of land in order to retain their land rights. He was comparatively well-off.

Poona was an exceptionally neat, tall, slim, distinctive-looking white-haired man. His uniform was always sparkling white. His wife was an *ayah* somewhere in Bombay. He had six daughters, poor soul, for whom he would have to find marriage dowries, despite the fact that dowries had been illegal for years. He was an excellent worker.

Tom was a great favourite with them all. He started off at the kindergarten section of the Cathedral School. This was very convenient, being just round the corner from the flats, next to the Anglican All Saints Church. Either Poona or Bauji would take him there every morning and bring him back at lunchtime, when the school closed. Manuel taught him how to make fairy cakes, pancakes and pastry. All three servants earned extra money by babysitting when we went out at night, which averaged about three times a week. This saved us having to employ an ayah. We also had a dhobi who came in twice a week, who did the ironing. I did the washing every day in the old twin tub machine in Tom's bathroom, and Bauji ironed all the clothes except on *dhobi* day. Jim also had a bank car and driver, which I used during the day.

When we first arrived in Bombay, we went on a tour of the city, Jim revisiting all his old childhood haunts and showing us where he was born (in Rashid Mansions – still there) and grew up (in a flat at Southlands in Colaba). It being the kite season, we soon came to a small hole-in-the-wall street shop that sold paper kites and wooden spinning tops. We stopped the car to go buy some and were immediately surrounded by a pack of urchins, all demanding a kite. They were very cheap – I think one rupee for ten – so we bought about five rupees' worth and distributed them to the delighted children, keeping a dozen for ourselves. More expensive was the bobbin of manja – the string steeped in ground glass that you attach to a kite and use to cut the string of any kite you have a fight with. The little wooden tops and string need some skill to make them spin.

We returned to Mayfair House with our booty to be met by the delighted servants, who soon departed with Tom up to the flat roof to fly the kites and teach Tom how to spin the tops. I don't know who enjoyed themselves more – but I don't think it was Tom.

If you live in a flat in Bombay, you do not have to go out to grocery shop – or for entertainment – as most people come to you. There was the storeman round the corner, who phoned every morning for your order and then delivered it.

Manuel went to the market most mornings, to buy fresh meat, fish, fruit and vegetables, and the street vendors went from building to building shouting out their wares, exactly as they did in Victorian London. The fish man – 'Pomfret, fresh pomfret'; the vegetable man – '*Subjee, subjee* (vegetables), *aloo* (potatoes), *gajar* (carrots), *piaz* (onions), *phoolkhobi* (cauliflower)'; the lady selling baskets of fresh strawberries, blueberries, mulberries and mushrooms from Mahableshwar; the monkey man with his sad-looking monkeys, a man with a moth-eaten dancing bear, shambling along led by a chain through a ring in his nose; the snake charmer, very occasionally a magic man; a fortune teller; the bird seller with a cage of small munias – supposedly 'tame' but actually drugged with a small piece of opium and a man leading a couple of ponies for the children to ride.

Tom and his friend John Issit had a ride on his ponies once and came back with their legs covered in flea bites. In the early evening, the street singer and her accompanist, who played on a one-string instrument with a bow, would perform – we always threw them down some money.

As it was so expensive to import goods, you soon learned to 'live' on what was produced locally. As India has always had a good manufacturing base, dating back to the days of the Raj, tinned goods and food were of quite a high standard, and we did not find this a drawback.

Cars were very expensive and only the very rich could afford to buy an imported car, so most people had a local car. There were only two main makes of local car, the Fiat 1000 and the Ambassador, so the traffic on the streets looked like something out of the fifties. The bank had Ambassadors. You had to put your name on a list to buy a new car, and it usually took ages, sometimes years, to get one. Jim's bank Ambassador was due to be replaced, and after we had been there a couple of years, it was. By this time, Tom had just gone to boarding school at Markyate, and the first time I returned to Bombay, the new Ambassador had just arrived. Jim decided to use it to collect me at the airport.

On the return journey to Bombay, in one of the most crowded suburbs, there was a loud explosion and great clouds of steam poured from the bonnet of the new car. The engine had blown up! One of the advantages of there only being two sorts of car in India was that every small garage knew how to fix them. We left the driver with the car to wait for the AA to turn up and returned to Mayfair House by taxi. The agents offered to repair the car for free, but Jim demanded a new one, which he eventually got. The problem was that some of the car part dyes at the factory were so worn that parts were quite often faulty, and new cars had quite a few teething problems.

Maharashtra is a dry state, so Bombay is a dry city – and has been since just after Independence in the late forties early fifties – the then governor of Bombay, Morarji Desai, being teetotal (unlike the governor of Bengal in Calcutta, who, my father said, drank like a fish). When we first arrived in Bombay, Morarji Desai was prime minister. Every morning, he drank a glassful of his own urine – reputed to keep you very healthy. This liquid is the same colour as a gin and lime, which was known in Bombay society circles as a 'Morarji Desai'. You needed a permit to be able to have a drink in public: this was easily obtained; you visited the local permit office and signed on as an alcoholic.

Drink was available at designated shops but at a very inflated price. The result was that most people had a bootlegger. A bootlegger's liquor was normally half the price of that in the liquor shops. However, it was important to get a trusted bootlegger if you wanted to ensure that your liquor was unadulterated. We normally bought Scotch for entertaining and occasionally some brandy. Imported wine was rarely served in Bombay, and anyway, by the time we left, the local rosé was quite palatable.

Local gin, vodka, rum and beer were fine, but the local whisky gave you a dreadful headache – even if you drank just a little of it – so we always served Scotch. We inherited our bootlegger from the Goulds. His name was Harilal. He would telephone Jim at about ten o'clock at night, just as we were dropping off to sleep and whisper down the line, 'This is Harilal. I have got two dozen bottles of Johnny Walker Black Label!' Jim would usually buy half a dozen bottles. Harilal could never understand why we didn't buy more. The bottles would turn up at the back door a day or so later; they normally had the name of some Middle Eastern embassy stamped on them – usually Saudi Arabia.

Harilal only let us down once, when at a dinner party, we discovered we were serving local hooch instead of Scotch. Unfortunately, Jim was drinking rum that evening, so did not realise this until his boss, who was one of our guests, told him about it. As the bottle was authentically sealed, I have no idea how the hooch came to be inside. Harilal got a flea in his ear.

Bombay had one official dry day a week – Wednesday, if I remember correctly – when hotels were not allowed to serve alcohol. They would, however, serve you a Bloody Mary, as it just looked like tomato juice – or a Bullshot – consommé and vodka – but not a Morarji Desai.

We had a large selection of friends from various Bombay communities, but my favourite community had to be the Parsis. Bombay has the largest Parsi community in India. The Tower of Silence, where the Parsis give their dead a sky burial, is on Malabar Hill – not far from the flat. That is to say, Parsis expose their dead on the top of the tower, the corpse being eaten by scavenging birds – vultures, hawks and carrion crows.

Because of this, all the old blocks of flats on Malabar Hill were shorter than the tower, but some new blocks were taller. This resulted in odd parts of human remains, say a finger or a couple of toes, sometimes being dropped by passing carrion onto the upper-storey verandas of the new flats – much to the dismay of the residents This caused quite an outcry; however, the Tower of Silence authorities maintained that the builders had been warned what would happen if they built higher than the tower.

Since 1990, there has been a scarcity of vultures throughout India due to the dosing of cattle with diclofenac. This anti-inflammatory drug is poisonous to vultures, rendering their eggs infertile and this has led to a shortage of the birds. Vultures are essential in India as they scavenge on corpses, carcasses and other rubbish, helping to keep the fields and streets clean. Dead bodies are unclean and left to rot where they die, as only people of the untouchable Dom caste can touch corpses. I digress.

Our neighbour across the landing was a Parsi widow called Freny.. Freny would often appear unannounced in our flat, through the back door and always seemed to know what we were doing.

"How does she *always* know what I'm doing?" I asked Bauji.

"Oh! She asks us!" he replied.

"Well, please don't tell her!" I said.

One day, I was ill and in bed when Freny appeared in the sitting room. "Mrs Kemp, Mrs Kemp, are you awake?" she called.

"No!" I replied. "I am fast asleep!"

"Oh, good!" says she, coming into the bedroom to tell me what she wanted.

If I wanted to see her about something, I would ring her bell and her ayah would let me in. "Is Nallaseth *memsahib* in?" I would ask her.

"*Ha,*" she would invariably reply, "she is praying in her prayer room."

One afternoon, as I came in, Freny appeared out of her prayer room. "Come and see," she said.

I went into this long, narrow, closed-off bit of corridor. There was a shelf running round the walls on which she had displayed every god you can imagine. There were pictures of the Sacred Heart, a statue of St Anthony of Padua and Our Lady of Lourdes, portraits of the Parsi prophet Ahura Mazda, statues of all the Hindu and Jain gods – Shiva, Saraswati, Vishnu, Brahma, Ganesh, Ram and Sita, Krishna, and the Sikh Guru Nanak. She saw me looking at this astonishing array with wonder. "My dear," she said to me, "I'm taking no chances!" I have often since thought what a good idea that is.

Freny was about eighty and an astrologer of some renown. Every evening, she would remove her nightie and housecoat, don her wig and make up and a white sari or trouser suit, shed about twenty years and go down to the Taj Mahal or Oberoi Hotel, where she had many foreign clients – mainly German, as far as I could make out. I think her husband was the manager of the Taj before he died. She was a real character! She had no car so always wanted a lift. Originally, she got a lift with Jim when he went into the office, but after a while, the driver returned to the flat later and later and often was not there when I wanted him for an appointment.

"Why are you always late?" I asked him one day. "Oh," he replied. "Nallaseth *memsahib* asks me to take her shopping!" Of course, he was unable to refuse her, so the upshot was that Jim refused to take her into town any more. Freny was not pleased! Jim had quite a few run-ins with her.

One day, Freny decided that she had only five years to live (according to the stars), so she let her son and his wife move into her flat and commandeered a storeroom on the roof, which she renovated and moved into. This was so that her son and family could become sitting tenants in the flat when she died, as no way would they be able to afford the market rent of her flat. This was, of course, not strictly legal. She then complained that our servants were taking 'women of ill repute' onto the roof at night.

Jim objected to her moving onto the roof – it was not only illegal but also a fire hazard. It made no difference! "That horrible man!" she called him. When we left, she said to me, "I am sorry to see you go – you are very nice – but your husband – he is a horrible man!" I did not let Jim forget that for a while! I believe she did actually die as she had foretold, but we had left Bombay by then.

One hot, sticky Saturday May morning, the leaden sky heavy with the coming monsoon, I called to Tom, "Hurry up and get dressed and let's go to the market before it gets too hot!"

We had inherited a fish tank from the Goulds, and despite an oxygen bubbler, our fish did not survive very long. I think we overfed them, as whoever was passing the tank was inclined to put in a pinch of fish food, and we lost at least one fish per week – so most Saturday mornings found Tom and me visiting Crawford Market to replenish the tank.

Tom was soon ready, looking cool in his shorts and bush shirt – why do children never seem to feel the heat? The perspiration was already trickling down my back, and it was only eight thirty! We climbed down the first two flights of stairs, got into the rickety lift, pulled the steel shutters closed behind us and juddered noisily down to the ground floor.

Tom bounded out of the lift and went to rub Ganpat's tummy for luck – he did that every time he went in and out of the flat – then ran out to meet our driver, Ravi, who was waiting for us with the Ambassador. We clambered into the back seat, Ravi turned on the air conditioner and off we set.

We drove down Malabar Hill, past the Hanging Gardens and the Jain temple, the rent-a-baby beggar at the bottom of the hill and along Marine Drive. The sea was grey this morning, but there were still a few people walking along the beach and sitting on the sea wall before the day got too hot. Wait till evening, when all of Bombay flock to Chowpatty beach, and the vendors and entertainers are out in force. Magicians, snake charmers, roundabout men, acrobats, sellers of ice creams, balloons, paper windmills, drinks, candy floss, coconuts, hot gram and savoury snacks, all vying for custom. Down past Victoria Terminal, the railway station, weaving in and out of the cars, bullock carts, handcarts, horse gharries and rickshaws that constitute Bombay traffic and at length turned into Crawford Market.

The steps teemed with shoppers, beggars, children demanding baksheesh, market coolies to carry your shopping, street vendors of multi-coloured sticky drinks, sliced fruit, nuts, T-shirts and various delicious-smelling curried snacks and Indian sweets, all guaranteed to give you instant diarrhoea.

We left Ravi to park the car and climbed up the steps. Kiran, my market coolie, was waiting at the top with his basket. "Salaam, *memsahib*, salaam, *baba*," he said.

"Salam, *Kiran*," I replied. "Storeman and fruit stall first, Kiran, and then fish stall." Kiran grinned knowingly.

"Tom baba's fish die?" he asked. Tom nodded.

We made our way to Mr Perreira's stall for my weekly grocery shopping. The stall was piled high with a great mountain of groceries. Bags of rice, sugar, flour and various dhals stood on the floor. Banked behind them rose stepped shelves of tins of jam, milk powder, vegetables, soups, washing powders and soaps, packets of tea, coffee and every other kind of grocery item you can think of.

Mr Perreira sat in one corner of the stall by the telephone, with his order book. He took my list and called out the items to his shop boys, "One kilo Basmati rice, quarter kilo raisins, six cakes Moti soap, one packet Digestive biscuits, two packets strawberry jelly, one kilo sugar..." As he called out the list, one boy scampered up and down the back of the stall collecting the goods, and the other weighed the rice and sugar and handed them all to Kiran, who put them in his basket. Tom was jigging up and down impatiently. At length, the list was completed. Kiran lifted the loaded basket onto his head, and we set off for the fruit stall.

The fruit seller sat on a dais in the midst of his stall, surrounded by fruit of every kind. There were red apples from the Kulu Valley in Kashmir, oranges from Nagpur – both green for juice and yellow for eating, sweet limes, sour limes, custard apples, watermelons, papayas, bananas and many varieties of mangoes, for it was the start of the mango season.

"Salaam, *memsahib*, salaam, *baba*," said our fruitman. "*Ap kysai hai? Aj boht garam hai!*" (How are you? It is very hot today!)

"*Ji ha!*" I replied. "*Boht garam!*"

"Mangoes good, *memsahib*," he said. "You like to taste?" He cut one open and offered us both a slice. They were delicious!

"*Kitna dahm*? How much?" I asked.

"For you, *memsahib*, special price!" said the fruitman, and the bargaining began! "Sweet limes good, papaya good – apples too expensive!" he said. "Baby, you like banana?" He peeled one for Tom. We bought some sweet limes, mangoes, a papaya and some small yellow bananas called '*cheeni champas*', which means 'sugar sweet'.

I paid for the fruit and looked down to see Dilip smiling at us waiting for his weekly tip. Dilip was a young, legless beggar who wheeled himself round the market on a little wooden trolley. He had a curved spine, a humped back and long thin arms that dangled loosely by his side. He propelled himself along on his wrists. He never asked for baksheesh, just smiled and salaamed. We always gave him a few rupees. He was lucky this morning, as the fruitman handed him the rest of the mango he had sliced for us. Dilip was pleased. He salaamed his thanks and rolled off with his booty. Kiran added the fruit to the load in his basket, and hoisted it back onto the top of his head. Next stop, pet shop!

This part of Crawford Market is both fascinating and repellent. The stench is indescribable: a mixture of stale straw, rotting food, urine, excrement and sweaty bodies combined with that of animals closely herded together in small cages, all bubbling together in the sweltering heat.

You can find almost any kind of animal here: rabbits, guinea pigs, hamsters, cats, chipmunks, snakes, monkeys, dogs and birds of all description. Pigeons, guinea fowl, bright green parrots and parakeets, cockatoos and cockatiels, hummingbirds, munias, various 'tame' birds, doped with a little opium, which sit on your finger, but become extremely wild by the time you get them home, baby chicks dyed bright orange, red, green or a bilious blue, hens, ducks, turkeys and, of course, fish. All sorts of fish, from the exotic Siamese fighting fish to the common or garden guppy.

I know nothing about fish, and we once were sold two Siamese fighting fish, which we took home and put in the tank – within minutes, they had killed each other. Surely, I should have known better, as the clue was in the name of the fish – fighting fish! It always took Tom ages to choose his fish, and we always bought more than we intended. We were good customers of the fishman.

We picked our way through the steaming mounds of rotting rubbish shimmering in the heat and rounded the corner to the fishman.

I stopped short in surprise. There, chained to one of the wire cages, was a silvery-grey Sidney Silkie (an Australian Yorkshire terrier, only grey).

"Why look, Tom, there's a Sidney Silkie!" I cried in surprise. We went up to the small dog. He was friendly and licked my hand, looking at me out of his bright black eyes. He had one ear up and one down. Tom looked at me pleadingly. The dog looked at me. "How much?" I asked.

"Five hundred rupees, *memsahib*," said the pet man.

"Nonsense – too much! I'll give you three hundred rupees!" I said.

"*Aacha, memsahib*," came the instant answer. I immediately knew I had been done! Nothing for it now, I would have to pay up.

Only I did not have three hundred rupees – we would have to get it from the bank! I asked the pet man to keep the dog and said I would return with the money.

Tom could hardly contain his excitement. "Now look, Tom," I said. "We shall have to go to the bank and get the money from Daddy. Don't say anything about the dog! Let me tell him first!" I did not think Jim would be too thrilled about our purchase.

We drove to the bank, Tom telling Ravi all about the new dog on the way. He dashed into the bank, raced through the door into Jim's secretary's office, straight past Tammy and into Jim's private office where he was holding a meeting with half a dozen businessmen. "Daddy, Daddy, we need three hundred rupees, Mummy's bought a dog!" he cried. So much for breaking the news gently! The men all burst out laughing as Tom excitedly told his story.

"Well," Jim said, "we'd better get that money!" Tom rushed off to tell Tammy all about his dog, while we waited for the money to arrive. "Better get him checked by the vet first thing! You never know where he might have been or what he may have, apart from the market fleas! And see that he has all his inoculations!" said Jim.

We collected our money; Tom and I got back into the car and drove back to the market and the pet man.

I counted out the money, and the pet man handed Tom the dog. We trooped out of the market, the little dog trotting in front of us on the end of a large, rusty chain more suitable for an Alsatian, without a backward glance.

Ravi grinned when we arrived with the dog. He helped Tom into the car and put the dog on his lap. Tom sat cuddling his dog, fish forgotten! After we had lost our last animal, we had sworn, 'no more dogs!' He could not believe his luck! "Next stop, vet, Ravi!" I said. "Do you know a good vet?"

"*Ha, memsahib!*" said Ravi, and off we went.

"Where did you get this dog?" queried the vet.

"Crawford Market," I replied. He looked shocked.

"That is no place to buy a dog, Mrs Kemp," he said.

"If you had wanted a dog, I could have got you a good Sidney Silkie – one with a kennel club pedigree!"

I weakly tried to explain that I did not want a dog at all; we had been shopping for fish! The vet was unimpressed. "Crawford Market is not a good place for buying dogs!" he repeated sternly.

"How old is he?" I asked, trying to change the subject. "The pet stall man said he was a year old."

The vet examined the dog's teeth. "Oh no!" he replied. "He is at least nine!"

We returned to the car armed with flea shampoo and doggie vitamins.

Once inside the flat, we let the dog off the lead. He trotted round inspecting the lounge and veranda and chased a couple of visiting crows. They flew onto the veranda wall just out of his reach and sat there laughing at him.

Once more round the room, and then he spied the grand piano in the corner of the lounge – *ah*, a good, cool place to lie. A corner from which he could survey the front door and most of the comings and goings of the household. He flopped down in it.

"What shall we call him?" asked Tom. "What about Tuppence Ha'penny, because he's so small?" I suggested. Tom agreed. We looked over into the corner. Tuppence had fallen asleep. He was here to stay.

Tuppence ruled the roost! He liked Manuel (food), Poona (walks) and particularly Bauji, who liked dogs. He did not like Freny and used to growl at her from his corner. The feeling was mutual, and Freny was scared of him. Bauji used to encourage Tuppence, and I saw Bauji one day when Freny had come uninvited through the back door, encouraging Tuppence to growl. "Tahpence, Tahpence," he was whispering out of the side of his mouth, "kill, kill!" I scowled at him and tried not to laugh. However, once Tuppence had a bone in his corner, he could be very fierce and would attack any passerby, so we stopped giving him one. I was sure that he had been in some well-heeled household, as he was so at home in the flat and must have either been stolen or strayed. We were also sure he must have known some tricks, but try as we may, we could not get him to beg, give a paw, turn on his back or do anything.

One day, we came home to be met by a grinning Bauji who opened the door to us. "*Memsahib*, look, look!" he said to me. He bent down to Tuppence and said, "Tahpence, sheking, sheking!" The little dog sat up on his hind legs and offered Bauji a paw! Obviously, Bauji had found the correct magic words!

Every night before he went to bed, Tom and Tuppence would chase each other round and round the couch with Tuppence jumping up and pulling down Tom's pyjama trousers. Tuppence's arch enemies were the crows. They would fly onto the veranda and tease him. Tuppence would chase them, and they would alight onto the wooden plant steps, which were full of pots and baskets of phlox, just out of his reach, cock their heads to one side and open their beaks, laughing at him. He would bark furiously and jump up and down trying to catch one but never did!

I had been in Bombay for about a week when I was invited to coffee to meet some ladies, one of whom was a Parsi called Jean Moos. We became very good friends. When she learned I sang, Jean told me her sister Tehmie was a pianist, one of the official accompanists for all visiting musicians to Bombay and offered to introduce me. This she did, and I would often go round to Tehmie's flat in Cuffe Parade to sing. When Tehmie was studying at the Royal Academy in London, she was one of the official accompanists so an excellent accompanist and much admired by all the visiting musicians.

Not long after, I met another Parsi lady, Zenobia Vakil-Patel, a graduate of the Mozart Academy in Salzburg, who also offered to accompany me. She came to our flat once a week. Zenobia was also a palmist and was often uncannily correct when she read your palm – one being your 'past' and the other your 'future'. She told me things about my past that she could not have possibly known.

I also met the talented young organist of All Saints Church, Elizabeth Thomas. Elizabeth was about eighteen and was going to a music college in America. She wanted to practise her accompanist skills, so *she* also came round once a week. I have never had so many wonderful accompanists – except in Madras and I was in seventh heaven.

I joined a very friendly, active ladies' group called INDUS – a mixture of Indian and expatriate ladies of many nationalities. INDUS ladies' interests spanned many activities, including religion and philosophy, music (both Indian and Western), dramatics, travel, yoga, cookery, arts and crafts, history and so on.

Each section had a monthly meeting. One month, the meeting would have an Indian theme, and the next, a Western one. Each group had an

Indian and expatriate chairman responsible for the meetings. I ended up as deputy chairman, which meant I produced the monthly newsletter together with Jean Moos. I think the membership was restricted to approximately two Indian members to one expatriate – something like that anyway! They had a long waiting list for the Indian ladies.

About the second time I attended a meeting, one of the ladies said to me, "Oh, Noreen, you sing; we have a new English member who is also a singer; perhaps you can sing together!" I smiled a bit warily, there being many types of singers, not all of whom go together and turned round to be introduced to a tall, striking blonde.

"This is Kate Nicholls," she said. "She is a soprano." I was a contralto, so this sounded promising. Kate looked at me just as warily – we had both been in this position before.

We chatted briefly, and it was immediately obvious that we liked the same kind of music. I suggested she join me the next day for a session with Zenobia. This she did; we blended beautifully together and were soon in great demand, often singing a 'voluntary' at the services at All Saints and giving recitals all over town.

We had a variety of programmes, duets and solos, usually starting with some Bach, Handel or Mozart, then progressing to German Lieder – Schubert, Schumann and a lot of Brahms for me – ending the first half of the recital with some opera. After the interval, we would have some English songs – art songs, folk songs – finishing with some operetta or musical numbers. We were quite popular, and as we both had a powerful voice, the whole street was treated to an involuntary concert most mornings – Rod saying to me one day, "You do realise, Mother, that we can hear you and Mrs Nicholls right at the end of the road."

And Freny, in her inimitable way, commented, "I can hear you singing clearly in the flat – you are quite good and getting better every day!" I took that as a Freny sort of compliment.

Our biggest recital was for the Time & Talents Club at the Homi Bhabha concert hall. It was both well received and attended, and I felt we had finally arrived when I overheard an American member of the audience say to his wife, "They were very good and easy on the eye as well!"

However, the most memorable concert we had was, I think, for the International Women's Club. Zenobia had asked us to do a concert at their Christmas meeting, which was held in an old Parsi house in the middle of

Bombay. The house had been unoccupied for some time, due to a family feud, over a will, which had been going on for years. We were to sing in a huge lounge.

The room had a badly cracked black-and-white marble-tiled floor and contained a pipe organ as well as a grand piano (in tune, but tinny through non-use), lit by an immense Czech crystal chandelier, covered in dust. At one end of the room were two tatty gold thrones, which we were told were used by King George V and Queen Mary when they visited India for the Delhi Durbar in 1911, where they were declared 'Emperor and Empress of India'. There was also a glass cabinet containing a mixture of souvenirs – some priceless Doulton and Chinese ornaments (Ming perhaps) side by side with a spray of artificial flowers and an old chocolate box. What was their story, I wondered. There was no one to tell me. So sad! There was a huge highly decorated Christmas tree in the middle of the room, underneath which was a mound of presents.

We had prepared our usual Christmas programme for the members – a mixture of Bach and Handel, Mozart, carols ancient and modern and Christmas music, which we had given at several venues with great success.

When the members started to arrive, we realised they were not our usual mix of ladies, and indeed, the only international ladies present were Kate and I. Not long after we started, I realised that this was completely the wrong programme for them, and anyway, they were far more interested in the presents under the tree. Halfway through the performance, the chairman got up and said, "Thank you, ladies, for a lovely performance…"

"Hang on," interrupted Kate. "We haven't finished yet!"

She sat down again, and we ploughed on valiantly to the end of the programme before the poor ladies could get their presents. *We* never received one! I was highly amused, but Kate was cross. "Don't ever do that to us again!" she said to poor Zenobia, who, it turned out, was not one of the international ladies either.

Our last concert was actually a revue, which we did for INDUS, who every year had an 'entertainment' at their AGM. Kate was music chairman that year – which was great for me as she asked me to do a recital at one of the meetings. I did an illustrated talk on the British art song, which included songs by Elgar, Howell, Vaughan Williams, Roger Quilter, Ivor Gurney, Arnold Bax, Benjamin Britten, et al, accompanied by Zenobia, which went down very well – much better than I had expected, given that most of the composers were unfamiliar to the audience.

When Kate was asked if we would provide the 'Entertainment' for the AGM, she said, "Leave it with me!" and we decided to do a revue. We had both done a lot of revue, and between us had quite a selection of skits, monologues and suitable songs to include. We asked one of our American members to join us and produced a programme which ended with a selection of music hall numbers – a favourite music genre of mine. This revue went down a bomb, and when I returned on a visit to Bombay in 1998, older members still remembered it, telling me how much they had enjoyed it – which was very satisfying.

Kate had two boys, David and Philip, who were about the same age as Roderick, now sixteen and at boarding school at Haileybury. Philip was fifteen and David eighteen, both at the time at Bedford. They all got on well together, which was great. The Nicholls lived in the Yacht Club down by the Taj hotel. Because of the difficulties and expense of renting a flat in Bombay, Kate and Colin decided to rent a suite at the Yacht Club – thus, Kate could then come and go at will to and from Bedford. It was cheaper, and they did not have to bother with servants, setting up a house, etc., and could just lock up and move out.

I was also a member of the 'Time & Talents Club' – a group of very erudite ladies, mainly Parsis, who organised concerts from visiting 'artistes' in Bombay. At the time, there were strict currency regulations in India, so the Time & Talents could not afford to pay the artistes much of a fee. Instead, they arranged concerts for them all over India – Bombay, Calcutta, Delhi, Madras, Poona and Goa – where the visitors were billeted in local people's homes, had all their internal travel and expenses paid and were paid a small fee. We had some wonderful concerts by some very famous people.

I was on the entertainments committee. This committee arranged the accommodation in Bombay for the artistes and was run by a formidably efficient Parsi lady called Korshaad Bilimoria. She was so efficient that after attending one meeting, I said to her, "Korshaad, just tell me what you would like me to do, and if I can, I shall do it!"

So she would phone me up and say, "Can you house so-and-so for one or two days on such and such a date?" and I would say yea or nay! In this way, we had quite a few artistes to stay! They took over Tom's bedroom, and Tom slept in Mhairi's passageway during their visit.

Our first visitors were an Italian flautist and her Spanish lady impresario – since they spoke little or no English and I not much French and no Spanish, communication was difficult and limited to Italian musical terms – not very successful! They just wanted to sunbathe round the pool at Breach Candy and asked Korshaad if they could have an Indian vegetarian meal. She arranged for one of her Gujarati ladies to have them to lunch, but "I know they will not like it!" she said to me. They didn't! But the Gujarati lady had laid on such a fantastic spread – enough for about a dozen people – it was difficult not to taste at least a bit of everything.

They were a very attractive, easy-going pair, who insisted on washing their smalls themselves and then hanging them up on my veranda clothesline, dressed in a miniscule pair of shorts – even Manuel appeared in the lounge to have a look. The concert was unremarkable – I don't think lying all afternoon in the sun before performing is very conducive to good flute playing.

Our next guest was a Canadian pianist called Anton Kuerti, who appeared at the flat door, looked very disappointed to discover that I was not an Indian and immediately announced that he was a vegetarian. As we were having roast beef for dinner, this was not a good start. However, I sent Manuel next door to borrow some tomatoes from Freny and he had an omelette instead (we still had our roast beef!).

The next day, he asked if he could phone Canada, which was fine, but Bombay telephones were often out of order and he could not hear too well! He therefore dismantled my phone to try and fix it – despite being told it had nothing to do with the instrument but would be the exchange. He then sat down at the piano to practise. He was a powerful pianist and sort of attacked the instrument, which clearly did not impress him. Before I knew it, he had the insides out on the floor while he tinkered about with the action to my visible dismay. "Don't worry," he said to me. "I'm an accredited piano tuner." I was unimpressed!

Unfortunately for him, there was a *hartal* the day of the concert. This is a general strike – the whole of Bombay was on strike, and you are not supposed to be out and about. The concert was great, but most of the guests who should have been at the dinner went home instead to avoid any trouble. He was not an easy guest!

Our last guest was a drummer from a Modern Jazz Quartet (can't remember their name) called Ashley, who stayed a couple of days. I shouldn't really call him a drummer; he was a tympanist and had nine cases of instruments. The quartet was composed of a flautist, lady violinist, pianist and drummer. They rehearsed at the flat and were giving a jazz workshop in the morning, with an avante-garde classical concert the evening before. This last at the request of the Time & Talents. "Are you sure that is what you want?" they asked the ladies.

"Oh yes!" they replied, having no idea what it entailed! The programme consisted of pieces by John Cage (the one with the two-minute silence in the middle of it) and other ultra-modern composers. Bombay audiences had no idea what to make of it all!

John, the pianist, had the Time & Talents' prized Bosendorfer opened, plucked the piano strings and hit them with a hammer – which brought shocked gasps from the ladies, the piano being irreplaceable – and Ashley sat amidst his nine cases of instruments, which he played beautifully. At one stage, he immersed a large Chinese gong in a zinc bathtub of water on the stage (to stop the sound), much to the amusement of the audience, who were fidgety and some of whom left. They were very clever and talented folk – John was, I think, a Doctor of Philosophy as well as a pianist; Ashley a timpanist and publisher, but the superb flautist and violinist 'were only musicians', according to John.

The next day was the jazz workshop. They traced the life of jazz from its beginning. I followed most of it, but when they came to the ultra-modern section, where all the instruments went their own way, most of the audience, mainly young people, was flummoxed. "How do you know when one will stop and the other start?" I asked. "Do you have a time limit as in an Indian raga?"

"No," they replied. "We just know because we have played so long together." They were delightful, and I was very sorry when they left.

The Metropolitan Opera singer Joanne Grillo and her daughter also visited Bombay, and Joanne gave a memorable concert at the Homi Bhabha. She was one of the leading mezzo-sopranos at the Met – a large lady with a huge creamy voice, which easily filled the hall. She did not stay with me. After the concert, one of my Parsee friends said to me, "She was very loud, wasn't she!" I often think people don't know what to make of large female voices – apart from asking the singer to sing softer, which they are unable to do! I asked Korshaad to request her to give the Bombay singers a masterclass, which she did. About six of us joined. I sang, *'Che Faro'* from Gluck's 'Orfeo' and the *'Habenera'* from 'Carmen'. She was very complimentary, so I was extremely chuffed with that.

One day, Korshaad rang me up and asked if I would like to have tickets to a pop concert. "Some pop group called 'The Police' are coming. The BBC are going to televise the concert and have asked if we shall put it on. It will make us a lot of money, as they are paying for everything and giving us a big donation as well for our charities." I said pop music was not really my scene, and I had no idea who the pop group were. However, the children were arriving on holiday the day before, so that would probably amuse them and I would buy some tickets.

Rod arrived the next day, and on the way home from the airport, I told him that I had bought some tickets for a concert by the Police. "Oh gosh, Mummy," he said. "I don't want to go and hear some police band giving a concert."

"No, no," I replied. "It's not the Bombay Police band, it's some pop group called the Police."

His mouth fell open. "You mean THE Police?" he asked.

"I don't know if they're THE Police," I answered. "I just know they are a pop group called the Police!"

"Wow," he said, "they're only the top pop group in Britain. Fantastic!"

I got more tickets from Korshaad and arranged for the Nicholl boys, the Issit children, Mhairi and Katherine Gould to join him.

We were hosting a cocktail party that evening, so I took the children, minus Katherine who was late, to the venue – a large open-air stadium down a narrow lane. I arrived to find the lane crowded, and Korshaad standing inside the wire fence round the stadium looking very hot and bothered. She had had no idea what a pop concert would be like – neither had I – and had been unable to clear some of the band's instruments through customs. Sting was sitting on the stage, apparently refusing to perform until all the instruments arrived. It was getting near the concert's starting time. Poor Korshaad said to me, "That man Sting is just sitting there and refusing to perform until all the instruments arrive – if the concert starts late, I shall have a riot on my hands!"

I deposited my load of teenagers and said I would be back with Katherine. By the time I returned, the lane was packed with people. I think every hippie in Bombay had come out of their hole to go to the concert – not the T&T's usual audience. Katherine and I could not get near the gate. Eventually, I asked two large, burly, waistcoated, long-haired English hippie men if they would mind if we stood between them as we were getting squashed, and if they would make their way to the gate. This they smilingly did. Katherine and I went in to stand with Korshaad, still looking worried. An old Parsi couple of about eighty, who came to all the T&T concerts appeared and were ushered to their seats (rows of benches).

"They're not sitting in the front row," I said to Korshaad, aghast.

"Yes, they insisted on their usual seats." she replied.

"Oh dear! They won't like it! It will be too loud." I said.

The crowd appeared very good-natured; however, it was getting perilously close to the concert starting time and they would soon get restive. At that point, much to Korshaad's relief, the lorry with the instruments arrived, the ticket holders were let in and the band started tuning up. However, the lane was still packed with non-ticket holders. Half an hour late, the concert began – the noise was horrendous – indeed, I reckon it was better to be in the lane than at the concert. I now had to get back to my party at the flat. Just as I turned to go, the old Parsi couple appeared on their way out.

"This is a disgrace!" the old man said to Korshaad. "How could you let this happen?"

"Sorry, Uncle. Sorry, Auntie," replied Korshaad, looking very crestfallen and wringing her hands. "Believe me, we won't do it again!" she said, looking suitably chastened.

They staggered out through the crowd, which respectfully parted to let them hobble past, leaning on their sticks. (Would that ever happen in Britain? I think perhaps not.) "I shall never ever agree to have a pop concert again." Korshaad said to me. "Never! No matter how much the BBC pay us!"

I made my way back to Ravi and my guests – I had also never been to a pop concert. Truth to tell, I rather wish I had been able to stay – with earplugs. The children thoroughly enjoyed themselves. Sting signed all their programmes, had a chat with them and we even caught a fleeting glimpse of Rod waving his arms around in the audience on television when the BBC showed the concert as part of a programme they were doing on The Police's tour.

One afternoon the telephone rang. "This is Coomy Wadia," the voice said. "I am the conductor of the Paranjoti Choir. We are going to perform Bach's '*B Minor Mass*' at the Homi Bhabha hall with the Shri Rajneesh Ashram from Poona. We shall have a combined choir and orchestra – would you like to sing the contralto part?" *Would I?* How often do you get an offer like that – especially given my peripatetic lifestyle. I jumped at the chance.

The Paranjoti Choir was a Bombay choir, named after their original conductor, Victor Paranjoti. They went on tour all over the world and performed in Europe, particularly in Germany. At our first rehearsal, I was talking to the choir members and asked them what they sang. "Oh, we sing all the usual classical composers," they replied, "BachHandelBrahmsMozartHaydandofcourseacappella," running it all together

"Who's he?" I asked, thinking this was a modern American composer I had never heard of. They looked shocked.

"You know," they replied, "without the piano."

"Oh," I said. "You mean unaccompanied." I did know that – it was just the way they had run everything all together. Oh dear! They must have thought I was terribly ignorant!

The concert was to celebrate the silver jubilee of the death of their founder, who had been dead twenty-five years, and of whom they spoke as if he had died yesterday. This is one of the charming things about India – they do speak like that of people who have been dead for a considerable length of time. When I went home, I said to Jim, "You know, I'm sure I sang *The Messiah* in Madras with Handel Manuel and the Madras Musical Association in 1970 at an anniversary of Paranjoti's death." When I looked up my old programmes – yes, I had!

The Shri Rajneesh Ashram was a sect, a bit like the Hari Krishnas, whose guru, Shri Rajneesh, preached a doctrine of free love (only it wasn't free; you had to pay to join it) – who had a huge ashram in Poona. His followers were called Sanyasins, most of whom were Europeans and Americans, all looking for something (love), plus a few locals. They all wore red robes – any shade of red, from pink to maroon. There were all sorts of expatriates there – Shakespearean actors, public schoolmasters, painters, musicians, bakers, teachers, chemists – all sorts. They had a huge orchestra – the flautist was from the New York Philharmonic, and the oboist who accompanied one of my solos, from the Amsterdam Concertgebouw.

As I understood it, when you joined the ashram, you had to give them most of your money, were given a new name, were allocated a place to stay and did communal work. Asmito, the oboist, was cleaning the toilets. They did not do drugs (so I was told), but all had a strange peaceful look in their eyes. "Join us," they said. "You would make a good Sanyasin."

"No, thank you," I replied. "I couldn't afford it." I could just imagine Jim's face if I came home and said I wanted to be a Sanyasin.

I took Asmito home with me for a private rehearsal. Bauji opened the door for us. His face was a picture of disapproval. Not many Indians approved of the hippie-type population – whether Rajneeshis or Hari Krishnas – whose ashram in Bombay had just been involved in a very nasty murder. I had to ask him twice to get Asmito a drink, and when he left, Bauji very ostentatiously dusted the armchair on which he had sat. "Asmito," I asked him. "Why are you wasting your time here? What will you do when your money runs out?"

"Yes, I knew you'd say that," he replied peacefully. "I shall return to Amsterdam, make some more and come back!" There were a lot of Dutch Rajneeshis in Poona, most of whom lived in a big old white house known as the Dutch Palace.

Asmito told me he lived on the veranda. "What do you do when it rains?" I asked.

"Oh, I just go inside and stay with one of my friends till it clears up," was the answer.

"You know, Coomy," I said later to the conductor when we were discussing the Rajneeshis. "It's not so bad, Asmito tells me he has a room on the veranda."

"Noreen, don't be so naïve," she said witheringly. "He means he has a bedspace!"

A bit of the orchestra and the soloists had a rehearsal one Saturday morning in St Andrews Scots Kirk, a vast old church with high ceilings, famous for being the first church in Bombay to have air-conditioning. It had a huge basement, which, on a Sunday, was filled with ice blocks, on which fans blew – sending the cold air up through the wooden floors of the church and cooling the congregation. I think this air-conditioning was installed pre-war. However, no air-conditioning whatsoever was in evidence at this rehearsal. It was stinking hot, and the perspiration was running down my back, despite the ceiling fans turning full pelt, churning the hot air round and round.

Jim and Mike Issit dropped me off at the rehearsal – they were going sailing. They came in, took a pew and sat down to listen. The orchestra took their places and struck up. The leader of the orchestra was a lady violinist and the very well-endowed, plump lady cellist – both wearing the Sanyasin red robes, tuned up. They were flapping their long skirts up and down trying to cool themselves, and the cellist was having trouble trying to find a comfortable place for the neck of her cello. We went through a few numbers, and I looked up to find Jim and Mike still sitting, listening. Later, I said to Jim, "You and Mike stayed a long time – I didn't think you cared too much for Bach – were we very good then?"

"Do you know," he replied. "Those two girls didn't have a stitch on under those robes – not a stitch!" I never did find out what he thought of the singing.

The concert was a great success – a one hundred-strong choir and a huge orchestra – nine cellos – I definitely couldn't compete with that. Coomy halved them for me. "Come and see us in Poona!" the Rajneeshis said to me when they left. I did but never saw any of them again.

We did go to Poona quite often, as a customer of Jim's, Shiamak Marshall's family had a screw/nut and bolt factory up there. Shiamak's father, old man Marshall owned the factory, and the family had a villa in Poona, which they went to most weekends. Shiamak and his wife, Maki, were good friends of ours. His sister and her husband ran the Poona factory, and Shiamak ran the office in Bombay.

Mr Marshall senior also grew roses in the Poona garden, which he sold to the Taj in Bombay – a very profitable little sideline. He also had a farm at Deolali – where in the days of the Raj, there was a large lunatic asylum, hence the expression *'he's going Deolali'* – where he raised hens. We bought all our eggs from him. Jim often went up to Poona on 'inspection', and Tom, Tuppence (who came everywhere with us) and I would accompany him and have a most enjoyable weekend in Poona, which, being higher up the Ghats than Bombay, is much cooler in the hot weather.

We would set out with Mr Marshall in his large air-conditioned Studebaker, accompanied by a Czech colleague of Mr Marshall called Tony Ziss. Halfway up the ghat, we would stop for breakfast and a couple of pilseners and a nip of slivovitz from Tony's flask. We usually spent the whole weekend eating. Mr Marshall was a firm believer in children having hearty meals, so Tom always had to have at least one egg for breakfast – no excuses. Mhairi and Roderick came with us on one trip, not long after the Rajneesh concert, and I said to Shiamak that I would like to visit the ashram. At that time, I think almost half the economy of Poona depended on the Rajneeshis.

On the Sunday morning, I said to Shiamak, "I'd like to go to the Ashram."

"I'll come with you," replied Shiamak, "because I have never been." SoShiamak, Mhairi and I went to the ashram – it was enormous. When he was in town, Rajneesh, whom the Sanyasins called 'Bhagwan', which in Hindi means 'god', used to give a lecture to his followers every day. Once in Hindi and once in English. If you wished to attend one of his lectures, you had to be fragrance-free – that is to say, you must not wear any perfume or use perfumed products – deodorant, soap, shampoo, talc, etc. therefore on Sunday morning, none of used any perfumed products and tried get into the hall.

Before you were admitted into the lecture hall, you had to run the gauntlet of 'the sniffers' – two Sanyasins who sniffed you as you passed through them. Unfortunately, we did not pass their scrutiny, Shiamak having used some sort of fragranced soap! This, according to the guru's doctor, whom we met later at the Marshalls, was because Rajneesh was highly allergic to any sort of perfume. I was quite disappointed – however, we did a tour of the ashram.

They had all sorts of things there – a vegetarian restaurant, a bakery run by an Austrian, they made their own fragrance-free cosmetics and soap, run and made by an ex-Helena Rubenstein employee and everything was produced on the premises. There were masses of unruly children rushing round everywhere, whose language would make a sailor blush – I have never heard such swearing before or since. This was presumably because everything was free – not financially, as you had to pay for whatever you bought – but emotionally, without any restraints. I did not see any of my musical friends. "Can we go now, Mummy?" Mhairi asked me after about an hour. "I don't like it here – it feels evil!" We left.

We also visited the seven-hundred-year-old shrine of the Sufi saint, Hazrat Qamar Ali Darvesh, in the village of Khed Shivapur, just outside Poona. All castes and creeds of people are welcome at this shrine – except women, as the saint died at eighteen and was unmarried. However, they let Mhairi and me in, as, being feringhees (foreigners), presumably we did not count.

There is a holy stone there that levitates. Normally it is immoveable, and the saint could not lift it, but if eleven or more people put out their index fingers and shout the name of the saint – Hazrat Ali Darvesh – with the emphasis on the first syllable, they can lift the stone. However, if anyone stops shouting, the stone will fall and injure them. We all went forward to lift the stone. Roderick stopped shouting, and the stone fell, missing his bare sandaled toes by a millionth of an inch. He visibly went several shades whiter. "See!" he was told. "You must always have faith!"

Shiamak and Maki invited us to their daughter's Navjote ceremony, which I thought was something like a Jewish bar mitzvah. First, there was a private ceremony at their flat, with just the family – we were most honoured to be part of this – and then there was a big dinner and celebration for friends and extended family – which in the Marshalls' case were very numerous.

This must have been sometime in 1977, as it coincided with the newly elected Prime Minister Indira Gandhi's Austerity Programme. Mrs Gandhi thought that the elaborate and extortionately expensive Indian weddings (and other celebrations) were far too ostentatious, getting out of hand and should be cut down in size, as it stressed the very visible disparity between the rich and poor. Weddings could go on for weeks, with trains and planes being hired to get guests to the occasion. This policy suited Shiamak, who was railing against the expense of the Navjote and was all for having a smaller celebration.

All Shiamak's family were most upset and Mrs Gandhi's policy backfired spectacularly. She was accused of singlehandedly ruining the livelihoods of millions of people connected with the wedding industry. There were the jewellers, the cloth merchants, tailors and embroiderers, hair and make-up artistes; the shamiana (marquee) employers – those who rented out the shamianas, the erectors and the electricians; the caterers – table and chair renters, cooks, waiting staff, food and drinks purveyors, bullock cart owners, taxi drivers and rickshaw wallahs who brought all the paraphernalia and guests to and from the wedding; entertainers of all sorts – dancers, singers, musicians, actors, tumblers, band; priests, bridegroom's horse hirers, sweepers, venue hirers, clearer uppers, dishwashers… right down to the beggars who waited outside the gates for leftover freebies, which would keep them fed for many days.

Mrs Gandhi more or less retracted her policy. Shiamak was over-ruled and the dinner ended up by being for about three thousand guests, at a huge wedding venue on Marine Drive – there being four sittings for the dinner. We were at the first sitting, and our wonderful food was served on banana leaves (which, being disposable, was eco-friendly – not that anyone bothered about that in those days), which made it taste all the more delicious. Once you had eaten, you just got up and left, and someone else took your place. A truly memorable occasion.

Though it is a huge city, it was relatively easy to get out of Bombay into the countryside – unlike Calcutta, which seems to go on for miles and miles – and there are many places you can visit for a weekend or even a day. I guess it is not so easy now.

The bank had a beach hut at Marvi, a township on the beach just outside Bombay. We sometimes went there for a weekend with the Issits or some other friends. Not often, as it took ages to get there, and you had to go through Marvi itself, which was a very poor and congested area through which you could only drive very slowly. The beach was not that great and the mosquitoes were huge. I am sure the sea was highly polluted, though we preferred not to think of that – we did not come to any harm anyway. We also had to take all our own food and drinks with us.

We also spent a couple of weekends at Matheran with the Issits. This is the smallest hill station in India – just a small hill about two thousand six hundred feet above sea level. Cars are banned in Matheran, so people go up the hill in the toy train – a narrow-gauge railway built in 1907, or you can walk up the hill – which Mike, Jim and the boys did. Christine, Tuppence and I went in the train.

We stayed in an old-fashioned Parsi hotel, which consisted of a long line of rooms for rent. What I remember most was the monkeys – what a pest they were – you could not leave any fruit or food anywhere. They were aggressive – especially towards Tuppence, who was smaller than they were – we had to keep a good eye on him.

There were some wonderful views of the ghats, which you could see from various view points which we walked to. Poor Tuppence, who was a city dog, was worn out and eventually just sat down exhausted amongst the forest leaves and refused to budge. Christine took pity on him and carried him back to the hotel. Matheran is closed during the three months of the monsoon.

Elephanta Island sits in Bombay harbour and is a UNESCO World Heritage Site, with its collection of rock art cave temples, all dedicated to Shiva. This is a short boat trip out from the city. Temples such as those at Elephanta, Karla, Ajanta and Ellora were neglected and almost forgotten until being rediscovered and restored by the Raj. I believe Elephanta is now very popular and crowded, but in the 1970s, not many people went there.

The Karla Caves are on the way to Poona from Bombay, at a place called Lonavala. They are a series of ancient rock-carved Buddhist caves, the oldest shrine of which dates back to about 160 BC, set up a hill. We climbed up some two hundred steps to get there – quite a climb – going down being much harder than going up.

Jim, Tom and I also went to Aurangabad, where we hired a taxi and a guide (a professor of history) and visited the temples at Ajanta and Ellora. Ellora is also a UNESCO World Heritage Site located in the Aurangabad district of Maharashtra. It is one of the largest rock-cut monastery-temple cave complexes in the world, featuring Buddhist, Hindu and Jain monuments and artwork, dating from the 600–1000 CE period. Tom was quite an authority on Hindu mythology, learnt through the medium of some marvellous Hindu comics, which told the stories of the Mahabharata. We all read them. By the end of the trip, the history professor was obviously fed up with all our questions and just answering 'Yes' when we asked him, "Is that Brahma?"

"No!" piped up Tom. "It's Shiva – see the rat under his seat? That means it's Shiva!"

"Yes," replied the professor. "He is right!" He had wandering hands, and after the first stop, we ensured Tom was sat in the back seat with us.

One of Jim's sub-branches was in Goa, so of course we accompanied him there. The bank was in Vasco de Gama, the 'capital' of Goa, but we stayed at the Taj hotel in Fort Aguada. This was a couple of hours' drive from Vasco. So, whilst Jim went off to do his inspection, Tom and I went in a taxi to visit the shrine of St Francis Xavier in Old Goa.

As the taxi stopped at the Basilica, an old Goan gentleman came up to the car and asked if we wanted a guide. I said, "Yes," and he took us round the Basilica and showed us the relics. I had told Tom the story of St Francis, and he was fascinated. "Do you think we shall see his body?" he asked. I said I did not know, but supposed all we would see was the casket it was in. I could not have been more wrong. When we got into the church, there, on the top of the side altar, was a silver and glass coffin with the body of St Francis inside – like *Snow White* after she had eaten the poisoned apple in the Disney film. Our guide obligingly turned the spotlight on the casket, and we could clearly see the saint's mummified corpse. Tom was very impressed and listened attentively whilst the guide told us the story of St Francis.

St Francis died of a fever and was buried on Shangchuan island off the coast of China. Sometime after his death, his followers decided to dig up his body and take it to be buried in Goa – where he had spent years doing missionary work. When they disinterred it, they found that the corpse had not decayed, so they carefully transported it to Goa, where they put it on display and, after St Francis had performed several miracles, wrote to the Pope asking for him to be canonised. The pope asked for proof of the body, so his followers cut off St Francis' big toe, which they put in a 'matchbox', according to our guide, and sent off to Rome. After St Francis had performed the required number of miracles, the pope duly canonised him.

We also saw a large wooden cross hanging on the wall, with a figure that, in the 16th century, was said to have cried, tears running down the Christ's cheeks and blood pouring from his side. "How did they work that?" queried Tom, thinking that someone must have been behind the cross, pulling levers. Our guide assured him it was a miracle.

Tom was so impressed that when we returned to the Taj and Jim came in, he regaled him with all the stories and insisted that we return the next day, Tom this time doing all the guiding. Unfortunately, our visit was marred on the last day by Tom being stung by a jellyfish whilst swimming in the sea at the beach. The hotel, which was in the middle of nowhere, had no first aid box and the sting was excruciatingly painful. We did all the usual things to it – washed it, rubbed sand on it and eventually rang Jim's officer in Vasco, who was coming for dinner that evening, to ask him to bring some antihistamines with him. Fortunately for us, the officer's son was an asthmatic, and his mother had some Piriton with which we dosed Tom.

This relieved him somewhat, but he had an ugly red lash mark round his ankle where the jellyfish had stung him for months. I wrote on the Taj's 'comments' card that I thought they should have a basic first aid kit, but the card was too large to be posted into the comments box. This drew a second comment card from me suggesting that either they had smaller cards or put a larger slot in their box.

Halfway through our tour, Jim contracted some sort of unknown virus and was hospitalised for a week in Breach Candy Hospital. This hospital was originally set up in the 1930s for the British staff of the large British firms in India. In 1978, of course, it was self-funding and arguably the best private hospital in Bombay. However, I was not too impressed with the cleanliness of the room – especially the bathroom. Once he was installed, I returned to the flat where I picked up Poona, some phenyl and a tin of Vim and set Poona to giving the en-suite room a deep clean.

Jim later told me that the sweeper came in every morning to 'disinfect' the room with a pail of phenyl, water and a dirty cloth, which he dipped in the phenyl and then liberally waved around, splashing the walls with the water, which disinfected the room. Poona and I returned every morning to give the room an added clean.

After Jim recovered, the doctor said he had to have some 'recuperation leave', so London head office said he could either fly Home by himself for a week or go with the family to the nearest hill station for a fortnight. This was a no-brainer, as we had tenants in our house in St Albans, and anyway, what would Jim have done on his own in the UK – so we chose the latter option and decided our nearest hill station was Kashmir, which is right at the other end of the country.

Tom, Jim and I flew to Srinagar. Jim had arranged for us to spend a week at Gulmarg at Nedou's Hotel, the Highland Park being full, four days at Pahalgam, and two days at Nedou's in Srinagar. We only lasted one night at Gulmarg, as the accommodation and the food were so dreadful. The hotel room was a log cabin, with a wood-burning stove in it. It was cold, so we lit the stove, which belched forth clouds of thick smoke. The smoke was so thick that you could not see across the room. This was no good for my hay fever, and I spent the night coughing and spluttering. We therefore returned to Srinagar and reorganised our stay so we could go early to Pahalgam and spend the extra time in Srinagar, where we elected to stay on a houseboat, as I said to Jim that we could not possibly go to Kashmir without staying on a houseboat.

The hotel room at Pahalgam was quite acceptable, and we spent our time walking, horse riding (mainly Tom) and roller skating. Pahalgam was a real tourist resort, and some entrepreneur had fixed up a small temporary roller skating rink at the edge of the town, on which I taught Tom how to roller skate. I learned to skate at school in Darjeeling in the 1950s, as the school had a skating rink but I had not been skating since. Though I was never much of a skater, I found I could still get round the rink. Tom loved it, and we spent most afternoons there. At the end of our sojourn, he was a pretty good skater and could go backwards and forwards and round in circles.

We rode and walked most of the way up one of the mountains – Khilanmarg; Tom rode all the way. I think all of India was holidaying in Pahalgam that year – there were Indians from all over the country – especially young people – Keralans, Tamils, Goans, Gujaratis, Marathis, Bengalis, Punjabis, Sikhs, people from Delhi – all going up Khilanmarg. Halfway up, there was a small patch of snow, with crowds of people waiting to have their photograph taken on it – the first time most of them had seen snow.

As we went up, we passed a huge Punjabi lady riding up on a small pony. She must have weighed about eighteen stone and was overflowing the saddle of the poor little horse, with a *sais* (groom) supporting one buttock on each side. I have no idea how on earth she got down the steep hill.

Kashmir is not really known for its cuisine, the meat being tough, fish, mutton – possibly goat – and chicken. It was difficult for Jim to get something tasty to eat, as he was on a restricted diet, and unable to stomach curry, spicy or fried food – so his choice was limited. After a couple of days, I said to the bearer, "Can the cook make *nothing* but roast chicken?"

"Oh yes, *memsahib*," came the reply. "You like grilled chicken?" We were quite glad to leave for Srinagar.

Here we were rowed out in our own *shikari* (small boat) to our own houseboat on Dal lake. We should have gone there sooner. It was beautiful, and we had our own cook. The inside of the houseboat had a four-poster bed with Jacobean patterned woollen crewel work embroidered curtains and every inch of wood that could be carved was. Of course, the Kashmiris are known for their wood carving. The houseboats were beautifully kept – a relic of the Raj – but the lakes were little more than open sewers, with water lilies floating in them.

We did go on a 'tour' of the seven lakes, but it was a progression from sewer to sewer, I'm afraid. Still, we thoroughly enjoyed ourselves. We bought a walnut carving of a shikar for Tom, who spent his time sitting on the boat's veranda, polishing it with a special stone (as instructed by the cook). The flower shikari came round every morning, heavily laden with all sorts of gorgeous flowers which, of course, we never saw in Bombay – delphiniums, roses, all sorts of lilies, cornflowers, tuberoses, gardenias – all with a most heavenly perfume. I could not resist filling our houseboat with them.

We went to the bazaar where we tried to buy some papier-mâché bowls from a very famous shop called Suffering Moses. We met Suffering Moses himself, but he would not sell us any of his work, most of which were museum pieces. Particularly not an exquisite small black bowl that I fancied, with a Moghul hunting scene painted on it – both inside and out. The artist, Moses himself, had to paint the inside of the bowl holding the paintbrush upside down. Moses claimed he needed it to show at an upcoming exhibition and promised to send it to us via one of Jim's Bombay officers who was due in Srinagar the following month, but Moses changed his mind after we left, so I never received my bowl. We left our houseboat with great regret to return to Bombay, Jim being greatly refreshed and quite well again.

Not long after we left, the trouble between India and Pakistan reared its ugly head once more, and Kashmir was more or less closed to tourists. How lucky we were to have been able to visit, and how I feel for the luckless Kashmiris, whose main source of income was the tourist industry.

Still, later in his tour, Jim attended a chamber of commerce meeting in Delhi – wives were invited as well. We went up for a week. I had the best of that trip, as the ladies were well looked after by the Delhi Chamber of Commerce wives, whilst the men had to attend some very boring meetings. The ladies took us on guided tours all over Delhi, and we visited all the famous landmarks – the Red Fort for a Son e Lumiére, Akbar's pillar, Humayun's tomb, the Old Delhi market and all the tourist spots, culminating with a trip to Agra to see the Taj Mahal and look across the river to the Kala Mahal – made out of black marble, where Shah Jehan was locked up by his son Jehangir, who subsequently put his eyes out – but before that, he could look across the river and see his beloved wife Mumtaz Mahal's tomb.

Our very modern, pretty, young Punjabi guide asked me if my marriage was a love marriage or an arranged marriage. I said, "Love. What will you have? Love or arranged?"

"Oh, arranged," she replied, "because I know my father will pick a very suitable boy for me."

I asked my hostess about Muradnagar, about twenty-five miles outside Delhi, where my father spent the war helping to build an ordnance factory, and was told that it was now the biggest ordnance factory in India. Unfortunately, it was too late for them to arrange for me to visit it. I wish I had known that when we arrived, because I would have loved to have gone there. My sister was born in New Delhi during the war, whilst my parents were posted in Muradnagar.

Whilst in Bombay, Christine Issit and I used to visit a home for abandoned babies. These babies were all foundlings – mainly girls – and were found discarded in the streets, in dustbins, just anywhere really by their unfortunate mothers – probably prostitutes – who were barely able to keep themselves, let alone a baby. The babies were all seriously underweight (and certainly in Britain would have been in an incubator), plus they all had scabies and vomiting and diarrhoea. The baby home staff did their best to get round all the cots, feeding and changing the infants, but they had no time (or inclination) to cuddle the infants. Quite a few expatriate ladies visited the home and helped the staff feed the infants and cuddled them.

You could apply to be a foster parent and fatten the babies up so that they could be put up for adoption – this some of the ladies did, including Christine, who I think had three babies during her time in Bombay, which were then adopted by suitable families. This was an amazing undertaking – she got scabies from one of them, I remember, and she was up most of the night as they were fed every two hours, until they put on some weight. She had them for about three months, and the transformation from thin, weak infants into bonnie bouncing babies was heart-warming.

"You must not get too upset if the baby dies!" the paediatrician warned her every time she had a new baby. None of them did. She would take them to the pool at Breach Candy in the afternoon, where they got a lot of attention from everyone, which they loved.

The adoptive parents went through a stringent adoption procedure before they were allowed to adopt the baby, and the home authorities made every effort to ensure that each baby was placed with a suitable family – Hindu babies with Hindus, Muslim babies with Muslims and Christians with Christians. I don't know how they knew which was which.

There are plenty of beggars in Bombay – every traffic light has an assortment of them. This is a highly lucrative and organised business. Apart from the horde of children begging for baksheesh, you will only ever see one of each kind of beggar at one set of lights – i.e. one blind man, one leper, one man with a rent-a-baby (probably borrowed from a prostitute), which the beggar will pinch to make it cry, one one-legged/armed beggar and so on. There is a beggar king (as there was in Paris in the 17th and 18th centuries) who gets a large proportion of whatever the beggars make, as rental for his 'patch'. You would be courting big trouble if you tried to beg in the streets of Bombay without the patronage of the king! So, the moral is, do not give money to street beggars, no matter how much they pester you – give it to one of the numerous well-deserving charities in the city.

Christine and I kept packets of glucose biscuits in the car, which the driver doled out to the beggar children – much to their disgust. But at least they had something to eat. I once bought a sandwich at the airport to give to a beggar child who was importuning me (which cost more than I would have given her), to the disgust of her mother, who was watching her from the sidelines and gave her a hard slap! But at least she got to keep and eat the sandwich.

We were members of the swimming club at Breach Candy – most members of the expatriate community were. This was a club started in the days of the Raj by large British companies, for their British staff and for visiting seamen. You could become a member if you were a resident of Bombay, or, if visiting from other parts of India, you could buy a day's ticket. Breach Candy was on the seafront. It had two pools, an indoor Olympic competition-sized pool and a huge outdoor saltwater pool, which was fed from the sea. There was also a restaurant/café that sold delicious pomfret and chips, English breakfasts and a variety of popular Indian/Western dishes. It was the meeting place for all the expat children in Bombay, and a popular venue for the children who came out from the UK on holiday.

Mike Issit was the president whilst we were there and Jim was the secretary. They made a good team. There was an Anglo-Indian superintendent called Mr Parks who ran the club extremely efficiently, and a lady swimming coach who taught all the children how to swim. Mr Parks was on the verge of retirement, and just before we left, had the shock of his life to discover that his wife, whom he had thought was extremely ill, was in fact pregnant. He was extremely worried about how he was going to manage financially once he had retired. We unfortunately left before the good lady had her baby, but I have always wondered how they got on and whether Mr Parks was asked to stay on by the club committee, which I am sure he would have appreciated.

The first New Year's Eve we were in Bombay, I was sitting at the pool with three or four other ladies, when I casually asked, what everyone was doing to celebrate New Year, as we were doing nothing. They all replied, "Nothing!"

We had quite a few teenagers between us, so I said, "Well, we have quite a large sitting room at the flat – why don't you all come over and we shall have fish and chips and then the children can be with us." Between four families we had about ten teenagers and John Issit and Tom, both seven, so there were quite a few of us. We had a great time that evening, saw the New Year in, and introduced the teenagers to some Scottish country dancing – Gay Gordons, Eightsome Reel and Dashing White Sergeant – which they loved. The outcome was that they asked if I would hold Scottish country dance classes at Breach Candy. This I did once a week until the holidays were over.

Our impromptu party had proved so popular that many more people wanted to come, so the next year, we decided to hold the New Year's party for members and their families at Breach Candy – setting the lower age limit at eight because of John and Tom.

Mike, Christine, Jim and I arrived early at the club to check all was in order for the evening, only to find it practically deserted. It was about six thirty, and the party was due to start at seven thirty p.m. Eventually, we found a bearer and asked him where Mr Parks was, to be told that someone had died! It transpired that this was so. Apparently, some sailors from a Norwegian ship had come ashore for a swim, had lunch and a couple of beers.

They had then all gone into town, leaving one of the crew behind, who elected to stay and continue swimming – and drinking. He was a large Norwegian blonde sailor, well over six feet tall – a young man of about twenty-five. At about five thirty, one of the members and his son were having a meal in the upstairs restaurant when the boy said to his father, "Daddy, look at that man sitting there (they were the only other members in the club at the time). There's something the matter with him." The member called one of the bearers over and asked him to check that the sailor was all right. The bearer went over to the sailor, touched him on the shoulder and saw that he was dead. Panic ensued!

Mr Parks was summoned. Breach Candy Hospital was next door, but when Mr Parks phoned them, he was told that they could do nothing if the sailor was dead – not even send an ambulance, as in Bombay there are special ambulances that carry dead people only; otherwise, a normal ambulance would be contaminated. Mr Parks sent for that.

Meanwhile, time was creeping closer for the party – there were about one hundred people coming. With great difficulty, Mr Parks got about six of the bearers to carry the sailor down the narrow staircase and into his office, where they laid the body out on the floor, whilst he tried to contact the captain of the ship. The problem for us was, should we cancel the party? As we did not want to upset all the children coming, and as the guests had now started arriving and nobody knew the sailor, we decided to carry on with the party. The captain arrived not long afterwards, together with the 'dead' ambulance and a couple of members of his crew and they departed to go through all the formalities with the authorities. The sailor had apparently died of a heart attack, brought on, presumably, by a combination of too much sun and alcohol. We did not tell anybody of the traumatic drama being played out during the evening, and I have to say the party was a roaring success. I do hope the young sailor would have approved – I rather think he would have!

As the Bombay population is such a diverse mixture of people of all castes, colours and creeds, and India being a secular state, there are many public holidays, celebrating every religion's high and holy days – and in 1978, one of the things I liked best about Bombay was that everyone appeared to celebrate everything with great gusto and to treat every religion with great respect.

Thus it was that one of the big Catholic churches in Bandra had a regular novena to Our Lady, which was attended by people of all faiths, praying for their own special intentions – whether it be for someone to pass an important exam or for a girl/boy to make a good marriage. Every year, there was a large Easter procession in Bandra, with the East Indian Christian population and the Goans vying for the honour of carrying the cross.

We went to the Roman Catholic cathedral in Bombay, and Tom made his First Holy Communion there, instructed by the South Indian Parish priest, Father John. Father John was in his late thirties but quite an old-fashioned style of priest. He gave long sermons during which my mind, never very attentive to sermons, was inclined to wander. I remember him haranguing his congregation one Sunday about controlling their wayward teenagers. "You must keep her in," he said. "And if you have to break her leg, break her leg!" (No mention of what to do about teenage boys, I noticed – I guess they were permitted to be 'wayward', or perhaps I missed that bit.)

I shot out of my reverie. "He can't be serious!" I whispered to Jim. "Oh yes, he is!" was the reply.

Anyway, we arrived home one Saturday afternoon to be met at the front door by Bauji in a great state of excitement. "*Fadder Jahn ayah, memsahib* (Father John came)," he said. "*Aur au bhot burra puja benayah* (He performed a big ceremony)."

"What on earth did he do?" I suspiciously asked Jim. It transpired that he had brought some holy water and blessed the flat, which was very nice of him. This won great approval from Bauji, as opposed to his blatant disapproval when I brought home a Rajneeshi. I am sure Manuel would also have been very pleased, though we got no comment from him.

The Hindus had many processions, taking the relevant gods down to the beach at Chowpatty, where they carried them into the sea – Ganesh (also called Ganpat), the elephant god, is particularly popular in Bombay. The statue of the god is paraded through the streets down to the beach at Marine Drive, where their followers take it down and immerse it in the sea, letting it float out on the tide until all that is left is a garland of flowers. And, of course, the holiday season peaks in October/November during Diwali – the festival of lights and Hindu New Year, when the Bombay night skyline is twinkling with the light of oil lamps set up on the verandas of all the high-rise blocks of flats (including ours). I think this is everyone's favourite festival.

Many of Jim's customers would arrive at Diwali bearing *dhallis* (baskets) full of fruit, dried fruit, nuts and Indian sweets. I would keep some of the fruit and nuts, make marmalade from the oranges, apricot jam from the dried apricots and mincemeat from the dried fruit for my mince pies and Christmas cake. The rest went to the servants. They all loved Diwali.

One of Jim's customers, a Mr Jain, bought and sold silver. He bought silver from the village women, who often sold their wedding jewellery, probably to pay off family debts. This would be melted down and sold to the film industry. I thought this was terribly sad, as many of his necklaces, anklets, bangles, etcetera were quite old and probably family pieces.

At Diwali and Christmas, he would bring his latest acquisitions tied in an old blanket to show me, and I could buy a piece if I wished. Many of my friends bought silver at the silver market in Bombay. Silver being sold by the weight, the amount of work on the piece did not count for valuation. You could, therefore, have quite a selection of silver jewellery, which you wore until you were fed up of it and then sell it back in the market for a new lot.

Some of the modern blocks of flats had an open-sided ground floor for parking, and during Diwali, troupes of young people came round dancing and singing. One of the dances was a type of stick dance, which reminded me of the Morris dancers' stick dance. Anyone could join in. All were welcome, and they thoroughly enjoyed teaching you how to do it.

Tom and I used to go round the Hanging Gardens during the Ganpat festival, visiting all the shrines on the various levels of gardens, eating and drinking all sorts of things we were offered, which should have made us very ill but never did.

At the end of our tour, before we could leave India, we had to get a tax clearance certificate. As corruption is rife in India, most companies have a 'Mr Fixit' whose job it is to facilitate any problems expatriate staff might have with government departments when they arrive and leave. So, the bank Mr Fixit informed Jim that in order to get his tax clearance certificate, he would have to buy the income tax inspector two suit lengths.

Jim was appalled. "No way am I going to bribe a government officer!" he said. "In that case," came the reply, "you will not be getting a tax clearance certificate, Mr Kemp, and you will be unable to leave the country. Not only will it cost you two suit lengths, but the tax officer requires them to be Binny (a local up-market cloth producer) suit lengths. One is in a navy blue stripe and the other a grey check. *Sah*, it is cheap at the price." Jim meekly agreed to buy the suit lengths and got his certificate with no further trouble.

Just before we left Bombay, Jim and I realised that we had taken hardly any photographs of the city – so, belatedly, on one of our last Sunday mornings, we loaded Tom, John Issit and a couple of his other friends (and Tuppence) into the Ambassador and went into a deserted city to take photographs around the bank in the city centre.

Just as we arrived at the bank, who should appear round the corner but the famous Indian film star, Shashi Kapoor, riding in a howdah on a highly decorated elephant, at the head of a very colourful 'royal' procession making a Bollywood film. All the children knew Shashi, who was a friend of ours and a member of Breach Candy. Indeed, Jim knew him quite well, as when he was posted in Chittagong in 1957, Shashi and his wife Jennifer Kendal, who were members of the famous touring theatre group 'Shakespearana', came to town.

This group, which toured all over the subcontinent, was owned by Geoffrey Kendal and his wife (father of Felicity Kendal), and Jennifer, Shashi and their little furry white dog, stayed with Jim at his flat. Jim vividly remembers this, as the dog ran away through the paddy fields, and though they searched high and low for it, they never found it. When he met Shashi at Breach Candy, he reminded him of this and Shashi also remembered the incident.

"Uncle Shashi, Uncle Shashi," the children called excitedly, nearly falling out of the car and waving frantically.

"Hi, kids!" the great man replied, waving back and completely ruining his whole 'take'.

"Cut!" roared the director despairingly. They would have to reshoot the whole scene! It could only happen in Bombay.

In 1980, our tour in Bombay came to an end. We said a sad, reluctant farewell to our many friends. Bauji, Manuel and Poona were in tears when we left, and so was I.

Jim, Tuppence and I set off for a new tour of duty in Doha, Qatar – the Middle East – which was completely new and unknown territory for both of us.

CHAPTER 11
DOHA, QATAR (1980–1983)

We were posted to Doha in Qatar in November 1980. Whilst on leave in St Albans, we tried to find out a bit about life there, as we had never lived in the Middle East, which was emerging into the modern world, with cities developing at a phenomenal rate.

Jim's sister Norah worked for the director of the School of Oriental and African Studies (SOAS) in London, and she kindly arranged for us to have lunch with one of the professors from the Middle East sector. This was a very interesting and informative lunch, and I recall at the end of the meeting the professor saying to us, "Just think of someone in the Middle Ages, being transported into the middle of the twentieth century and then winning the lottery." Generally speaking, this was a very good analogy.

Jim and I returned to Bombay to pack, and then caught the plane for Doha, together with Tuppence Ha'penny, our Sidney Silky terrier. As we approached Doha, flying low over the desert, I thought I had never seen so much sand – miles and miles and miles of ghostly silvery sand dunes as far as the eye could see. That was all. No sign of human habitation or a single trace of life.

We were taking over from Tim and Marion McCartney, who met us at the airport with the bank Mercedes. We had known them in Singapore before they were married, so we were old friends. They introduced us to Roderiquez, the driver, who loaded our luggage and Tuppence in his kennel into the bank Land Rover, and we all drove into Doha.

It was dusk, and my first recollection of Doha is driving through a blaze of brilliantly lit wide roads with not much traffic. This was a sharp contrast to Bombay's congested streets and heavy traffic, where electricity saving was high on the political agenda, power cuts and load shedding frequent and every household on an electricity quota. There were obviously no such shortages in Doha.

One of the bank bachelors had kindly lent us his house for the month's takeover period. We drove into the compound, and the Goan houseboy opened the gate. It was early December, quite cold and every light in the house was turned on.

We got out of the car and went round the back of the Land Rover to let Tuppence out of his kennel. He jumped gratefully onto the drive and was sniffing around when a large half Alsatian cross Saluki dog loomed out of the gathering darkness. Tuppence ran towards it in attack mode, barking furiously. The big dog picked Tuppence up by the middle of his back and shook him vigorously. Everyone ran towards them shouting, "Drop him, drop him!" which the dog duly did onto the hard concrete drive.

The dog belonged to the resident bachelor, who came running up out of the gloom and caught it. I knelt beside Tuppence. It was obvious that he was badly hurt, as he was bleeding from the mouth. Within minutes, the vet arrived – Tuppence was still on the ground, as I was afraid to move him. The vet examined him and shook his head sadly. "I'm sorry!" he said. "Something has burst inside." I picked him up and cuddled him.

He just looked up at me with his big brown eyes. The vet gave Tuppence an injection, and he went to sleep in my arms with a little sigh. Everyone was devastated. I am sure the dog, whose name I cannot remember, thought Tuppence was a rat (plenty of those in Doha). It wasn't really anyone's fault, just a terrible accident, and we *were* in the dog's house. He was a really friendly dog, and thereafter spent most of his time with us during the rest of our stay in his house. If Tuppence had not been such a feisty, brave little dog, who would attack anything, it would never have happened. If we had waited until we were in the house before letting him out of his box, if, if… It is easy to be wise after the event.

The children were due out within days – what on earth would I say to them – particularly to Tom, as Tuppence was definitely his dog. We sadly went into the house. This was not the best start to our stay in Doha.

The next day, Marion held an 'introductory' coffee morning for me at the bank house. The story of Tuppence had already spread like wildfire through the town, and I had the offer of two dogs at the party. When Jim came home that evening, he told me all his customers knew about it, were most concerned, commiserated with him and offered him umpteen replacement dogs, of all breeds and some of none, ranging from Alsatians to Pomeranians, both puppies and adult dogs. Arabs can be such kind people. We refused all offers, having decided yet again that we would have no more dogs. They cause too much heartache.

The bachelor's house was quite new and built on the edge of the town. It smelt strongly of sand – all the curtains and carpets were obviously full of it. Sand has a very distinctive, rather acrid smell. I recognised it immediately from the times I had spent as a child, sailing home on leave with my parents, passing through the Suez Canal in Egypt. I thought we would never be able to stay there, as four out of the five of us suffer from hay fever. I got the houseboy cleaning. Over the next day or so, I washed all the curtains, vacuumed and shampooed the carpets – everything shrank. Jim then had to find someone to come in to lengthen all the curtains and stretch the carpets back to the walls. Fortunately, with the amount of building going on in Doha, that was not a problem, and we were soon shipshape again.

I think we had been there about a week when the children arrived for the Christmas holidays. Sadly, we told them about Tuppence, but because everything was new and we were busy and occupied, they did not seem to dwell on it and were happy to accept and pet the 'attacker dog'.

The McCartney children also arrived for their Christmas holidays. Their young son was the same age as Tom, so that was a friend for him. We spent a lot of the time at the McCartney house being introduced to people and shown round. Marion took me to the embassy to be formally introduced to the ambassador's wife, who was a very pleasant lady and we had coffee with her. I guess this was rather like presenting my credentials as Marion's successor – a formal first for me. Jim also had a formal presentation to the ambassador in his capacity as the new Standard Chartered Bank Manager, Qatar.

The McCartneys had quite a menagerie of animals to dispose of which they offered us – an aviary of budgies and a tank of tropical fish – both of which I politely refused. I could see Tom's face getting longer and longer every time I said, "No, thank you!" Lastly, a gerbil – a genuine desert rat, called Sniffles, whom they had saved in the desert one day, from some local boys who were stoning him.

I opened my mouth to say 'no', not being fond of rats, but then I looked at Tom's pleading face. "Okay," I said, "we will have Sniffles." Tom's face lit up – he was over the moon! Sniffles was sweet – he was small, pink and furry with a long tail, and very inquisitive – he would come to the bars of his cage and nibble your fingers if you put them through the wires, which was quite endearing.

The first weekend we were there, the McCartneys invited us to go for a drive into the desert with them. When they arrived, Tim informed us we would first have to go to the bank, as there had been an attempted robbery. This was unheard of in Doha. We drove over, only to find that the police were already there. They had arrested the bank watchman – an Indian – and thrown him into jail. This despite the fact that he had protested his innocence, his alibi being that he had been at the mosque. Nonsense, they said – they knew he never went to the mosque but was sitting drinking coffee in the local coffee house. Anyway, he should have been guarding the bank.

It took Jim three months to get him out of prison – and then only after he had met the chief of police and requested his help. It struck me then what a dangerous place we were living in. The attempted robbery was extremely amateur. The robbers had tried to get into the safe by forcing the lock open using a blowtorch. Needless to say, this did not work. They had also left the imprint of a huge foot on the door as they tried to pull it open and fingerprints all over the place. I understand that a couple of Sikhs were eventually apprehended. The poor watchman was a nervous wreck by the time he came out of prison, and was, I think, repatriated to India where he retired with a good pension.

The McCartneys left just before Christmas and we moved into the house. Before we unpacked, I decided yet again to shampoo the carpets and wash the curtains. Lo and behold, the whole lot shrank once more, and we again had to call on the carpet fitter/curtain man to fix it. He was very amused and wanted to know when I was moving again, so he could get some more business. We soon settled in, and the children returned to school in the New Year.

One of the first things we had to get used to in Doha was the Middle East banking hours. The bank opened from seven thirty a.m. to one p.m. Sunday to Thursday. Our weekend was on Friday and Saturday. Sunday was a working day. Jim was in the office by seven a.m. on weekdays and home by one thirty for lunch; the rest of the day was our own. The shops all shut from midday during the heat of the day, and then re-opened from about four p.m. till about eight p.m. Jim would often go down to the souk of an evening and visit his shopkeeper customers. I have never seen so much of Jim, because in other postings, he would leave for the office at about seven in the morning and not return till about six thirty in the evening.

The bank house was a large, rented Arab-style bungalow. This was unusual, as normally the bank had its own property. In Doha, they were in the process of planning a new bank building and manager's house. This was one of the projects under Jim's management. Fortunately, he enjoys overseeing the building of new properties. It was about five years since we had left Kuala Lumpur, where he had overseen the building of the 'houses on the hill' project.

In common with all the properties in Doha, the house was in a walled compound. At the right-hand side of the house, we had a bit of green lawn, which was rare in Doha, water being scarce, more expensive than petrol, and lawns having to be watered. The rest of the compound was tarmacked, with a huge purple bougainvillea tree hanging over the side wall into the next property.

It was a flat-roofed concrete bungalow, designed in the Arab style. Half a dozen steps led to a big wooden front door, and into the hall or *'majlis'*; a very large room, furnished like a sitting room with a comfortable three-piece suite, a large television and, to my delight, a lovely new Yamaha piano against the back wall. Indeed, we spent most of our time in the *majlis*. At the back of the room were a few steps leading to a Romeo and Juliet-type balcony and then up a few more stairs to a door leading to the flat roof. No one ever went up there, that I can remember, except for maintenance. I have no idea what the indoor balcony was for; perhaps the owner just fancied it.

The house was not connected to the water mains; a large metal container at the back of the garden was our sole water supply. This was filled regularly by bowser, the water being pumped up to the roof tank. Marion warned me that during the winter, hot water ran out of the hot water tap, but during summer, the hot water was turned off and came out of the cold water tap – stinging hot, the sun having heated up the roof tank.

At the left of the majlis was a study and en suite bathroom, which we used as a bedroom for Roderick, who was now seventeen. Adjacent to the study was the main bedroom suite, then a passage leading down the side of it to the third and fourth bedroom and bathrooms. It was quite a wide passageway, as there was room in it for a table tennis table, on which sat Sniffles' cage.

At the rear of the hall, a door led into the kitchen, and on the right side of the hall was a large lounge/dining room with a wall-to-wall celadon green Chinese carpet with comfortable, squishy beige upholstered armchairs and settees placed round the walls. A row of wooden, glass fronted bookcases/china cabinets lined the lounge wall adjoining the hall. It was a lovely room. A door led from the dining room to the kitchen, which was quite spacious and modern. The back door led outside, and by the back compound wall were the servants' rooms. The whole house, including the servants' rooms, was air-conditioned.

The first night we were in residence, I woke around midnight hearing a terrible noise going *gudk, gudk, gudk* – which I took to be a faulty air conditioner. The next morning, I said to Jim, "There's something wrong with the air conditioner – it's making a dreadful noise – kept me awake all night." The air conditioner man duly came out and checked the machine, to find nothing wrong.

The next night, the noise began again. "There *is* something wrong with the air conditioner," I said to Jim, "It's clanking away as if something is loose inside and it's going to blow up!" Back came the air conditioner man – nothing wrong.

The third night, the noise started up again. This time, I put on all the lights and got up to have a look. I walked over to the air conditioner and put my ear to the machine – it was running silently. Up started the noise again – this time I followed it; it seemed to come from the passageway outside the bedroom. Sure enough, when I got into the corridor, there it was louder and clearer than ever. I discovered it was Sniffles running round and round on his exercise wheel – the faster he ran, the louder the noise. I had forgotten that gerbils are nocturnal creatures. We moved him slightly further back on the table and the noise vanished.

In an Arab household, the bedroom area would have been the women's side of the house, and male guests would go through the hall into the lounge/dining area so that they did not have to meet the ladies, who could remain in '*purdah*' if they wished.

We had a house staff of two. Parras was the houseboy, and there was a cook called Peter. They were both Catholic Goans. Unfortunately, Peter, who I understand was a fabulous cook, retired due to ill health just before we took over, so we were cookless for a while until we could get a replacement from Bombay. Fortunately, Parras had learnt to cook from Peter and was a more than adequate cook.

An Arab friend of ours found a cook for us, but when he arrived, we discovered his cooking was not really up to scratch. We put up with him – he was all right for everyday cooking but not for entertaining, when I would borrow Simpatio – also Goan – from a friend whose husband worked for Cable & Wireless. Simpatio was a great friend of Parras, which was just as well, as Parras did not get on with the new cook whose name I have forgotten. This was because Parras and Peter had worked together for a long time, and the new cook did not come up to Parras's exacting standards. I'm not sure that we did either.

I found the Middle East very different from our previous postings and always felt I was living 'on' the country rather than 'in' the country, and was very much an 'expat'. For the first time ever, I had more expatriate than local friends, which I thought was very strange, but one did not really meet the local Qatari ladies as most of them were very orthodox. Indeed, I felt very privileged to meet a Qatari family whose ladies actually visited my house, though they would not eat or drink. They spoke no English and I no Arabic, but we communicated through their husbands and, with a bit of my fractured Hindi, we got along very well if conversation was somewhat limited.

The family owned an estate somewhere near Rochester, which they visited quite often. It sounded huge and very grand. The ladies did not go out much, and when the men visited London on business trips, they would shop for the ladies – mainly at Marks and Spencers in Oxford Street, bringing back armfuls of nightdresses and slippers in every available colour for the women to wear round the house.

I admired the ladies greatly, especially for their piety and strict adherence to their religion. They were Shias, and during Muharram (and I guess also Ramadan), they watched no television or videos whatsoever for a whole month. As this seemed to be their main occupation, and they were virtually housebound, I cannot imagine how they did without them for an entire month. They were very devout. I understand one of their husbands had never ever seen his wife's face without her *betullah* – the black eye mask the ladies normally wore. Indeed, she only took it off to wash her face, and with the passage of years, the black dye from the mask had stained the skin all around her eyes.

There was a very large and varied expatriate community in Doha. Most of the jobs, from manual labour to top executive positions, were filled by expatriates of one sort or another. There was a large Indian, Pakistani and Korean labour workforce, Filipino domestic and hotel staff, various Europeans and British working for the oil company, embassies, banks, Cable & Wireless and other major and minor companies.

Qatar was then undergoing major development. There were no street names, and directions to your house were given via various landmarks. *'Go to the centre (the new only shopping centre in Doha), turn left after four streets, then past the mosque and two streets further along on the left-hand side is our house!'* Nowadays, of course, Doha is a huge metropolis. In 1980, there were two hotels, the oldest being the Gulf Hotel, with a German general manager, and the newest Sheraton Hotel, with a Swiss general manager. The Sheraton was still under construction when we arrived.

We had not been in Doha very long when an Arab friend, Akbar, said to me, "Noreen, you like animals. I have a lovely bird that I shall bring you."

"Thanks very much, Akbar," I replied, "but I don't really like birds in cages."

"Never mind!" says he. "You will like this one."

Oh dear! I thought. Anyway, nothing happened for about six months until one day, the doorbell rang, the gate opened and in came Akbar, carrying a large greater sulphur-crested cockatoo in a gilded brass cage (from Harrods, no less).

"Here," he said, thrusting the cage at me. "You have him – he bit me!"

"Thanks very much, I think!" I said. "What's his name?"

Akbar thought for a moment. "Benjamin!" he said.

"That's a good Arab name!" I replied, laughing. We called him Benji for short.

We put Benji's cage on a tall table in the corner of the hall, by the kitchen door, where he could see whatever was going on in the house and keep himself amused. He was a great character, vocal and very destructive. We were completely novice bird owners. When we returned from shopping one day, we found he had pushed his water bowl out of the cage onto the floor, put his head through the hole and chewed a huge lump out of the teak door jamb – there was a mound of sawdust on the floor. Thereafter, we kept his water and food dishes wired in and carefully turned away from the door jamb.

Benji regularly chewed through his broom handle perch. I was always buying new broom handles. He could be extremely noisy and screeched like an express train whenever he got bored, which was quite often. It was very disconcerting to suddenly hear an express train running through the middle of your sitting room. He could keep this shrieking up for hours. Fortunately, though he hated Parras, who was apt to tease him, he liked the cook – so when he had one of his screeching fits, we would relegate him to the kitchen, where he talked to the cook. Actually 'Benjamin' was really 'Benjamina', as we discovered after we had had him/her for about six years, when he suddenly laid an egg. He was a bird of uncertain temperament – he quite liked Jim and me, hated Rod, who teased him and loved Tom. Mhairi didn't pay much attention to him.

We occasionally let Benji out of his cage, and he liked to sit on the railing of the Juliet balcony – until we found that he was quietly demolishing the wooden bannister! It was difficult to catch him and return him to the cage. You had to chase him around the room, throw a towel over him, then grab him – squawking loudly and trying to bite you through the towel – and push him back into the cage.

He would only eat sunflower seed hearts, which, according to our bird book, were very bad for him, as they made his beak and claws grow very fast and long. We once asked the vet to come and cut his nails – what a performance. The vet turned up unannounced at about five in the evening – I had dinner guests arriving at seven! We could not get Benji out of the cage. I can't remember quite how it happened, but we ended up with the cage rolling sideways on the floor minus the food dishes, with Benji perched outside the cage on the bars and the vet trying to cut his nails through the bars while Benji was trying to bite him – an impossible task.

"Put a sock over his head!" said the vet.

"*You* put a sock over his head!" I replied, struggling unsuccessfully to prize him off the bars. Eventually, we managed to throw a towel over him, remove him from the bars and I held him whilst the vet cut his nails. What a carry on!

On another occasion, Benji escaped outside and flew into the purple bougainvillea hanging over the wall. He would not return, so I got my towel and the kitchen steps and climbed up to catch him. Whenever I got anywhere near him, he would cock his head and jump a little higher and further along the branch, just out of reach. Eventually, he hopped well out of reach. I gave up and thought exasperatedly. *Well, just let him go – I'm fed up with him! The crows will get him, and it will be his own fault!* Benji flew off, and I wondered what I would tell Tom when he returned for the holidays!

Five minutes later, Parras ran up to me saying, "*Memsahib, memsahib,* backside maid say, Benji in her garden!" I charged round to the house at the back with my large towel, and the maid let me in. There he was, sitting on the last sunflower of the season, happily munching the seeds in the middle of the flower. I threw the towel over him and prized him off the sunflower. Benji was very cross, biting my finger through the towel. He didn't just bite – he sort of ground your finger as well, as he would a seed, and would not let go. Neither would I!

"Quick," I said to the maid, my finger by this time dripping blood. "Get something to put him in!" She dithered around for a while – meantime, Benji carried on crushing my finger, and blood was pouring all over the towel. "Hurry up!" I yelled.

After what seemed an age, she appeared with a plastic laundry basket, which we managed with difficulty to put him in, and I returned home triumphant and managed to get him back into his cage. My finger took months to heal, and I still have the scar! *Who wants birds?* I thought. *Even if they do come from Harrods! Give me a dog every time!*

There was no official church in Doha. When we arrived, there was a Catholic priest, a tough ex-service padre, called Father Kevin, who had special permission to say mass in the football stadium. He left within weeks of our arrival. During this time, the law regarding assembly was altered, large gatherings being prohibited.

Sean Cooper, the captain of the Emir's yacht (a sizeable passenger vessel) and Jim obtained permission from the Emir to replace Father Kevin, with the provisos that they would take full responsibility for the conduct of the new incumbent, all services to be held within private houses and no assemblies of any sort to be allowed outside. The new man also had to have an alternative profession in order to obtain a work permit.

The replacement was Father Gerald Dunn, a tall, balding, thin Mill Hill priest, and a very gentle man, who was also an educationalist. He had spent the last few years in Sabah, living with the Dyaks, so this was a great change for him. He stayed with Sean and his family.

Father Gerry had his work cut out for him. He had a large and varied congregation of several thousand, consisting of Catholics, mainly Filipino and South Indians, plus members of the Eastern Orthodox Church. He was granted special permission from the Pope to give communion to the many Coptic Christians working in Doha. Mass was held in private houses, including ours. Because we had a large reception area, which could hold about sixty people standing, one of the main masses was held at our house at festival times such as Easter and Christmas.

At the time, the authorities stipulated that crowds could not gather in the streets, so we supplied soft drinks and biscuits after mass inside the house. There was plenty of room for everyone in our compound, but despite repeated requests, we could not persuade some of the congregation to desist from spilling over onto the street for a chat before they dispersed, and had to keep Parras and Roderiguez, our driver, on duty outside to ask them to move on. In my experience, you can never rely on crowds, even small ones, to do as requested, despite the fact that they know it is dangerous and that the authorities could well arrive and arrest them all. There was a large mosque in the next street. I found this scenario quite nerve-racking sometimes.

I played the piano for the service, so we could have carols at Christmas – which I played at a cracking pace to the astonishment of the congregation, who were inclined to sing at what I call a 'slowly is holy' funereal tempo. But I must say, they kept up.

"Wow! That was fast!" said Father Gerry. He said mass back-to-back all week during the Christmas and Easter season, and about three or four masses in various houses every Friday, Saturday and Sunday and once a day otherwise. He must have found this extremely tiring, especially as there was no substitute priest, plus he visited the sick and did everything else that a Parish priest would normally do. I don't think he ever had a day off. I did not envy him his job.

There was an official Catholic church in Bahrain, with an Italian bishop and a few other priests, whom Jim used to visit when he went there on business. They invited him to lunch one day, which was cooked by the bishop. When the dessert, which was Italian ice cream, was served, the bishop asked Jim if he would like a blessing. *Strange,* thought Jim. *Halfway through a meal!*

Of course, he said, "Yes!" (you can't have too many blessings, can you?), whereupon the bishop produced a large bottle of Benedictine, which he proceeded to splash liberally all over Jim's ice cream, amidst much hilarity from the other priests – clearly, this was a very popular joke.

We had been in Doha for about three months when we were invited to a cocktail party. We arrived with some other guests, and as the door opened to welcome us, a dirty grey ball of fur sped in through the open door and hid quivering under the host's dining table.

"Get that dog out of here!" yelled the host.

"Wait a minute," said Jim. "If it doesn't belong to anyone, we'll take it!"

I could hardly believe my ears, he having adamantly said we were not having any more dogs after the Tuppence debacle. There was another couple behind us who also said they would take it. "No, no," Jim said, "we'll have it!" We picked up the frightened creature and deposited it in the car, with Roderiquez.

We were going out to dinner with one of the bank staff after the cocktail party, and when we arrived, I asked if I could bring the dog in. "Wait a minute," said our hostess Moira when she saw the animal. "I know that dog, and I think I know who owns it. I'll let you know tomorrow."

We took the little bitch home, and the next morning I gave her a really good bath. She was about the size of a West Highland terrier, snow white with long silky fur, and absolutely terrified. Halfway through the morning, Moira phoned. "I found the owner," she said, "a British couple, and they're going to call you." Half an hour later, I had a phone call from the owner.

It transpired that they had rescued the dog and her brother from some local youngsters who were stoning the two pups on some waste ground. They kept the little bitch, which they called 'Pola', because they said she looked just like a miniature polar bear – she did – and gave the dog to a friend. The couple moved from a house to a fifth-floor-flat, and because the wife was very pregnant and could no longer go up and down stairs to take the dog out, they gave her to a friend. The friends were obviously not too keen on the animal, as they said she was dirty.

One day, Pola escaped, and they made little effort to find her. Pola's owners did not want her back. So, would we like to keep her? There was a cat that went with the dog. Would we like the cat as well? "Okay!" I said "We'll keep the dog and have the cat as well." thinking that might make

Pola feel more at home. We did not think Pola was dirty – just very nervous and frightened. If you raised your voice, she would run away, trailing a little wee behind her. She couldn't stand newspapers rattling – especially if they were rolled up. She had obviously been hit with them.

About an hour later, Pola's previous owner appeared with the cat. He was the ugliest tabby cat I have ever seen – thin and scrawny – the spitting image of Tom from the Tom and Jerry cartoons. Pola was dozing on the top step. She looked at the cat coming up the stairs, shook her head, did a double take and pounced on it.

The cat strolled nonchalantly past her into the house. He stalked round the room, shaking his feet, investigating his surroundings, accompanied by Pola, who kept leaping at him and nudging him. Eventually, he went up onto our Juliet balcony, where he made himself at home and sat there washing his ears, followed by Pola, who lay down next to it with a contented sigh – d there they stayed.

The cat stayed with us for about two months, seemingly settled, until one day he just vanished without a trace. We searched all over the streets for him. All we could think of was that he had perhaps eaten some rat poison, which the municipality used to put down regularly in the streets, and gone off somewhere to die. Pola did not even appear to miss him. Perhaps that was because the children arrived for their holidays, and she attached herself to Tom. She replaced Tuppence as his dog

Pola went everywhere with us. She was an extremely friendly dog and loved children. We never had any trouble getting someone to look after her when we went on our annual leave – in fact, the only trouble we had was getting her back. She was nine months old when we got her and eventually died in St Albans at the grand old age of nineteen, by which time she had travelled with us from Doha to Karachi to St Albans to Johannesburg and back to St Albans.

We had a busy social life in Doha, both with our expatriate friends and Jim's local customers. He was invited out to the desert quite frequently by the sheikhs at Wakra to attend a 'mutton grab'. This event was male-only. Jim and his accountant, Alastair Ramsey, would be driven out to Wakra, where they would sit cross-legged on the ground for dinner with the sheikhs. This would be roast mutton.

A whole sheep dripping with grease would arrive wrapped up in a hairy blanket and be plonked down in front of you. You then broke bits off the carcass, which you ate with your right hand fingers – hence the title 'mutton grab'. Occasionally, one of the hosts would pass you a tasty titbit – like one of the sheep's eyes – which you were expected to eat with relish. After the meal, there would be a bit of singing and dancing and the sheikhs would then discharge their rifles into the air with great gusto. No one ever got shot, but I thought this must be a bit hairy, as what goes up must come down somewhere.

Every couple of months or so, we would go for dinner to one of Jim's favourite customers, whom we called the Rolls Royce sheikh because he had the Rolls Royce franchise in Qatar. The sheikh was a small wiry man of about seventy, with a young, attractive wife (the one we met anyway, I think he had more than one), and a young son of about ten, plus an adult son.

We would start off the evening in his *majlis*, which was a very large hall, carpeted a couple of feet deep with miscellaneous carpets, ranging from expensive old Persian ones to cheap Belgian tat. At the entrance to the majlis, at the side of the wall, were three cars parked on the carpets. The Rolls Royce the queen had been driven in when she visited Qatar, a large American Panther and a big Pontiac. Opposite them were a Louis XV-style couch, and then various expensive-looking armchairs, ending with an Ercol suite at the far end of the *majlis*.

The sheikh, who was a Bedouin, also had a large tent in his garden, where he moved whenever he felt hemmed in by the house, which was often. He told me he liked to live in his tent and look up at the stars at night, rather than stay cooped up in a house. We would have soft drinks and small eats here and then adjourn to his eldest son's house for dinner.

We would be ushered into the dining room, which was quite small – largely because at one end of it was a large electric organ. This, the young son would play for a while. I don't know who the organist in the family was, but it definitely wasn't him. You couldn't hear yourself think, let alone carry on a conversation. We would then sit down to dinner. On our first visit, I took my place at the table and was obviously squirming around a lot on my seat, as the next thing I knew – *whoosh* – I disappeared under the table! Everyone was most concerned, but I was unhurt and sat on the floor laughing. The chairs had newly arrived, and someone had forgotten to screw the seats onto the frames. After dinner, we moved to the lounge, where we all watched a video of the Queen's visit to Qatar, driving along in the sheikh's Rolls Royce. He was so proud of this; we saw the video every time we came to dinner.

At the end of another of our visits, the sheikh, who spoke Hindi, as did Jim, so they were able to communicate without an interpreter, said to Jim, "Kemp, I like you very much and I am going to give you a gift."

He spoke to one of his servants, who scuttled away. *Oh no!* thought Jim, having heard stories of how the sheikhs sometimes gave you very expensive gifts, such as Rolex watches – even an expensive car. *How will I be able to refuse the present without offending the old man and maybe losing his very lucrative account?* The bank did not allow its employees to accept expensive gifts. Eventually, the servant returned carrying a half-full bottle of Eau Sauvage cologne, which the Sheikh presented to a greatly relieved Jim, who thanked him profusely. We all thought this was hilarious. To make matters worse, when we got home, Rod saw the bottle. "Oh," he said, grabbing it. "Eau Sauvage – my favourite – you don't want it, do you?" and commandeered it. So poor Jim got nothing at all.

One of Jim's major customers, whom we called 'the Pirate' as he had a patch over one eye, which made his tall, hawknosed, imperious figure look very dashing, told Jim that a very wealthy sheikh (who banked elsewhere) was ill in the London Clinic in Harley Street, and if Jim could arrange a visit from someone in the London office with some flowers, a box of chocolates and felicitations, this might result in some lucrative business. Jim rang up head office, who sent around one of their officers, whom we called 'Gorgeous George'. George, who was always very dapper and smartly dressed, arrived at the hospital with a huge bouquet of flowers, a big box of chocolates and a large basket of fruit. His visit was a rousing success, resulting in the sheikh opening a large deposit account.

We made quite a bit of music in Doha. There was a group of four teachers who played the recorder, an excellent German concert pianist, Karl Heinz Loeblin, who worked at the embassy, another bank manager, George (I forget his other name), who was a lovely light tenor, a soprano, Valerie Dodd, whose husband Philip worked for Cable & Wireless and myself. a mezzo contralto.

Since I was the one with the piano, we hosted a couple of house concerts, with a varied programme. Elizabethan music for the recorders, a couple of solos from Karl Heinz, who also accompanied us and a mixture of baroque, lieder, opera and English songs from the singers. We invited an audience of about fifty, which we could seat comfortably in our *majlis*. The concerts were very successful. The only fly in the ointment was Benji, who at the rehearsals, insisted on joining in with Valerie! Fortunately, during the performances, he got stage struck and just sat in his cage as if he was stuffed.

Valerie worked for Qatar Radio, where she ran a classical music programme for an hour every evening at about five o'clock and also had a 'Desert Island Discs' programme once a week for a season or two. She invited me to participate in the 'Desert Island Discs' programme, where I spoke about my schooldays in Darjeeling and had a most enjoyable time choosing my 'discs'. After much agonising, I chose Mozart's horn concerto, Telemann's trumpet concerto, Paganini's violin concerto, 'Dieu parmi nous' from Messiaen's organ nativity suite, Janet Baker singing 'The Swimmer' from 'Sea Pictures' and Benjamin Luxon singing 'Break the News to Mother' – a tear-jerker Edwardian ballad.

I have always loved Edwardian ballads because they usually tell a story – as indeed do most songs – in this case about a general's young son who, though underage, enlisted in the army during the Boer War and is killed saving the flag. Oh dear how sad! My mother used to sing loads of Edwardian ballads to me when I was a little girl – though not this particular one. She had a vast repertoire of songs, which she passed on to me, many of which I have sung in concerts at the end of a programme. Most audiences seem to thoroughly enjoy them. I expect my choice of discs would now be quite different, though these are still some of my favourite pieces of music. Valerie's programmes were extremely popular.

Quite a few of the wives worked in Doha, and after seeing an advertisement for a computer course, Jim suggested that I take it. Rather reluctantly, I did. It was a week's course on a Philips computer. Once I had completed it, I started to look round for a job. As I had not worked for a good few years, I then rather tentatively joined a recruitment agency as one of their temporary staff and set out on a temping career in Doha. I worked with various companies during term times, ending up with a stint at the Sheraton Hotel, who were just opening, working for the hotel manager, a charming Palestinian.

The Palm Court Orchestra, made up of musicians from the Bournemouth Symphony Orchestra, arrived for the opening, stayed for a couple of months and gave us all tremendous enjoyment. It was so good to be able to meet and talk music with the orchestra members, who were all charming and a lot of fun.

Jim, meanwhile, was busy overseeing the construction of the new bank building. This involved quite a bit of marble tiling, which proved problematic for the contractor. Jim contacted an Italian marble expert, Ricky Bertelli, who was involved in building the new palace for the Emir and pressed him into service. Ricky gave him and the contractor a lot of advice and solved their marble problems. Whilst with us, Ricky asked me if I would like to see the Emir's unfinished palace. I jumped at the chance, and we went down to the site.

"Gosh," I said when we came to the bathrooms. "Gold-plated taps!"

"Gold plated!" said Ricky. "These are solid gold!" We became extremely friendly and visited Ricky some years later in Italy. The new bank was still incomplete when we left Doha, but Jim was invited by the bank to return for the opening ceremony.

On a Friday, Jim and the children, when they were on holiday, went fishing with Daniel Appramaniam, whose niece Maral was Jim's secretary. Daniel owned a thirty-two-foot motor launch with twin Volvo Penta motors, and the family spent many happy hours fishing with him. Sometimes, Daniel and Jim would go spear fishing, but without aqualungs, as Daniel thought that aqualung spear-fishing was unsporting and extremely unfair to the fish. I usually stayed at home, as I got terribly seasick.

The first time they persuaded me to go with them, they told me Daniel had a 'large' boat. When I saw it, I wanted to know where the 'large' boat was – anything smaller than an ocean liner being 'small' as far as I am concerned. I had taken a seasickness tablet and was fine, if a bit drowsy. I would have been better if they had stopped asking me if I was okay all the time!

All my family loved fishing with Daniel – especially Mhairi, who one day caught a huge ten-pound garoupa on her line – the fishhook had caught on its upper lip, and the men netted it, as it was too large for her to reel in on her own. They normally went out early in the morning and would throw a net overboard, to catch prawns, which they would uplift, throw into a large wok, cook and eat there and then – delicious!

The bank also owned a boat and a Land Rover for the use of their executive staff. The staff took it in turns to have use of them at the weekend.

As we already had the use of Daniel's boat, I don't think we ever used the bank boat, but we always took our turn in the Land Rover for trips in the desert.

For safety reasons, you always signed out at the yacht club if you went out in the boat, as '*shamals*' or sudden storms, which were quite dangerous, could suddenly blow up. Also, for safety reasons, we always carried several lengths of stout rope in the Land Rover in case we got bogged down in the sand – no AA in Doha – an extra four-gallon plastic jerry can of petrol, two jerry cans of drinking water and a compass. This was before the days of satnav, and it is very easy to get lost or disoriented in the desert, as everything looks the same. Miles and miles of identical sand dunes as far as the eye can see.

Some people went 'dune buggy racing', where they drove over the dunes at breakneck speed. This was an extremely dangerous sport, as you never knew what was on the other side of the dune – the sand shifting all the time, often just disappearing and the buggy facing a sheer drop of perhaps fifty feet or more. This is how Derek Nimmo, the actor, who often visited Doha, broke his back – he went over a dune at speed, and the buggy turned turtle. He was lucky to escape alive. I have always found the desert quite spooky – it is beautiful, deathly quiet, with a distinctly menacing and unfriendly atmosphere. Something to be treated with great respect.

Early in April 1982, the navy paid a courtesy visit to Doha. As is customary on these occasions, the crew were all invited out by the local Brits, and we asked to have a dozen ratings. "Would you not prefer officers?" I was asked.

"No!" I replied. "The ratings are more fun!" Our problem was then finding enough beer for our guests.

Though alcohol is officially prohibited in Qatar, the expatriates all had a generous alcohol allowance. This was far more than we drank, and Jim arranged for a couple of trunks to be stored in the bank, in which everyone could put their surplus booze quota at the end of the month if they wished, so that we had extra supplies to call on for official entertaining. The problem was that beer was expensive in terms of units. A bottle of beer cost the same amount of units as a bottle of spirits, which made it an expensive drink. However, by mixing the beer with non-alcoholic beer, we managed to eke out our supply without anyone being any the wiser.

I arranged for us to have a BBQ on our little patch of lawn; alas, when the day arrived, it was pouring with rain. I was absolutely flabbergasted. This was unheard of in Doha – the last time it had rained was apparently about five years earlier. It really bucketed down like a monsoon! To make matters worse, our flat roof leaked, and the water poured in through the sitting room ceiling into a zinc bathtub, which we had put in the middle of the celadon green carpet to catch the deluge. However, we decided we would still have the BBQ and moved the brazier onto the small covered porch by the front door. We then discovered that most of the boys sent to us were cooks – the last thing they wanted to do, was cook! We delegated Parras to do the cooking.

There was a howling gale outside, and as soon as Parras lit the fire, great clouds of smoke blew into the house, choking everyone. One of the boys, who was a Yorkshireman, said to me, "*Ee*, when I coom 'ere I thought this were a right posh place, but now (looking at the waterfall going into the tub and the smoke blowing everywhere), *Ah* 'm not too sure!"

Anyway, they seemed to have a good time. Tom, who was eleven at the time, was sitting next to one who was a Sparky (radio operator). "Are you into heavy metal?" the sailor asked. Tom nodded vigorously, and I left them to it, chatting away nineteen to the dozen. I had no idea what heavy metal was!

The destroyer left Doha early to sail to the Falklands. Unfortunately, I can't remember the name of the ship, but we often thought of them all through the Falklands campaign and sent up a prayer that they would all come through it safely.

We spent three years in Doha and only had another three years left to do with the bank before Jim was due to retire. In 1983, we were posted to Karachi. We were sorry to leave Qatar but looked forward to returning to the Indian subcontinent where, as Jim was to be 'Manager Pakistan', we hoped to be able to travel and see a bit of Rudyard Kipling's 'Kim's country', with Lahore coming under his jurisdiction.

We left Doha just before Easter in 1983. Unfortunately, before we left, I had news that my father was terminally ill with liver cancer. The children had just arrived in Doha for the holidays, and I thought that if I could get everybody to Karachi, I could then return to Arbroath with the children to spend some time with my father before he died.

Unfortunately, it was not to be. We had barely arrived in Karachi when I received a telephone call from my cousin advising me to return to Arbroath immediately, as he was in hospital and not expected to last long. With a heavy heart, we left Doha and our friends behind.

CHAPTER 12
KARACHI (1983–1986)

We arrived at Karachi Airport with all our luggage, Pola and Benji. The bank 'fixer' was there to greet us and facilitate our passage through the customs. The customs officer was totally uninterested in Pola, who was looking through the bars of her kennel wagging her tail furiously, but very intrigued by Benji. Daringly, he put his fingers through the cage bars to tickle him. Benji, who was sitting in his gilded cage like a stuffed parrot, looked at him balefully and speculatively out of one eye. *Oh, please, dear Lord, don't let Benji bite the customs man!* I prayed silently – Benji was a bird of uncertain temper who could give you a very nasty bite! Fortunately, he just sat there silently, never moving a feather.

The day we arrived June McPherson invited the children and me for coffee. As we were staying at the Holiday Inn, I asked if Pola could come too. "Oh," she said. "I don't know if Pickles would like that." Pickles was June's cat. She had adopted him from the streets in Bombay, as a scrawny, underfed kitten, and he had grown into a massive beautiful sleek tabby cat. I remembered Pickles from our stay in Bombay, the Macphersons having been there at the same time as us.

"Oh," said I. "Pola loves cats – she used to have her own cat in Doha before she came to us." So Pola came.

June loved cats and I think fed all the cats in Bath Island; saucers of milk were placed for them all over the garden. When we arrived, Pola leapt out of the car and, in seconds, had treed a couple of passing cats – fortunately, not Pickles, who was sleeping somewhere inside. We retrieved Pola with difficulty. By the time I returned from St Albans, all the saucers of milk had disappeared, Pola was comfortably installed and the cats had all vanished!

The day after we arrived in Karachi, I managed to contact Grace, who said to come immediately as my father was worse. Jim booked the children and me on a flight to Edinburgh that evening. The McPhersons had organised a staff party for us at the bank house. The children and I left straight from the party to the airport to catch the night flight to Edinburgh via Heathrow.

At Edinburgh, I rented a car and we drove to Arbroath, but unfortunately, my father died earlier that morning. My sister Linda, who had flown from Johannesburg, also arrived just too late. Fortunately, Linda's friend Fiona, whom Dad was very fond of, was with him when he died, so he was not alone. We made the arrangements for his funeral guided by cousin Grace and dealt with the business side of things, including selling the house and contents – a traumatic experience for everyone.

After a six-week stay in Arbroath, Linda returned to Johannesburg and I to Karachi. By this time, the McPhersons had left, Jim was installed in the house at Mary Road and had his feet well under the table at the office.

The house at 1 Mary Road, Bath Island, Karachi, was a large two-storeyed old yellow sandstone building, built in the early 1900s. The first sight of it from the bridge over to Bath Island was not inspiring. There were quite a number of old colonial style houses on Bath Island visible from the bridge, one which had its rear festooned with pipes and two 'Buckingham Green' water tanks hanging off the back. I devoutly hoped this one was not ours. It was!

Actually, the house was rather nice. I liked it. Entry to the compound was to the rear of the house through a big wooden gate, opened by a *durwan* (watchman). There was a large 'elephant' (or probably 'camel', this being Karachi) porch over the front door, and the drive exited further down Mary Road through a spectacularly beautiful purple bougainvillea avenue, which, with judicious pruning, remained in flower most of the year.

You entered the house up four steps, through a massive wooden door, into a large hall. Immediately to the right was an air-conditioned study, and on the left, a cloakroom. A wide grand staircase on the left led to the upper floor. The ground floor was all tiled with terrazzo tiles.

Beyond the study on the right was a large dining room, and on the left, a door leading to the pantry and kitchen. At the end of the hall was an air-conditioned drawing room running across the width of the house. All the rooms were large.

The air-conditioned dining room had a teak table with eight chairs upholstered in a sort of salmon, ecru curtains at the doors and a different pink pair of short curtains at a window overlooking the veranda. Double doors opened onto the veranda. There was an old cream, green, yellow and brown patterned carpet on the floor.

The drawing room was carpeted wall to wall with beige carpeting. Double teak doors led to the veranda, and a further pair of teak doors into what had been part of the veranda at the far side of the room, which had been enclosed and made into a bar. To my joy, this contained an upright piano that Jim had found in the bazaar and bought for me.

All the walls in the house were painted magnolia, and the skirting boards were of dark brown teak. The house was full of utility 1920s-style heavy dark teak furniture – brown again! This made the whole of the ground floor very dark, dingy, gloomy and crowded with a mishmash of furniture.

During the past ten years, the bank had sold off two or three houses, and it looked as if all the unwanted furniture had been dumped in Mary Road. I later learnt this was indeed the case.

There was, for instance, a light with a hundred-watt bulb fixed onto the underneath of the staircase, shining on a large table. "What," I asked Mohammed, our bearer, "is that for?"

"Oh, *memsahib*," he replied. "That was where Pickles sat."

A large, deep veranda ran along the front of the house, overlooking the lawn, with double doors leading into the study, dining room and drawing room, and big green wooden shutters that were closed at night. Three steps led down into the garden.

In our first year, I cleared out a lot of the furniture, which I sent to the bank godown. I had all the downstairs magnolia walls and dark brown woodwork painted white and bought some light cane furniture that I painted aquamarine with matching print cushions for the bar room. I also recovered the main suite in the drawing room in an aquamarine print, replaced the carpet with a celadon green one and the heavy brown brocade curtains with white net ones in both the sitting and dining rooms. The whole downstairs was transformed.

On the veranda, I painted the heavy but comfortable cane furniture bottle green and covered the cushions with a red poppy with dark green foliage printed cotton, giving it a more modern look.

The door to the kitchen ran off from the bottom of the staircase into the pantry, past a large lockable walk-in store cupboard tucked away on the far side of the stairs. This was where I kept all our tinned goods, flour, oil, rice, tea, coffee, etc., plus liquor. It is essential to lock all these dry goods up everywhere in the subcontinent, so that you can keep an eye on how much you use. Every housewife does so. Every morning, I opened the cupboard and doled out what we would need for the day. All the servants expect you to do this and would rather you did so, so that they are not accused of pilfering.

The pantry was big, with wall-to-floor cupboards containing an astonishing amount of crockery and crystal. We had a huge amount of china – three dinner services for twelve, two Doulton and one Noritake, a couple of tea services for twelve, also Doulton and two Shelley breakfast sets for two – years later, I saw an identical set featured on the Antiques Roadshow – and sundry white plates, etc., for large parties. I could have a buffet party for seventy-two with all our own crockery and tea for one hundred and fifty! Unfortunately, though the kitchen was spacious and well-planned, it was not large enough to cater for that amount of guests, so when we had large parties, we catered out.

Upstairs were three large air-conditioned bedrooms with a veranda running the length of the house in front of them, overlooking the front lawn.

The main bedroom had two bathrooms, but Jim had one made into a dressing room whilst I was in St Albans. This held two wardrobes (called '*almirahs*' in the subcontinent), plus a chest of drawers. The bedroom had a couple of *almirahs*, two chests of drawers, two single beds pushed together and two bedside tables with lamps. We closed off the veranda just outside our bedroom as a bedroom for Tom, and he used our bathroom. As all the children were at boarding school, their bedrooms were only used during the holidays.

The 'guest suite' at the other end of the house had been recently refurbished with a new bathroom suite. This we designated 'Mhairi's room', whilst the middle bedroom was for Rod – his bathroom was across the landing and in need of a complete refit, especially the plumbing.

All the plumbing in the house was questionable; the flat roof was crisscrossed with a maze of pipes, with no pipe ever being removed when a new one was installed. The result was that no one knew which pipe served which purpose. We removed a vast amount of redundant piping, but to tell the truth, you could not see much difference to the lines of piping crawling all over the roof.

As you entered the compound, there was a line of double-storeyed servants' quarters and a garage on the right-hand side. These were originally the stables.

The garden surrounded the house. As you drove in under the elephant porch, there was a flower-bordered lawn to the right, then the bougainvillea avenue, beyond the left of which was the lawn in front of the house veranda, going down to the compound wall bordered by tall trees. When we arrived in May, the lawns were scruffy and brown, as it was just before the monsoon and Karachi is on the edge of the Sindh desert. As bits of the city are very green, it is sometimes hard to remember this.

Continuing down the side of the house was a cement tennis court, then more garden at the back of the house. Not lawn this time, but a packed earth courtyard with a vegetable bed by the back door, leading into the kitchen.

Next to the kitchen, there was a windowless room containing a generator for use during power cuts. Fortunately, we did not have many of these, as once you switched on the generator, the room filled with highly toxic fumes. We put in a window and some vents so that the gas had somewhere to escape.

Whilst I was in St Albans, Jim had a huge wooden and heavy-duty chicken wire cage built for Benji under a large shady tree by the side of the house, near the servants' quarters. It was about four feet square and six feet high on feet, so that it could be moved – a sizeable room. There was already a huge aviary under the tree, home to a couple of dozen budgies who lived in some luxury, with perches, nesting boxes, swings, a couple of old tree branches, lots of little clay pots with food and water in them – everything a caged budgie could wish for.

Benji's cage was placed next to the budgies' aviary. He had only been in it a day when he managed to snip a hole in the chicken wire at the side of his cage by the aviary, fly out and cut a hole in the wire of the budgies' cage. Benji had a field day! He slaughtered half a dozen budgies. The remainder escaped out of the aviary hole and vanished, never to be seen again – no doubt victim to all the crows and hawks in the garden. Benjie then systematically vandalised the cage – drilling through the perches, smashing the clay pots and generally causing mayhem – before he was discovered and returned to his cage in disgrace. We did not replace the budgies.

To prevent him from escaping again, though he did his best to do so, we rewired his cage with even thicker wire that he was unable to clip through. He then started to chip away at the wooden bottom of the cage. This we then lined with a thin sheet of aluminium, which we regularly replaced, as he would pull it up by pecking at the corner of the sheet with his beak, loosening a bit, then peeling it back – just like a tin opener opening a biscuit tin or a can of sardines.

Benji was later transferred to the budgies' aviary, where he could fly around and try to destroy the large tree branches. The aviary was cleaned daily by Panchoo, the sweeper, who got into it with a twiggy besom called a *jaroo* and hosed it down. Panchoo was justifiably terrified of Benji, who would chase him and the *jaroo* round the aviary, pecking at the twigs. Panchoo normally enlisted the aid of one of the other servants to distract Benji.

Benji could see the entrance to the house from his aviary and made a magnificent watchdog – no one could enter or exit the compound without him letting us all know. He extended his vocal repertoire from 'Hallo, Benji, good boy, Benji' and his imitation of an express train to mimicking the cawing of the crows and all the bird songs in the garden.

We had a staff of eight, which we took over from the McPhersons, plus, of course, a *dhobi* (washerman) who came twice a week and did not really count as a servant, as he was a 'visitor'. There were two bearers, Saeed the cook, and Panchoo the sweeper, Noor the driver, plus a Pathan *durwan* (gatekeeper), whose eldest son was the head gardener and another gardener. Having such a large staff means having a large headache – and the more family and hangers-on they have means an even bigger headache, as there are more problems to solve and deal with. Life was much simpler in Malaysia with just two *amahs*.

When we arrived, the number one bearer left to work elsewhere and Jim hired a new bearer, Mohammed. Mohammed had been unable to find employment as a bearer for about five years and had been employed on a building site when Jim hired him. He was an excellent bearer – a regular jack of all trades. He knew all sorts of people – if you wanted to know where to get something or to find someone to do something, all you had to do was to ask Mohammed. A real Mr Fixit! He was also willing and able to turn his hand to all sorts of jobs that were not strictly within his remit.

Mohammed had a room in the servants' quarters but did not live on the premises. His family was very poor. He had six children, a house in one of the slums in Karachi and travelled home every night. His two eldest boys, aged ten and twelve, worked in a garment factory and contributed to the family expenses. He was very proud of this. His father, Ahmed, was an excellent cook and worked for some British friends of ours in Grindleys Bank. Later, during our tour, Ahmed fell ill whilst his employers were on leave, with a kidney complaint. We counted him as part of Mohammed's family, so we paid for him to have an operation and allowed him to recuperate in one of our empty rooms. Unfortunately, he never recovered and died soon after at home.

When we were in Sandakan, we had had some very strong wooden crates made for our baggage. After we unpacked, Mohammed asked if he could have the empty crates. "No," I said. "They are expensive, and we shall use them again when we leave. Anyway (thinking he wanted to sell them), why do you want them?" He explained that the roof of his hut had blown off during the last monsoon, and it leaked, so he wished to use the wood from the crates to fix the hut. We gave him the crates. Jim also bought him a 'bank' bicycle so that he could go home every day, public transport being quite unreliable.

Panchoo, the sweeper, had worked at the house for years. He was a thin, bent old man, nearing sixty, which is old in Pakistani terms, blind in one eye and almost blind in the other. The bank paid for him to have an operation to restore a bit of sight in his better eye, and he wore a patch over the blind eye giving him a jaunty, slightly rakish, piratical air.

Panchoo lived in a room in the quarters, which he kept spick and span. I threw out Jim's old cotton kimono-style dressing gown one day – it had a distinctive pattern of black spider's webs on a white background printed on it. Panchoo retrieved it, cut it up and turned it into six very smart cushions, which he scattered around his room. Panchoo was a Hindu, a bachelor and very prominent in his community. He often asked his friends round in the evening to sing *ghazals*, play the *tabla* and make music. This was very unusual for a person of his low caste.

Though Pakistan is a Muslim country, shades of the caste system remained from when it was part of India; there was a great divide between various sects and classes of people. Before partition, for instance, the Karachi sewage system was maintained by the Hindus of the sweeper caste (untouchables). Sometime after Partition, it was decided that, as they were Hindus, they should all be repatriated to India. However, as no one else would service and clean the drainage system, it was not long before the drains overflowed onto the roads and they all returned.

Saeed, the cook, was a British India-style cook schooled in the traditions of the Raj. He, too, was about sixty – tall, imposing and an excellent cook. He did not live in but was not as poor as Mohammed, having spent some time working in the Middle East, where he earned a good salary, most of which he sent back to his family in Karachi.

Noor Mohammed, the driver, and his family, composed of wife, father and two toddlers, lived in the quarters. Noor was very smart and an extremely good driver. Having taken Jim to the office in the morning, he was normally at my disposal for the rest of the day. He spoke little English. When we first arrived, he tried speaking to me in English but was unintelligible, so, as I speak Hindi, we communicated in Urdu – at least he did, and I spoke Hindi, which is basically the same language. For a while, I tried unsuccessfully to improve his English, and he tried unsuccessfully to improve my Hindi/Urdu grammar and would shake his head helplessly at some of the things I said.

As everyone understood my Hindi and I had been speaking like that for most of my life, he gave me up as a bad job and we decided to communicate in Hindi. One of my Pakistani friends, when she discovered that I was a Scot and had spent my childhood in Bengal, said to me one day, "*Ah*, Noreen! I have never been able to place your Hindi accent, but now I have it – you are a Bengali Scot!" I think she was being kind, so I took that as a compliment – I was obviously never going to change.

The watchman, or *durwan*, was a Pathan; he and his two sons also lived in the servants' quarters. His eldest son worked as our number one *mali* (gardener) and was a good, quiet, competent worker. As we had no number two bearer at the time, I suggested that Mohammed teach the durwan's nineteen-year-old son how to be a bearer; that way, his family would earn more money, and we would have less hassle finding a suitable new bearer and introducing him into our staff quarters.

The boy learnt quickly, and I thought he was doing well until one Friday, we came home unexpectedly from the yacht club, to discover that he was having a video party for six of his mates in our study. Friday was our Sunday in Karachi and the servants' day off. As we usually spent all day at the yacht club, only the number two bearer was on duty. Of course, he lost his job. However, being Pathans, this was a slight on their honour, so they all left – including my nice gardener.

I then discovered that the other servants had been scared stiff of the Pathans, who thought they had a hold over everyone else as three of them were employed in the house and had been bullying the rest of the servants mercilessly. After that, Jim got a firm to supply the security for the property, and everyone was much happier.

We then employed another number two bearer who was a Hindu called Puran. He was a widower and lived in the quarters with his young daughter of about twelve. I can't remember where we got him, but this was his first bearer job and Mohammed taught him the ropes. He was short, pleasant, quite lazy and not over-bright, but I was sorry for him and the daughter, as they were homeless.

We also employed another *mali*. This one was between fifty and sixty years old and dyed his hair jet black. We knew this as, over the weeks, the dye would gradually fade, then he would suddenly reappear one morning with his hair jet black once again. He was a good *mali*. As we needed a number two gardener to assist him, we recruited Noor's father, who, though sixty-ish, was able to do the work and was helped by Noor when he was not driving. This gave Noor's family a bit of extra money and meant we did not have extra people living in the quarters. The new *mali* did not live in. Jim said that I was running a home for old men.

All the servants, whether they lived in or out, had a lockable room in the quarters, where they could sleep in the afternoons and keep their belongings in safety. There were also ample washing facilities and toilets. We still had some spare rooms.

All our servants had uniforms. The house staff wore white short sleeved-shirts and long trousers, and the two bearers had a white linen *atchkan* (a jacket with a Nehru collar), which they wore when we had guests and were serving at the table. Panchoo and the gardeners wore a khaki short-sleeved shirt and shorts. Noor wore a smart pale blue safari suit with a peaked hat in summer and a navy-blue outfit in winter.

All the servants received three new suits of clothes at Christmas every year. The three house servants also received a monthly tea allowance, consisting of a kilo of tea and a kilo of sugar each and a five-pound tin of milk powder shared between them. Despite this, I was aware that they usually drank my tea and coffee, but as long as they did not go overboard with it, I turned a blind eye.

I also supplied all the servants annually with a pullover just before the cold weather. Karachi gets cold from November to March – especially in the mornings and evenings, and plains people feel the cold. There was not much in the way of knitwear in the shops, and it was expensive and of inferior quality, so after asking around, I discovered there was a large second-hand market in town.

This enormous covered market sold a wide selection of clothing, shoes, curtains, pots and pans and bedding – all donated from various charities around the world, particularly from the United States. Some of the clothes were of excellent quality, better than the new ones in the bazaar and there were quite a few designer labels – Pringle and Gucci sweaters, for instance.

I knew that my presence would ruin their bargaining power, so I gave Mohammed a couple of hundred rupees and sent him and Noor off in the car to purchase suitable jumpers for everyone. They were delighted and returned not only with the sweaters but also a couple of large plastic bags full of goodies, which they had purchased for their families for a song. Everybody was happy – me too, as I had outfitted them all for a bargain.

Thereafter, every November, I sent them off on their own on a second-hand shopping trip. I also went to the market and bought two designer sweaters for my boys, and some hall curtains for Rod, who had just moved into a flat in Bournemouth. He had them for years.

As Manager Pakistan, Jim's job involved a lot of public relations, building relationships with local businessmen, state and federal government ministers and politicians both in Karachi and Islamabad, the capital.

The president was General Zia ul Haq, who had been in power since 1977, after declaring martial law and hanging President Bhutto. General Zia was an Islamist. He remains a polarizing figure in Pakistan's history, credited with preventing wider Soviet incursions into the region from Afghanistan, as well as bringing in economic prosperity, but decried for passing laws encouraging religious intolerance. As a legacy of his Afghanistan policy, there was a large refugee camp in Peshawar.

General Zia had a mentally handicapped daughter and did a lot for mentally handicapped people in Pakistan simply by allowing her the freedom of the presidential palace. It was apparently not unusual for her to appear in the middle of a cabinet meeting. In Pakistan, the general public believes that if you have a handicapped child, it is Allah punishing you for some past misdeed, so they are generally hidden away.

Our London office appeared to have a bit of difficulty regarding the distance between Karachi and Islamabad, often asking Jim to 'pop up to Islamabad to see the minister', until one day he said to them, "You do realise you are asking me to go from London to Rome!"

"Oh!" was the reply, and he was not asked to go to Islamabad for quite a while.

Pakistanis are incredibly hospitable, and we had a hectic social life – business and social events being inextricably mixed. Much business was conducted at dinners, which were usually buffets. The men congregated at one end of the room and discussed business and politics, and the women at the other, discussing topics of female interest.

Occasionally, we sat down to a formal dinner. I recall once being seated between the CEO of the oil company and the minister for oil at one such dinner, during an oil supply crisis. I may as well not have existed, as they discussed the problems of the matter across me. I just kept quiet and listened, as it was extremely interesting.

When I got home, I asked Jim, "Did you know about so-and-so…?"

"Yes, as it happens, I do," he answered, astonished.

"But how do *you* know? This is highly confidential information."

I told him about my dinner companions and regaled him with the rest of the conversation, which he found both very interesting and extremely useful.

We were out to dinner most nights or had guests – so much so that we eventually refused to accept any invitations on a Friday night, so that we had at least one evening at home. 'Out to dinner' meant that you arrived at the venue just after eight o'clock, but dinner would not be served until at least ten. After dinner, everyone would go home. As time wore on, it became more and more fashionable to eat later and later at night, and often we would get no dinner until about eleven, with hostesses seemingly vying with each other to see how late we could eat. On one memorable evening, it was nearly midnight before we ate and one of the guests said to the hostess, "Amina, are we going to eat tonight?"

"You should talk," came the reply. "We only ate at twelve o'clock last time I was at your house!"

Jim and I would normally have scrambled eggs or something when he came home from work, as he had a sandwich for lunch and I knew it would be hours before we were fed. He would then have something in his stomach before consuming any alcohol. I'm afraid, at our house, guests were invited for eight p.m., and dinner was served at about nine p.m. – nine thirty at the latest. I was always conscious, that on weekdays, most of the men were in the office by about eight a.m. or earlier. After dinner, guests were welcome to stay for as long as they liked.

Though Pakistan is a Muslim state, unlike the Middle East, alcohol was sold in shops and you did not have to have a permit to buy it. However, it was not available to the Muslim community, who could be imprisoned if they were found drinking or with it in their possession. Beer and spirits were freely available, but for some reason, wine was not. Only embassies had access to wine, and normally, we did not bother to serve it – nor did our guests expect us to do so. Occasionally, if we were just entertaining friends, we would serve our own homemade variety. This was a hit-or-miss affair.

We made wine from the abundance of local fruit available. Some of it was successful, but some we threw away. Our plum wine was a quite drinkable red, the apricot brandy was excellent, but the best wine we made was from cape gooseberries and parsley. I sowed a packet of parsley seeds, and every seed must have germinated, as we ended up with a huge bed of parsley, which we did not know what to do with. So, we decided to make some wine.

The result was a very drinkable dry white wine with a tinge of green and a slightly herbal flavour. This was surprisingly popular with our guests. The cape gooseberry wine was also a nice dry white. All the homemade wines tasted innocuous but packed quite a kick with an alcohol content of about seven per cent or eight per cent proof.

We soon realised that the only way we could reciprocate everyone's hospitality was to have several large parties a year instead of small dinner parties, and that is what we did. We had about four parties a year for about one hundred people each time and got one of the large five-star hotels to cater for them – usually the Avari Towers. We always had one on New Year's Eve, which was very popular.

This was a hassle-free way of entertaining. We would erect a *shamiana* on the lawn in the front of the house. A *shamiana* is a large multi-coloured marquee with lovely colourful designs appliqued onto it. These are used for entertaining all over the subcontinent. In the cold Karachi winter, the *shamiana* would have charcoal braziers burning inside to keep the tent nice and warm and the mosquitoes at bay. The erectors would arrive at about five, and the tent would be erected within an hour or so. The caterers would arrive at about six, bringing the food, crockery and cutlery and set up the bar and food tables, and the guests would arrive at about eight.

The food was served buffet style, and the menu consisted of about four or five curries, *dhal*, three different *rotis*, two styles of rice, various side dishes like *paneer* and cucumber *raita*, followed by a selection of four or five desserts – fruit salad, ice cream, *oom ali* (a rich rice pudding with pistachios, raisins and other nuts in it – delicious), caramel custard (crème brulee), trifle and some sort of gateau.

There was not normally a cheese board, as there was no variety of local cheeses and only the embassies were able to source imported varieties of these. We usually set up small tables and chairs so you could eat comfortably sitting at a table instead of trying to balance a plate of curry on your knee. The next day, the workers returned at about nine in the morning and everything was cleared away by lunchtime.

The largest party we had was to introduce the Canadian ambassador to Karachi. Byram Avari, who was the agent for Air Canada, was asked by the ambassador if he could help by finding a venue other than a hotel to hold his introductory party. Byram asked Jim if the function could be held at Mary Road, and Jim was happy to oblige. There was a guest list of four hundred. We erected two large *shamianas*, the food was supplied by Avari Towers and the ambassador supplied the drinks. The party was a roaring success and the Canadian ambassador's store of alcohol was severely depleted.

Jim was on the board of a number of charities in Karachi, including the War Graves Commission, the Ex-Servicemen's Association (British Legion) of which he was the chairman, and the vice chairman of the United Kingdom Citizens' Association (Pakistan). He was also the treasurer of the yacht club. I was on the British Women's Association (BWA) committee and chairman of that for a year.

I found Karachi stultifying – probably because there was no Western music there, and I found no outlet for my singing. I still practised every day, but there is not much incentive if you have no performances to work towards. In fact, I thought Pakistan was a very sad place, whose many problems hung heavily over the country, and I missed the diversity of culture that there was in Bombay.

During our three years in Karachi, we went to two Western shows imported by the British Council. One was a one-man show called 'Nine Days to Norwich', which was all about Shakespeare's clown, who danced from London to Norwich in nine days. As the clown's name was Will Kemp, this was of special interest to us. He referred to Shakespeare as 'Shakerags', and the show was most amusing, educational and entertaining.

The other show was a concert by the Dorset Folk Duo, The Yetis – an odd choice, I have always thought. We were invited to the after-show party, and I had a wonderful evening sitting on the staircase in the British councillor's house, singing and talking music with them. As I have a large repertoire of folk songs, which I acquired during our sojourn in the Seychelles, we made a good trio and sang together for a good hour or so – to the astonishment of my local friends, who had no idea that I could sing. The Yetis were a delightful couple, wonderful musicians and acted as a balm to my music-starved soul.

I also taught Scottish country dancing once a week on our tennis court. We had about three keen dance sets, and I was soon able to deputise Jenny Habib, who was the bank architect, to take over from me on the countless evenings when I had to attend a dinner and was unable to teach.

Most Fridays, we went sailing at the yacht club, which is situated just outside Karachi harbour. To get to the yacht club, you parked at the quay, then took a small launch out to the club. The clubhouse was just a concreted, open-sided room floating in the sea. It had changing rooms, a bar with a variety of soft drinks and a cook on Fridays when you could get fish and chips and a small selection of snacks – baked beans on toast, egg and chips, cheese toast, samosas, spaghetti, omelettes, chocolate, crisps and nuts, etc.

There was a fridge and freezer, and the club had its own generator, but we did not keep much fresh food there, as if the generator packed up – which it often did – you would lose all the food. The cook marketed on Friday early morning and then brought everything with him to the club to cook for lunch.

Jim was a keen dinghy sailor, which is what the club sailed, and though we did not own a boat, he enjoyed crewing. He found sailing very relaxing. I am a terrible sailor, a poor swimmer and afraid of drowning should I fall in the water. I would sit in the clubhouse with the other non-sailors. This could get very boring, so I took along my Scrabble set and played Scrabble with my friend Amy Halai and the other non-sailors. We soon had four or six players.

There is a large Parsi community in Karachi, amongst whom we had many friends, several of whom were yacht club members, including the Avari family. Byram and Goshpi were excellent sailors and were members of the Pakistani team competing in the ASEAN Games in Colombo, where they won their dinghy race sailing an 'Enterprise'. Byram's family owned the Beach Luxury Hotel and the newest Karachi hotel, the Avari Towers. They had two boys, Dinshaw and Xerxes, who were slightly older than Tom, and a young daughter, Zeena. We had many happy times at the club.

There is not much for visitors to do in Karachi, so we always took our visitors crabbing in the harbour. This involved an early evening sail round the harbour on a large dhow. The captain and crew provided fishing lines, which you threw overboard and fished for crabs, which were usually plentiful. Once you had caught enough, he and the crew cleaned and cooked them for you, making a very tasty mild crab, cabbage and onion curry.

It was a lovely trip sailing round the harbour in the dhow at sunset when the light was dim, and the muddy water did not seem quite so dirty and unappealing. As Karachi harbour is little more than an open sewer, it is amazing that no one ever seemed to get ill after crabbing – apart from Jim, who did not like crabbing, only went once that I can recall, refused to eat the crabs and was violently sick that night, having eaten nothing but tomato sandwiches, which we had brought with us from Mary Road. The rest of us were unscathed.

We had been in Karachi about a year when the yacht club cook left, and the committee was searching for a replacement. I asked Saeed if he knew of a good cook, and he replied that he did and we arranged for his friend, Ahmed, to come to Mary Road for an interview with Jim. Ahmed was desperate for work, as he had a large family to feed. He had good references and Jim gave him the job on a trial basis. Ahmed was told to be at the market entrance at seven a.m. on Friday morning, and Noor would bring him to Mary Road and we would go to the jetty together. Saeed would do the shopping for the week, but Ahmed would do the cooking once we got to the yacht club and we would see how he got on.

On Friday morning, Noor went to the market as arranged, but there was no sign of Ahmed. Jim was annoyed and thought Ahmed had had second thoughts about accepting the job. Saeed came to the club with us and made lunch and we set about finding another cook.

On Saturday morning, I had a visit from Ahmed's wife, Ayesha, who had a harrowing tale to tell. Ahmed had been waiting for Noor at the market when a small bus came careering round the corner, ploughing into the knot of people gathered in front of the market and knocking over Ahmed and a coolie standing beside him. The bus swerved wildly and screeched off into the distance.

The crowd ran after it, shouting, but it disappeared down the road, swaying drunkenly from side to side – the driver probably high on qat. Ahmed lay on the ground with his arm badly broken, and the coolie lying beside him was dead. Of course, it all happened so quickly that no one had taken down the number of the bus, so there was no chance that the driver would ever be found. The police arrived, and Ahmed was taken to hospital, where he still was, having his arm set.

I was horrified at this story and said I would tell Jim. Though I did not think we could keep the job open for Ahmed, if he came to see me when he had recovered, I would see what I could do for him. I sent Ayesha away with some money and a large bag of lamb curry that we had in the freezer.

After three weeks, Ahmed returned to the hospital, where the doctor found that his arm had been set incorrectly and had to rebreak the arm, reset it and replaster it. Ahmed returned to see Saeed occasionally to report on his progress, and I would send him off with a bit more money.

A few weeks later, I said to Saeed, "What has happened to Ahmed, Saeed? He has not visited us for a long time."

"No, *memsahib*," said Saeed. "He has died. His arm did not improve, and he got a fever. Ayesha and he returned to the hospital, and when the doctors removed the plaster, they found the arm had gone bad (gangrenous) underneath, so they cut it off. He did not wish to live any more and be a burden to his family, so he turned his face to the wall, would not eat or drink and so he died."

I was appalled. "That's terrible, Saeed. What has become of Ayesha and the children?"

Saeed shook his head sadly. "I do not know, *memsahib*," he said. "They had to move out of his hut, as the *bunias* (moneylenders) came to take it when the family could no longer pay their debts. No one knows what has happened to them. *Inshallah*, Ayesha will be able to sell one of the children to a carpet factory – two of the girls are old enough now. Then she will have a bit more money to feed the family for a while."

I was aghast. "Surely that is illegal?" I said.

"*Ha, memsahib*," said Saeed. "But how else will they survive? The children will be glad to work so that they can eat." He shrugged his shoulders. "It is fate," he said. "Allah wills it!"

As General Manager Pakistan, Jim was in charge of four branches – two in Karachi, one in Lahore and one in Faisalabad. Every two or three months, he would visit Lahore and Faisalabad on inspection and I would usually go with him. We would spend a night in Faisalabad and a couple of nights in Lahore.

Faisalabad is an industrial city in Punjab about one hundred and eighty-two kilometres from Lahore. It is the third most populous city in Pakistan after Karachi and Lahore and the biggest textile producer in Pakistan. It is called the 'Manchester of Pakistan', and is twinned with Manchester in Britain. It takes two and a half to three hours to drive from Lahore to Faisalabad, or you can take the train, which takes two and a half hours. It is a hot and dusty drive, and the city is a grim, Victorian-style industrial city with its 'dark satanic mills' and very polluted atmosphere.

The first time I accompanied Jim on an inspection was not long after I arrived in Karachi. It was in the middle of Ramadan. I can't think why we went at that time of year, as Faisalabad is a very orthodox city, and really, no one wanted to know us as they were all fasting, but there must have been a reason. We stayed at the club, which was a very depressing, dark and dismal place, furnished with antiquated brown leather furniture and heavy brown brocade drapes.

In order to keep me amused whilst Jim was on his inspection, one of his officers took me to visit the nearby town of Chiniot. Chiniot is situated on the banks of the Chenab River – one of the great five rivers of Punjab – and is noted for its intricately carved wooden furniture, architecture and mosques.

Chiniot's metalworkers, along with those of Lahore, were considered to be the best in Punjab during the British Raj, and its artisans were employed in the construction of the Taj Mahal and the Golden Temple in Amritsar. I thought the city very quaint, with narrow streets passing between houses with intricately carved balconies and possessing a charm that was utterly lacking in Faisalabad.

Most of the furniture for sale was heavily carved or inlaid with brass and was a bit too ornate for my taste. However, I did buy a lovely French-polished coffee table in plain teak with a narrow inlaid brass border, plus two nests of tables and two small chests of drawers to match, which I still have.

The next time I visited Faisalabad was about halfway through our tour. This time, we were staying with a Swiss couple who worked for Brown & Polson. The firm manufactured products such as Knorr soups, custard powder, jam, etc., using the crops produced by the local farmers. Jim had met them on a previous visit and was invited to stay with them whenever he was in Faisalabad. A very welcome invitation, as it was so much nicer than the club.

In return, they stayed with us when they visited Karachi, which they occasionally did. She, unfortunately, had multiple sclerosis. It was a lonely posting for them, and visitors were always very welcome. They had a lovely house with a swimming pool – probably the only one in Faisalabad. They had a lot of contact with some Catholic nuns, who visited them regularly so that they could have a swim in the pool – a real treat for them. This is the only time I have ever heard of 'swimming nuns' – I automatically thought that would be the sort of activity that would have been forbidden.

We set out from Lahore in an Avis rental car with a driver. It was hot and sticky. About halfway to Faisalabad, we were driving through a very congested and populous small town when a little girl of about eight suddenly ran into the street, right in the front of the car. She was tossed up in the air onto the bonnet of the car, and her head smacked the windscreen with a sickening crack. She bounced off the car and was flung onto the side of the road. The car was going slowly, but there was no way the driver could have stopped.

Jim and I were both sitting in the back of the car – he was asleep and I was half-asleep when I saw her hit the car, then be tossed onto the side of the road on the left of the car. Jim was rudely jolted awake and realised immediately what had happened. A crowd had started to gather. "Stay in the car!" he shouted at me – but I was already kneeling in the road beside the unconscious little girl, surrounded by the crowd, putting her in 'recovery position' and trying to prevent anyone from moving her. There was no blood. The little girl was unmarked and looked as if she was in a deep sleep.

The poor driver was sitting behind the wheel in a state of shock, watching the growing crowd with mounting alarm. Drivers in accidents like this in the subcontinent are usually dragged from their vehicle, severely beaten up and often killed – as are sometimes any other occupants in the car.

Just then, a voice from across the road shouted, "It wasn't his fault, it wasn't his fault – I saw it all, I saw it all!" A thin, light blue safari-suited Pakistani man, being driven in a brown Mercedes, stopped his car and ran across the road to help. In the meantime, the little girl's father and a friend had arrived – no mother – I was the only woman. The men spoke together, and our rescuer translated, our Urdu was not up to understanding all that was said.

"This is an accident blackspot," he said, "and this man is the local headman. These other two are the girl's father and his brother. They shall pick up the girl and drive with you to the local clinic. There is a telephone there that we can use. I shall follow you with the headman so I can translate." We thanked him for his kindness.

The two men carrying the little girl started to get into the front of the car. I tried to persuade them to get into the back seat with her – her head was lolling alarmingly over the side of her father's arm – and to get them to support her head. She could have been laid out on the seat with the two men beside her, while Jim and I could have sat in the front with the driver. They would not have it. We all got into the car. I was worried about the driver, as I did not really think he should be driving after such a bad accident and was clearly in a state of shock. However, no one else seemed to be bothered about him, and I think he was just glad to be able to get away from the ever-growing crowd.

The father said to the driver that he knew a shortcut to the clinic that we should take to get there faster. We set off down a side road full of potholes and bounced slowly to the clinic, which took about fifteen minutes. I was so worried about the little girl, who was still being held by her father, with her unsupported head resting on the door as we bumped along the road to the clinic.

At last, we arrived to discover that the 'clinic' was just a large, roofed, concrete building without walls and empty except for a sweeper/caretaker. There was no other staff whatsoever to deal with emergencies. There were no beds or chairs and no equipment of any kind, barring an empty, rusty oxygen cylinder on wheels standing in a dusty corner, a table with a telephone on it and a gurney with a thin, green plastic-covered mattress, on which the unconscious little girl was laid.

Fortunately, the telephone was working, and Jim rang our Lahore Manager, Rana Ikram, who arranged for an ambulance to come and collect the girl and her escort and take them to Lahore hospital, where he would have 'the top brain surgeon in Pakistan' waiting for her arrival. He also arranged for Avis to send us another car with a driver and their manager, so that he could deal with our driver and all the formalities. Lahore was a good hour away from us at that point, and all this took a considerable length of time to arrange.

Our Pakistani friend had, in the meantime, been having a long conversation with the village headman. He informed us that the accident had happened at a notorious accident blackspot and that the headman would consult with the Avis manager when he arrived and arrange for the payment of 'blood money' to the father. Apparently, there was a scale of charges for accidents, ranging from the loss of a limb to death, with so much paid for a man, then a boy, then a woman and lastly for a girl – the lowest of the low. There was about one accident a week, most of them fatal, as the vehicle – usually a lorry – would be driving along much faster than our car. This was no doubt why the crowd had not assaulted our driver but had just gathered round to see the *tamasha*.

After about an hour, the Avis manager arrived with another driver and joined in the compensation consultation. Fifteen minutes later, the ambulance arrived – a rickety old vehicle that had seen much better days. Everything was explained to the father and his brother, including the fact that they would be driven in the ambulance straight to the hospital, where the surgeon would be waiting. The little girl was loaded into the ambulance – still unconscious, joined by her family and the ambulance men – and off they rattled down the road to Lahore.

The Avis manager now took control of the situation – we were ushered to the new rent-a-car with a driver. Our driver was now going to drive his boss, who had now successfully concluded negotiations with the village headman, back to Lahore. Avis would pick up the bills. The driver was still looking dazed. Our Pakistani friend bade us farewell, and taking our heartfelt thanks with him, went on his way.

The Avis manager had spoken to Rana and would give him a progress report on returning to Lahore. Rana had spoken to our Swiss friends in Faisalabad, explaining what had happened and would speak to us when we reached Faisalabad. We drove on to Faisalabad, where we spent the night with our friends, Jim inspected the branch and the following day we returned to Lahore. I was very distressed by the whole affair.

True to his word, Rana got the little girl into hospital, where she received the best available scans and where they were waiting for her to regain consciousness before any further treatment could be given. I went down to the hospital with one of Jim's officers but was unable to see her. However, I did see her father, uncle and her mother sitting patiently on the grass outside the hospital, along with many other patients' relatives, waiting to see when they could visit their loved ones. There was really nothing more that we could do.

For me, the rest of the visit passed in a bit of a blur, and we returned to Karachi, leaving Rana to keep an eye on things. He did, and the little girl died about four days later, never having regained consciousness. We never knew what she actually died of – probably a massive bleed on the brain. This depressed me for weeks, as I could not stop thinking of that so-called clinic, and it brought home to me how all these poor people did not have access to even the most basic medical care and facilities. I never returned to Faisalabad.

In contrast, our visits to Lahore were always very pleasant. The ancient and historic city of Lahore sits on the river Ravi, a tributary of the Indus. It is Pakistan's second-largest city after Karachi and capital of Punjab. There is much to see here. The city consists of an old city area, flanked on the southeast by the newer commercial, industrial and residential areas. The most notable sights include the Wazir Khan Mosque, built in 1634, and the Lahore Fort, both steeped in history; the Badshahi (Imperial) Mosque, built by Aurangzeb, which is one of the largest mosques in the world; the Shahdara gardens containing the tomb of Jahangir; and the magnificent Shalimar Gardens – eighty acres of terraced walled gardens with about four hundred and fifty fountains, laid out east of the city by Shah Jehan as a refuge for his family; and the fourteen-foot Zamzamma or 'Kim's gun', which famously features in Kipling's novel '*Kim*'. The fort and Shalimar gardens were collectively designated a UNESCO World Heritage site in 1981.

The Anarkali Bazaar is also worth a visit. It is one of the oldest surviving markets in the subcontinent dating back at least two hundred years. It gets its name from the nearby mausoleum, thought to be named after a courtesan named Anarkali, who was chased out of town by Akbar for having a love affair with his son, Prince Salim, who later became the Emperor Jahangir. The market is divided into two sections: the Old Anarkali Bazaar and the New Anarkali Bazaar. The old bazaar it noted for its traditional food and the new bazaar for its traditional handicrafts and embroidery.

Jim's family had a special connection with Lahore, as his great-uncle-in-law was John Stephenson, a noted surgeon and zoologist who worked for the Indian Medical Service. Stephenson was a fine Oriental scholar who spoke fluent Persian and Urdu and became Professor of Biology at Government College Lahore in 1906. He spent thirteen years in Lahore. In 1912, he was appointed Principal of the College, a position not previously held by a member of the Indian Medical Service. In 1918, he became Vice Chancellor of Punjab University, where he stayed until 1929 when he retired. There is a large portrait of him hanging in the university, and he is still remembered. Jim even met an old lecturer who professed to know Stephenson slightly when he was a young man.

Part of Jim's job was recommending loans to various customers. In Pakistan, many businesses employ children for various jobs, and he told me about two factories he inspected that did so. It was May when he was in Lahore, in the middle of the hot weather, just before the monsoon broke and extremely hot.

The first factory made soap, and Jim said that he was taken inside the building, where great vats of boiling liquid were bubbling away, being stirred by men, with children running errands and toting things from here to there. Steam was rising from the vats, and it was like something out of *Dante's Inferno*. There were no safety precautions being followed as far as he could see. They did not get their loan.

The next factory made screws and bolts and also employed children who were engaged in sorting out the various sizes of screws into heaps. By contrast, they were housed under a large roofed room – no walls and plenty of light – where they sat on the floor sorting the screws and laughing and talking as they worked. They did a morning shift, got a midday meal and had school in the afternoons paid for by the factory owner and were obviously well cared for.

Children were frequently employed in garment and carpet factories – in fact, in Karachi, the nuns ran a carpet factory employing children. Again, they were well cared for, got a meal, schooling and working conditions were strictly monitored. The nuns welcomed visitors, and I remember taking some visitors unannounced with me one day to find the factory deserted and no children.

"What's happened – where are the children?" I asked the Sister.

"Oh, they were very naughty today," she replied. "So I sent them all home!"

A harsh punishment, I thought, as they would not have been paid and their families relied on their wages. I don't know what they had done, but it must have been quite grave.

Our Lahore manager, Rana Ikram, was a most gregarious and hospitable host. Lahore was his hometown, and he was a very proud Lahori who revelled in taking guests round the town to see the sights. He was a very interesting and knowledgeable guide. Rana lived in the Lahore bank house with his wife and four daughters, all of whom he was trying to marry off (very expensive) and all of whom were first-class cooks. Their specialities were various types of sweetmeats – *burfi, jelabies, gulab jamoons, rosagoolahs, ladhoos,* all made from milk supplied by their buffalo who lived in the garage and also supplied plentiful manure for the garden.

Rana was very well known and popular in the Lahori community. They were a charming and very pleasant family.

"When you retire, Rana," I said to him. "You must become a tourist guide; you are so good!"

"I will, I will!" he beamed back at me. Rana did not seem to take much part in Jim's inspections, as he always appeared available to shepherd me around the city on my visits.

I well remember the time when Rana, Tom (who was about thirteen at the time) and I went to visit the Zamzamma – Kim's gun. The three of us were walking along, absorbed in Rana's story, when suddenly – *whoosh* – Tom just disappeared. One minute he was there, and the next – gone. Rana and I stopped abruptly. "Where's he gone?" I said. We turned round to discover that he had fallen into an open manhole just behind us. He was sitting wedged in the manhole with one leg stuck straight up in the air – supporting himself on his arms. Fortunately, he was unhurt. He looked so comical sitting stuck in the drain that I started to laugh, but it really wasn't funny. He could have been badly hurt and broken a leg or something worse.

As is normal in the subcontinent, a crowd was already gathering to see what was going on. With the assistance of some helpful bystanders, Rana and I eventually managed to prise Tom out of the hole – not without difficulty, as he was a big lad – and he emerged suffering nothing worse than a few bruises. Rana was extremely annoyed, railing against the stupidity of the municipality for having left the cover off the manhole with no sign, with the crowd all agreeing sympathetically with him.

It was very lucky that it was just before the monsoon, so the drain was bone dry; otherwise, Tom might have been stuck in a drain full of dirty water, with a year's worth of unspeakable filth and sewage floating about in it.

No trip to Lahore would be complete without a visit to Wagah, a town on the Grand Trunk Road on the Indo-Pakistan border, to see the Wagah-Attari 'Beating the Retreat' ceremony. This occurs every evening and has done so since 1959, when the Indian and Pakistani flags are lowered and the border gates are closed for the night. This is the only road crossing on the whole lengthy border between the two countries. The border post is manned by the Indian Border Force on the Indian side and the Frontier Scouts on the Pakistani side.

Since 1959, this ceremony has been staged as a symbol of co-operation and brotherhood between the two countries. The performance is witnessed by an audience on both sides of the border, all cheering for their own side and the two regiments, each in their dress uniforms, vie with each other as to who gives the best performance. The Indians are dressed in *khaki* army uniform and the Pakistanis in a blue/grey *shalwar kameez*. Both have elaborate turban headdresses, sporting a large cockade, which, as they march with an exaggerated goose-step, must be incredibly difficult to keep on the head – indeed, you can see it is, as several times during the ceremony, the soldiers having to save it from falling and push it back into place.

There is much posturing and such high kicks that occasionally the soldier staggers trying to keep his balance. A great spirit of rivalry pervades the atmosphere, and the ceremony lasts for about half an hour before the flags are both simultaneously taken down, folded and put away for the night. Rana loved this ceremony, and we visited it every time we went to Lahore and all thoroughly enjoyed the performance – none more so than Rana, who always asked, "Now who do you think was the best?"

As well as our trips to Lahore and Faisalabad, we went to the Swat Valley, which at that point was still reigned over by the *Wali* – The *Wali* of Swat. It sounded like something out of one of Edward Lear's poems, and quite romantic. However, it was anything but. Noor drove from Karachi to Islamabad, where he picked Jim, Tom and me up at the airport. We spent the night in Islamabad, and then drove to Swat, which was a long journey.

The Swat Valley itself, which I thought was supposed to be full of beautiful orchards with peach, almond and apricot trees, was bleak and desolate, with hardly a tree to be seen, between bleak and desolate hills. There were not many people – just the odd Pashtun tribesman. Women were conspicuous by their absence. I don't think we saw a single one. We eventually arrived at the so-called four-star Swat Hotel for the night. All I recall about the hotel is the mushrooms growing out of the bedroom wall.

When we asked for a room for Noor for the night, we were told he could sleep in the car. As he had driven for about eight hours, there was no way Jim was going to allow him to do this. We eventually managed to get him a room, but the place was so depressing, we decided to return to Karachi instead of spending a few days there. We did, via the Silk Road, passing the beginning of the Khyber Pass, an extremely forbidding, barren and menacing-looking place. We stopped at the village at the entrance to the pass and looked up at the large black stone pillboxes guarding the entrance. It was easy to imagine the pass full of bloodthirsty Afghan tribesmen streaming down upon the invading forces.

In 1983, a new resort called Shangrila opened in Skardu, a Pakistani province way up in the north, surrounded by the *Karakoram*, *Himalaya* and *Hindu Kush* mountain ranges. For some obscure reason, I took a notion to visit Shangrila, which was supposed to be the place described in James Hilton's novel '*Lost Horizon*'. It sounded extremely beautiful, and in the 1980s, was also almost inaccessible.

There was a small propeller aircraft that flew from Islamabad up to Shangrila, but should the cloud ceiling descend, the flight had to be abandoned, as planes could then neither take off nor land in the valley. We tried unsuccessfully to get there three times. The first time we never left Islamabad, the second time we nearly boarded the plane and the third time we actually flew out of the airport for about half an hour before the cloud descended and we had to return.

As we were sitting in the airport waiting for the Karachi flight, we saw the British manager of Grindlays Bank in Karachi coming off the incoming flight looking very pale. We hailed him and asked what was wrong.

He informed us he had just deplaned via the emergency chute, as the pilot had forgotten to put down the landing gear and the whole of the runway was now churned up. Apparently, the pilot had had an exhausting weekend in Karachi, so the assistant pilot took over the flight. So that the pilot could have an uninterrupted sleep, the assistant pilot had switched off the red light and buzzer warning system, which reminded the pilot to put down the landing gear. He then forgot to switch it on again, with the result that the newly wakened pilot thought the wheels were already down. The plane therefore landed on its belly, and ploughed up the whole of the runway.

No one was hurt, but the passengers had to deplane via the emergency chute. As it was the only runway in Islamabad that could take a jumbo of this size, this put the airport out of commission for international flights for about a month. To add insult to injury, the lifting equipment required to clear the plane off the runway had to come from India. The authorities were not pleased. We did, however, manage to get our flight to Karachi.

Visitors were always welcome in Karachi. As well as the usual 'visiting firemen' from London, we welcomed quite a few friends, including a visit from a school friend of Roderick's – Louisa – who was on a gap year going round the subcontinent. She was travelling with another girl, and somewhere on their travels, they had joined forces with a boy who was supposed to be acting as their 'protector' on the Pakistani leg of their journey. They having been told that in Pakistan, girls could not travel on their own. This was true.

I am sorry to say I cannot remember any of their names, but we shall call them Louisa, Mary and Ian. Louisa and Mary were more than capable of looking after themselves, but I am afraid that Ian, who was a very thin, tall, weedy-looking chap, though nice enough, did not strike me as being able to look after anyone. Anyway, they arrived at the house and we were happy to look after them whilst they were in Karachi.

They stayed with us for about three days, and were, I think, very grateful to be fed and housed safely and have their washing done. I sent them off sightseeing with Noor in the Mercedes, as it is definitely not safe for young girls to take public transport in Karachi. No respectable young Pakistani girl would be allowed to do so.

To my horror, the girls announced that they intended to travel third class by overnight train to Lahore and then make their way by bus to Swat.

"No way!" I said. "It is not safe!" I eventually persuaded them to buy second instead of third class tickets and sent Noor with them to the station to purchase the tickets. I could not dissuade them from going on to Swat.

On the day they were travelling, Mary fell ill with a bad case of Karachi tummy. I stood over her, making her drink a dose of 'fleaseeds' – '*isaphagol*' – an extremely effective if obnoxious local remedy, with no taste, but a horrible, gooey and lumpy texture. These seeds form a glutinous mass when mixed with water. You must drink the mixture immediately, and it forms a lining in your stomach, greatly lessening your tummy cramps and diarrhoea.

I did not think she would enjoy an overnight train journey with diarrhoea, having to continually use a probably filthy squatting loo. I later discovered that Pakistan Railways had amalgamated second and third class, so my precautions were all in vain and they had, in fact, travelled third class to Lahore, which must have been a nightmare journey.

Jim phoned Rana and asked if they could stay with him and his family and if he would show them round Lahore. This, as usual, he willingly agreed to do, so at least I did not have to worry about them whilst they were in Lahore! Before they left, I kept saying to them, "Now don't forget, never allow one of you to be on their own. Always stay together!" They promised me they would do so.

Rana duly met them at the station and was appalled to discover that they had travelled second class. He was even more appalled to learn they meant to go to Swat. "Why did you allow them to travel second class, Noreen?" he said to me.

"Unfortunately, there was no way I could stop them!" I replied.

"I would never allow any of my daughters to do that! And that boy. He is a useless escort." he said.

The girls returned to stay with me before continuing on their journey to Goa and said how much they had enjoyed the Lahore leg of their journey, but that Louisa had nearly been raped in Swat. I gather Ian had disappeared sometime before they got to Swat.

"Whatever happened?" I asked. "In Swat, you were in the five-star hotel!" Apparently, Louisa had an upset tummy and retired to bed. Mary went down to dinner and met a delightful Pakistani family, who, on learning Louisa was ill, invited her to go with them on a picnic and drive the next day. This she did, leaving Louisa still ill in bed.

Whilst Mary was out, the manager of the hotel forced his way into Louisa's room and accosted her. Whilst warding him off, Louisa had the presence of mind to tell him that if he touched her, she would scream for help, that his reputation would be in shreds and furthermore, she would report him to the *mullahs*. He was dissuaded by the threat of the *mullahs*, backed off and begged her to say nothing of the affair.

"But I *told* you never to leave each other alone! You promised me!" I said.

"We know," they replied sheepishly. "But we thought we would be safe in the hotel."

"No respectable girl goes round unaccompanied in Pakistan, so if you do, the locals think you are a person of ill repute and fair game. You were very lucky to have such a narrow escape," I lectured.

"Yes, we know that now," they said.

"Even in India, you must be careful travelling round on your own. It is *not* a good idea," I stressed. "You *must* realise that when you are in foreign countries, you must abide by the local customs. This is *not* Europe!"

We sent them off on the plane to Goa, with my strictures still ringing in their ears. I guess they were glad to see the back of me.

About six months before the end of our tour, we had a visit from Tom's Beechwood Park Prep. School housemaster, Murdo White. Tom, by this time, had left Beechwood and gone on to public school at Rannoch in Perthshire. Murdo also went to Lahore and was shepherded around by Rana and told me he was extremely glad he had come on this holiday, as he had no idea of what kind of life his 'foreign' boys led. I think he was very surprised.

At the end of Murdo's visit, we had one of our large bank parties for about one hundred guests. Mohammed did not show up for work that day, which was very unlike him. The *shamiana* men arrived, and as I really needed Mohammed, who knew we were having a party, I sent Noor to his house to see what was wrong. I wish I hadn't. By this time, Jim had come home.

Noor returned without Mohammed, looking very shocked. "Oh, *memsahib*," he said to me. "Something terrible has happened. Mohammed got very drunk and high on drugs. He has beaten up and nearly killed his wife, and he is also injured. It is very bad. He has beaten his head against a wall, and his face is badly injured."

"Right!" said Jim. "Obviously, he is now going to lose his job as well. We cannot keep him if he behaves in such a fashion."

"Could we not give him another chance?" I pleaded. "He has six children to feed."

"No," said Jim. "I am responsible for everyone in the servants' quarters. What would happen if he behaved like that here? And if the police arrived and raided the quarters, what would happen if they found drugs? I cannot risk allowing him to continue to work here." He turned to Noor. "Go back and tell him not to return to Mary Road, but collect the bank bicycle, and tell him to come to the office to collect his wages. He is a very foolish man!"

Clearly, Jim was right, but I was very upset, as not only did I like Mohammed, I kept thinking of his wife and children. He was a most efficient bearer. I missed him terribly. With hindsight, I should have guessed he was on something, as he would appear in the morning looking very hungover, then disappear into the quarters for a 'coffee' and reappear all bright-eyed and bushy-tailed raring to go about twenty minutes later. I should have known he was having a bit of a pick-me-up.

Jim found another bearer, called Ahmed, who was about five feet tall. "Where did you find him?" said Rod, who was out on holiday. "He looks as if he comes straight from Hamleys and should be on wheels!" This was true, as he buzzed about importantly as if propelled by clockwork – so he became known as 'Hamleys' between us. He was not as efficient as Mohammed, but we only had another six months to go before we retired, so Hamleys was with us until we left.

We had been in Karachi for a year and had just returned from home leave when I noticed that Saeed was perspiring profusely all the time. It was the start of the cool weather, and not hot, so warning bells started to ring, and I sent him to the Dr to have a check-up, as I suspected he might have TB.

Sure enough, his test came back positive, and as TB is extremely infectious, he had to go on immediate sick leave. We sent him off on full pay, promising to pay for his very expensive medicines and said he could return to his job as soon as he got the doctor's all clear. I then had to try and find a replacement for him.

We had a procession of cooks, most of them purporting to be 'ship's cooks', some of whom could not cook at all. I came to the conclusion that all ship's crews must suffer terribly from upset stomachs, as everything they ate was swimming in grease. Eventually, we found an adequate replacement, though he was not nearly as good as Saeed. We had him for about a year when, thankfully, Saeed made a full recovery and returned to work.

Every year, the Ex-Servicemen's Association held a Remembrance Day Service, which was most efficiently organised by Jimmy Katrak, a Parsi businessman, who was the long-term secretary of the association, and Jim in his capacity as chairman. This was a very moving wreath-laying ceremony held at the British cemetery, attended by the UK Deputy High Commissioner, local and expatriate businessmen and various other dignitaries.

Among the expatriates was the German General Manager of Deutsch Gramophone, whose last name I cannot remember – Dieter…? When |Jim and he first met, without preamble, he asked Jim when he was born. When told 4th July 1931, he said, "So was I. Fate has brought us together!"

During the last days of the war, Dieter, a boy of thirteen, was conscripted into the German Army, given a rifle, sent to the front where the German Army was retreating before the Russians. Afraid and not fancying the thought of being a Russian prisoner of war, he hid for a time in a tree, discarded his rifle and made his way to the American front where he gave himself up.

He asked Jim whether the Association would allow him to participate in the Remembrance Day Service and whether they would also remember the German soldiers who had died in combat. Jim discussed this suggestion with his committee, who readily agreed that they would be happy to allow this. Dieter made a handsome donation to the Association. There were many very needy ex-servicemen in Karachi who greatly benefitted from this. Not long after, Dieter was unfortunately diagnosed with liver cancer and, sadly, died in Karachi. Jim and I attended his funeral.

The British Women's Association had two main functions in Karachi: one was to act as a meeting point for British women there, particularly those who were not there under the umbrella of a British company, and therefore found it quite lonely and difficult to know where to find things, knowledge about schools for their children, how to hire suitable servants, and often, to find suitable housing; and secondly, to collect money for various charities. We met once a week for coffee in St Mary's Church Hall to carry out the former and held various functions throughout the year to collect funds for the latter.

Quite often, we were able to complete various charitable projects without spending any money, through using members' contacts. For instance, there was a Catholic nun in Karachi, called Sister Gertrude, who ran a home for mentally handicapped children and young people. Sister Gertie told us how she started her home. She was a teacher, and one day went out for tea with the family of one of her pupils. Whilst the mother was making tea, Sister Gertie asked one of the children how many brothers and sisters she had. "Two sisters, one brother and one we don't talk about," the child replied. Sister Gertie was intrigued.

Later, she asked the mother what the child had meant. The mother burst into tears and took Sister out to the back of the house, where there was a mentally handicapped child sitting tied up to a pole, like a dog, on the floor of the back veranda. The mother sobbed that this was her punishment from God for some past sin – a common belief in Pakistan.

The upshot was that Sister Gertie opened a home for mentally handicapped children. She was given a two-storey house by a generous Pakistani and converted it for her needs. She ran the establishment with the assistance of about three local nuns, and some of my friends and I used to go down quite regularly to help her feed the children, many of whom were bedridden. Many local people gave her generous help and support.

At this time, she was raising funds to build a hospital for the children, as she said they were so badly treated at the local hospitals. She often went on fundraising trips to Holland and round the continent. She had received enough money to start the building and was now trying to furnish it. Her most urgent need was sheets for the children's cots. I enlisted the aid of Brian Parker, the General Manager of Coates in Pakistan and the Chairman of UKCAP, who put me in touch with Mr Farouk, the owner of the biggest cotton mill in Pakistan.

I wrote to Mr Farouk telling him about Sister Gertie and asking if he could let us have some sheets – preferably with brightly coloured designs on them, so the children would have something to look at when lying in bed. I had a charming letter by return, authorising me to go to any of his outlets in Karachi and get as many sheets as I required. I passed this generous offer on to a thrilled Sister Gertie who, I am sure made good use of it. Best of all, it had not cost the BWA anything, and we could use our money for something else.

On another occasion, the home had a problem with rats. After local weddings and celebrations, many Pakistanis donated their leftover food to the home. Sister Gertie was also often given sacks of sugar, rice, *dhal*, etc., which she stored in a garage with a wooden door. They were plagued with rats, which gnawed the wood at the bottom of the door to gain entrance to the garage.

The husband of one of our members worked for a pest control firm. I contacted John and asked him if he would come and have a look at the problem. This he did and fixed a wide metal strip across the bottom of the garage door so that the rats could no longer gnaw their way in but said that unless the foodstuff was put in metal/plastic containers, the problem would not be solved.

Now, Salim Habib, the Managing Director of Burroughs Wellcome, was a friend of ours, and as I knew the chemicals for his factory came in large plastic bins, I asked him if I could have some of his empty ones. He wanted to know why, and when I told him, Salim said that he would send Sister Gertie as many bins as she wanted, already scoured and disinfected, ready to store her food. Again, the problem was solved at no expense.

Once a week for about a year, I went to the School for Blind where I taught English to some blind boys – they were young men really, about eighteen to twenty. I found this quite difficult, as I am not a teacher and, of course, there was a language problem. Still, I did my best, and it was quite rewarding.

One day, I took my friend Pat with me. She had written a simple, charming story for them about a British boy who had newly acquired a guide dog and how it helped him on and off buses and so forth. The boys listened in silence, and afterwards, I asked them, "Well, what do you think of that – would you like a dog like that?"

"Yes," they replied, "*if* it is true!" This brought home to me the vast difference between our culture and theirs. Most dogs, which are considered '*haram*' by Islam, that they would encounter would be strays on the street, and they did not really believe that there was such a thing as guide dogs. Before I went on my annual leave, I persuaded Amy Halai to take over from me. This was ideal, as not only would Amy be a permanent teacher for them, but she, of course, spoke fluent Urdu.

While we were in Karachi, Jim was a member of the Sind Club. This is one of the oldest and most exclusive clubs in Pakistan and was established in 1871, primarily for the use of British Army officers and other senior expatriates in 'Kurrachee', as it was then called. After Partition, it opened its doors to local members.

In the 1980s, it was still for men only, though wives were tolerated in certain parts of the club. There was still a notice leading to the billiards rooms that stated 'Women and Dogs not permitted beyond this point'. Fortunately, that did not include the swimming pool, which was the main attraction for families – including us. Indeed, I think I only ever had one meal in the dining room in all the time we were in Karachi.

Tom had grown into an excellent swimmer and made good use of the pool. During holidays, we went swimming at six a.m. most mornings when Tom had a lesson with the excellent club coach, an elderly retired Army PT instructor. Tom joined the Avari boys, Dinshaw and Xerxes for the lesson, and between them, they won all the cups at the annual gala.

The coach wanted the three boys to swim for Sind in the national swimming championships, but it was during Tom's term time. Anyway, I was quite glad because the local public pool was not very clean, and the one time Tom and the Avari boys went swimming there, it was green, cloudy and they could not see the bottom. Goshpi and I decided they would be better off not going back, in case they got some sort of eye, ear or other infection.

The Sind Club also had a wonderful garden section, and around October, I would send our *mali* to their nursery to buy seedlings for our garden. I created a wonderful border at the side of the lawn, with lady's lace (cow parsley) at the back, rudbeckia in the middle and red salvia in the front. It was my pride and joy. I grew poinsettias in pots for Christmas, which I placed in rows of three up the front veranda steps, about five hundred pots in all, followed in February by pots of chrysanthemums. Nothing much grew in summer – just a few straggly zinnias and some balsam.

Jim and I always had breakfast at the far end of the veranda, looking out over the pots in flower to the big trees by the compound wall. The trees were always full of squirrels, geckos and birds, mainly crows. I daresay there were some snakes in there as well, but we never saw any.

I have always enjoyed watching the Indian crows with their distinctive grey beaks. They are so clever. One day, Tom was sitting on the veranda steps, idly shooting at the trees with his air rifle when suddenly a crow fell off the branch. I don't know who was more surprised – the crow or Tom, who was quite upset. All the other crows wheeled round, cawing madly and swooped down to have a look at the dead bird.

On another occasion, a baby crow fell out of a nest near the bed by the lady's lace. Again, all the birds wheeled round and swooped down, cawing loudly and swooping at Pola, who had gone to investigate. I got up and started to walk over, but the *mali* stopped me. "Don't go there, *memsahib*," he said, "or they will attack you!"

The most exotic thing I ever saw in the garden was a couple of peacocks. One morning, I was sitting at the hall table, talking to Jim on the phone when I heard a rustling behind me. I glanced round, and there, coming up the front steps, were a couple of the most gorgeous peacocks with their tails fully fanned out. I couldn't believe my eyes. Apparently, they belonged to the general who lived next door. Unfortunately, they only stayed about fifteen minutes before flying back next door, and I never saw them again.

After we had been in Karachi about two years, we acquired a beautiful Rhodesian ridgeback, which we looked after for a Pakistani friend who had been posted to London for a while. Her name was Tyche, and she was eighteen months old. Tyche was a lovely animal – friendly and sleek. She and Pola hit it off and played beautifully together. Though we had a large compound, it was not really big enough for Tyche, who would tear madly round and round it, followed by Pola in hot pursuit for about two laps before Pola gave up.

Tyche was quite destructive, basically because she got easily bored. You would see her wandering round the veranda, thinking, *What shall I do now?* before she would make off with one of the scatter cushions, which you then had to wrest from her in the middle of one of the lawns, by which time, if it was not torn, it was filthy! We started putting them out of her reach – quite difficult, as she was very tall when she rose up on her hind legs.

When she first arrived, Pola was definitely boss, but as time went on, Tyche became more confident until she and Pola had a couple of nasty spats. We decided it would be wiser to rehome her before we went on leave, as I did not feel confident enough to leave both dogs together for six weeks in the care of the servants, all of whom were frightened of Tyche, who could easily have killed Pola. We therefore reluctantly rehomed her with a colonel in Lahore. Tyche was in her element, as the colonel was a keen huntsman and took her on *shikar* with him.

Our three years passed quickly, and it was soon time for us to move on. Jim was due to retire on July 4th 1986, so this was our last posting. He was being replaced by Faroukh Bengali, who was the Pakistani Karachi manager, and as they had their own servants, I began the sad task of trying to find new jobs for all our staff.

This was not easy, as most people now had only one or two servants who were sort of 'maids (men) of all work'. Hardly anyone had a dedicated cook, but I managed to get a job as a cook/bearer for Saeed, for Puran (who by this time had learnt some cooking from Saeed) and Hamleys, who was quite versatile. The gardener and Panchoo were staying put. The difficulty was Noor, who not only was losing his job but his lovely home as well. Also, his father would now have to 'retire'. Eventually, Jim found him a job with a Pakistani friend, which had quarters attached.

During our sojourn in Pakistan, the country became steadily more Islamic, particularly in the northern areas around Peshawar. There were some ugly incidents involving expatriate women considered to be 'improperly' dressed who were verbally assaulted and their legs painted black. A friend of Jim's, whose wife often accompanied him upcountry, insisted that she wore Pakistani dress and hijab for her own safety.

A form of Islamic banking, albeit a truly local version, was introduced. Jim was the only foreign bank manager invited to attend the discussions on its implementation – quite a compliment. Jim gave me the short version of what this involved: no loans, no interest, only investments and partnerships. Partners were to be charged, strangely, at a percentage rate, on the sum invested. Wealthy partners of the bank were charged at a higher rate than smaller ones, with the bank and partner sharing any cost of failure, the Reserve Bank arbitrating in cases of disagreement.

When asked his opinion, Jim said he believed it could work, but only if there was total honesty between the bank, commercial partner and, of course, the arbitrator, the Reserve Bank. This brought a wry smile from the minister of finance, who remarked, "Yes, complete honesty is always difficult to achieve."

We started on our round of farewell parties, which went on for weeks.

Pola was despatched to St Albans about a month before us, to start her six months' quarantine in the UK before she could come home. We found her a nice quarantine kennel in St Peter's Green, near St Albans, where we could easily visit her.

Jimmy Katrak and his packers arrived and packed up the house, taking our luggage off to a godown (*warehouse*) to await shipping.

I now just had to watch Benji taken off to join his new household. Our Parsi friends, the Cowasjees, said they would like him, as I could not imagine him living in St Albans, where he would disturb the whole neighbourhood, who, I am sure, would not appreciate his imitation of an express train.

Ardeshir Cowasjee was a delightfully eccentric and prominent member of one of the most prominent families in the Parsi community. A dapper, cultured and well-read man, he would appear at our parties dressed in a lovely long-flowing, silk Persian kaftan-style robe, with an ivory walking stick with a carved handle. With his beautifully trimmed beard and moustache, he looked like something that had stepped straight out of one of the pages in the Bible. So, Benji was put in his 'gold' transit cage and taken off to the Cowasjees, who lived just two streets along from us.

Noor had told Jim that he would organise the transport of Benji's aviary from our garden to the Cowasjees', and Jim had agreed he could do this, thinking Noor would make a bit of extra money.

As I watched, a cycle rickshaw appeared and Noor informed me that this would be the aviary's conveyance to its new home. "But Noor," I said. "The cage is far too big and will never fit on the back of the rickshaw. Look at the size of it! Three rickshaws will fit inside the cage!" Noor reluctantly agreed.

He thought for a minute and then said that everyone in the compound would join in and they would all carry the cage to the Cowasjees. I looked at him in disbelief. What! All those old men – including Noor's seventy-year-old father, one-eyed Panchoo, fat Puran and little Hamleys? Shaking my head, I retired inside.

About five minutes later, I heard much shouting and groaning from the garden and came back out to find all the servants, plus the watchmen, plus a couple of next door's servants, all carrying the aviary down the bougainvillea avenue towards the main gates. There were about twelve of them, four to each side, plus a couple of spares and it was all they could do to get the thing about a foot off the floor. They tottered out of the gate, the cage swaying perilously between them and disappeared down the road. That was the last I saw of them. What a pantomime – it was like something out of the *Keystone Cops*!

I have no idea how they got it into Ardeshir's gate, which was not as wide as ours, or where Nancy wanted them to put it. But as they never returned, and I never saw the Cowasjees again, I presume the installation was successful. Last heard of Benji (mina), he was lording it over their household, running freely all over Ardeshir's desk and generally terrorising their two bassets, whom he would chase, nipping their tails! Very painful! Poor dogs!

It was our silver wedding anniversary on 10th June, and we decided to celebrate it by taking a long route home, stopping off in Turkey to stay with a New Zealand couple, who worked for Reuters in Karachi, then travelling to Italy to stay with friends in Rome before eventually going to St Albans.

We had kept our last evening free, but in the end had to attend our last farewell party. The day before we left, Byram Avari invited us to stay at the Avari Towers for the last night. I did not want to do so, but Byram was insistent as he and Jim thought that farewells would be less fraught that way. Eventually, I said to Byram, "Well, I will if we can stay in your best suite that night!" fully expecting him to say sorry, but it was booked!

"Okay," he said immediately. I therefore had to reluctantly agree.

So, I bid a sad farewell to my house, my lovely bougainvillea avenue and all my servants, of whom I was very fond, and we decamped to the Avari Towers, where we settled into Byram's VIP suite.

That night, at about midnight, having returned from the party and got undressed, ready for bed, there was a loud knocking on our suite door. "Who on earth can that be?" I asked Jim.

I opened the door to be blinded by a bright white light, a whirring video camera and a highly embarrassed hotel photographer. Knowing what an inveterate practical joker Byram was, we immediately looked to see where he was. Sure enough, there was the whole Avari clan hiding round the corner of the corridor. They all trooped in for a final drink.

The next morning, Noor sadly drove us to the airport and we caught the plane for Turkey and flew off into the blue beyond to start our new, totally different lives as bank pensioners.